CW00956233

THE LAUGHING BABY

THE LAUGHING BABY

The extraordinary science behind what makes babies happy

CASPAR ADDYMAN

First published in 2020

Unbound
6th Floor Mutual House, 70 Conduit Street, London W1S 2GF
www.unbound.com

Text design by PDQ Digital Media Solutions Ltd.

A CIP record for this book is available from the British Library

ISBN 978-1-78352-796-0 (hardback)
ISBN 978-1-78352-798-4 (ebook)

Printed in Great Britain by CPI Group (UK)

1 3 5 7 9 8 6 4 2

A special thanks to Pampers, a patron of this book.

Pampers

seek to lift up parents and care for their baby's happy, healthy development.

Thank you to Lindsay Addyman
and Imogen Heap for their generous support
of this book

For my mother

Contents

Contents

Introduction: What's So Funny?

Babies are such a nice way to start people.
— Don Herold, American humorist (1889–1966)

What a piece of work is a man! How noble in reason, how infinite in faculty! In form and moving how express and admirable! In action how like an Angel, in apprehension how like a god! The beauty of the world! The paragon of animals!
— William Shakespeare, *Hamlet*, *c.*1600, Act II, Scene 2

Even the morbid Prince of Denmark had to admit humans are a big deal. Thanks to Charles Darwin, we no longer think of ourselves as the single summit of evolution. We're one tiny twig in the tangled thicket of life. We occupy a niche as social, bipedal omnivores. Glance around the planet and we have many well-adapted cohabitants, each excellent at their own tricks. Eagles and sharks outhunt us. Cheetahs and even hippos can outsprint us. Elephants and whales outlive us. Ants outweigh us. Plants and amphibians have bigger genomes. And bacteria secretly rule the world. But no creature is as clever, as dexterous, as social, as collaborative or as emotional, let alone as artistic, as talkative or as musical as humans. We are amazing and yet we are born almost entirely helpless.

Every superhero has their origin story: Superman and Batman were orphans, Spider-Man and the Hulk went radioactive. As you will see from this book, babies are the origin story of our own superpowers. If human babies were not so helpless, we would not be so clever. If our babies did not need our support, humans would not be so social. Our connection to our offspring even gives rise to our creation of music and art. We are all superpowered and the first two years of life are our training montage. This is a feel-good film.

Babies are pure joy and this book celebrates their achievements and their delight. The two are closely connected. Babies work very hard in their first two years, but to them it feels like play. They learn a lot and they laugh a lot. Curiosity and glee drive them forward. Surprising discoveries and daily progress keep them going. Parents provide support and encouragement – meeting babies' basic needs and structuring their lives. But it is the babies who scale the mountains and stand triumphant at the peaks.

So, this book won't list the dos and don'ts of raising a superhero. It is not a parenting manual filled with advice or warnings – I am not a parent. It is a book about the science of being a baby. As a developmental psychologist I am interested in the baby's perspective. I want to know what they are thinking, how they are learning and why they have so much fun along the way. Being a baby is a great adventure, full of ups and downs. Parenting books help you avoid the downs, but I believe there's a lot be learned from the ups too.

I have been a baby scientist since 2005, but it was only in 2012 that I started taking baby laughter seriously. My younger sister had just had her second baby and my younger brother was stand-up comedian. I was wondering what we could all do together. Eureka! Max could make the new baby laugh and I could explain why. It turns out that stand-up comedians take laughter quite seriously, so Max thought the gig was too easy. But the idea was planted in my mind and I started to wonder if baby laughter was a suitable topic to study.

I discovered very little previous research. Laughter is spontaneous, which makes it tricky to study in a laboratory. This is especially true of babies: they may laugh often, but they can be enigmatic, laughing at the most unexpected things. Stand-up comedy for babies is harder than you might think. Few scientists had taken on the challenge of studying laughter, which was usually viewed was a marker for something else, such as a way to understand early humour and joking, or as an indication of a baby's temperament and positive mood. Rarely was laughter central to the story of development itself.

Laughter is abundant in babies' daily lives and universally appealing to everyone else. I felt it must be important. I created a website (laughingbaby.info) and designed a detailed survey of baby laughter. Journalists from all over the world covered the project and thousands of parents from dozens of countries completed my questionnaire. Hundreds more sent me short 'field reports' and videos of things that made their babies laugh. I started to take baby laughter very seriously indeed.

In the years since then I have concluded that my intuition was broadly correct. Laughter is important to our early development and the roots of laughter are planted deep by evolution. This does not mean babies who laugh more develop better. There is no recommended daily amount of laughter. Instead, think of laughter as a happy counterpoint to crying. When a baby cries, we do not focus on the crying itself: we stop what we are doing and try to fix the problem the baby is telling us about. Laughter is the opposite; it is a baby sharing its successes. I believe it is worth stopping to examine those triumphs. In fact, this may be the purpose of laughter.

As I studied laughter, my interests kept widening to consider all the ways babies thrive and how they strive to meet their wider goals. So this book is about babies' emotions, their connections, their learning and their curiosity. It covers the first two years of life in roughly chronological order, but I have avoided putting in too many milestones. They don't mean much. Each baby follows their own path. The book is about the journey not the destination.

We have plenty of growing and learning to do beyond the first two years. But the foundations we build are important. Studying our origins helps us understand ourselves better. Don't get fooled into thinking this book is going to be just about the fun and games of babies. It contains a lot of serious academic research, explaining many core concepts that apply far beyond babyhood. We will address such big questions as how the mind works, how we evolved, what emotions are and what art is. Along the way, we will see babies taking on intellectual giants like René Descartes, Sigmund Freud, Noam Chomsky and Ludwig Wittgenstein.

Ultimately, however, this book is intended to do the impossible, which is to make the adorable sound of a baby's laughter even more enchanting. If it fails, find a baby and let them entertain you instead.

A Note About Scientific References

Throughout the book I try to give credit where credit is due. Science is a collaborative and cumulative exercise. Isaac Newton famously declared in 1675: 'If I have seen further, it is by standing on the shoulders of giants.' Scientific progress happens through evolution. Revolutions in science rarely throw away what came before; more likely they refine it. We argue about the details, but we are all working on the same big picture.

Only a minority of the research in this book is my own and I rarely give more than a summary. It is important to credit the people who did the work and point out where to find the full, original versions. Popular science books often hide this information in footnotes or endnotes, or omit it entirely. I prefer to use the convention adopted by psychology journals. When referring to a study you give the names of the authors and the year of the publication like this: (Author & Author, year). For example, one early work on happy babies was written by Charles Darwin. 'A biographical sketch of an infant' was published in the journal *Mind* in 1877, which would be referred to as (Darwin, 1877). The message is that you can skip over these. But each time you see a reference like this be aware that those were the people who did the real work. The full title of the work and where it was published is given in the References section at the end of the book.

Likewise, I have avoided footnotes. Scientists are pedantic sorts, always pointing out exceptions, approximations and alternatives. It gets very exhausting for everyone, so I have not done that. (I even try to avoid parentheses.)

Chapter One: A Time Before Smiles

When the first baby laughed for the first time, its laugh broke into a thousand pieces and they all went skipping about and that was beginning of fairies.

— J. M. Barrie, *Peter Pan*, 1904

A baby's first laugh is a magical moment. Parents have no trouble remembering it, even years later. Happening anywhere from a few weeks of age to four or five months, those early laughs will very likely be small and subtle, a light and breathy chuckle. A tiny baby cannot coordinate the rapid contractions of the intercostal chest muscles required to laugh properly, but the sound is unmistakable nonetheless.

For the ancient Greek philosopher Aristotle, the first time we laugh marks the instant when our soul enters our body and the moment we become truly human. He thought laughter was what separated us from the animals. He was wrong, of course. Other animals can and do laugh and the boundary between us and other species is a matter of degree, a question of genes and culture. As for the soul, nowadays we would probably call it 'consciousness' and we understand that it dawns slowly.

A baby's first laugh is a very special event and one that feels transformative. Sometimes it is a spontaneous sound of well-being and satisfaction: 'I am warm and happy and full of mother's milk.' Occasionally it is a response to something the baby sees, like a shadow waving on the wall. Best of all is when it is the result of something a parent does – returning to the room or planting a ticklish kiss. However small the first laugh may be, parents will recognise in it the idea that 'a laugh is a smile that burst'. It is the first time a baby expresses their absolute delight with the world.

It is a memory that can stay with a parent for ever. When I ran a global survey of baby laughter in 2012, one parent, Mary, took the trouble to write and tell me about 'the sound of the angels' that burst forth when she kissed her tiny daughter's tummy. It had happened 42 years previously, but it still echoed in her memory and made her 'smile with JOY'. It was one of many similar stories. This is rather remarkable, given that adult memory is usually very vague and non-specific. What did you have for lunch yesterday or do on your last birthday? Not many events in our grown-up lives stick all that well. Even wedding days become hazy. But our children's first laughs, first steps, first words remain with us and raise a smile decades later. Memories of first smiles can be more elusive and uncertain. Parents have a hard time pinpointing the very first smile and more difficulty recalling it. There are several things happening here. Not only are first smiles more subtle and fleeting but very often parents have been taught to doubt their own judgements.

There is a much-repeated myth that all smiles before about six weeks old are merely trapped wind or the sign of a baby filling their nappy rather than a true expression of pleasure or contentment. This myth is widespread and persistent. I've even seen it on popular midwifery websites. It is one I completely reject. It is true that babies do pull funny faces when burping or pooping. They also smile with true satisfaction. The parents I've surveyed are convinced they have seen genuine smiles from very early on and I believe them. They are, no doubt, slightly biased, but they are also studying their own baby far more intently than anyone else does. No one doubts that first cries and first tears are real. A baby in distress is obvious to all. Yet, strangely, experts often deny that early positive emotions are valid, saying first smiles aren't 'proper smiles'.

Worse yet, here we have new parents being told by experts they are wrong about something so basic. As they're already uncertain of their own abilities, it is not a great way to reassure them. The key message of this book is that parents and their babies figure most things out for themselves. Nobody is ever properly prepared for a baby. But, equally, parents know more than they realise, and they learn fast. The first weeks of life are even more stressful and bewildering for the baby, but their little laughs and smiles are a sign they are succeeding. No one should take that away from them. Happily, we will find the parents are correct, not the experts, as babies are able to experience and express pleasure before they are even born.

There is another milestone for new mothers that it is often overlooked. When was the first time her baby made her laugh?

This is earlier than you think. Of course there can be big smiles at the very beginning. Perhaps the time when she first suspected she was pregnant. Perhaps when it was confirmed by that second blue line on a pregnancy test? Or maybe a little later, when seeing another mum with her new baby made the reality of her own future more concrete?

Secret Joy

But I am not talking about those moments. I like to think the first time a baby directly makes mother laugh is when she feels it moving inside her. A good friend tells me of laughing on noticing her unborn daughter had the hiccups. But it doesn't take something as comical as this to bring smiles to a mother's lips. Often it is just the joy of a tangible new reality.

In my favourite part of *Expecting*, Chitra Ramaswamy's book-length memoir of her pregnancy, Ramaswamy describes going out for dinner with friends to celebrate her birthday. At five months pregnant she can't enjoy the restaurant's adventurous food, and is distracted from her friends as her baby wriggles inside her.

> I sat sipping champagne that tasted more like cider, pretending to follow the conversation while the baby fizzed in my belly. I said nothing about this furtive firework display. I had no desire to talk about it. There was nothing for anyone else to feel, nothing for anyone else to understand. This was my secret Morse code tapping out its message on my insides. I felt flushed with joy. It was one of the happiest moments of my life, one I

can summon up whenever I want to, and often do. (pp. 84–5, *Expecting*, Chitra Ramaswamy, 2016)

Just as that private joy became one of the happiest moments of her life, Ramaswamy also relates how Leo Tolstoy makes this secret moment a pivotal scene in his realist masterpiece, *Anna Karenina*. Anna is pregnant with the child of her lover, Vronsky, but huge obstacles face them because she is already married. Anna has dreamed she will die in childbirth, and informs Vronsky, prompting another a fraught discussion of their doomed affair, but in the middle of this Anna experiences the great fears for her situation giving way to a sense of bliss when she feels her baby stirring inside her.

This first feeling of movement is known as 'the quickening'. For thousands of years it was the first major event of pregnancy. Before pregnancy tests and modern medicine this was the first time a woman could say with certainty that she was pregnant. Ancient Greeks and Romans thought this was the moment when the soul entered the child's body. They believed that these movements indicated the moment when the foetus became 'animated' with life – *animus* and *anima* being the Latin words for mind and soul respectively and both having their roots in an even more ancient proto-Indo-European word for breath or breathing.

The legal system also recognised the quickening as the point that divided life from potential life, as in the biblical phrase 'the quick and the dead'. In English common law abortion was permissible before this point, and assaults that caused a woman to miscarry after the quickening were treated as more serious. Until 1869 even the Catholic Church held this view; it accepted abortion before the quickening as the destruction of potential life, not of life itself. Legal definitions are now based on viability of life outside the womb. English law recognises a foetus as being 'capable of being born alive' from 24 weeks and a baby's legal status as an individual commences from the point they draw their first breath.

In the private history of any individual pregnancy, quickening is a big milestone. The very first flutters of movement are a tangible joy, literally a 'touching' moment. From here onwards a mother has a new connection with her little passenger and can start to infer their personality. Comparing the patterns of activity with the experiences of other mums-to-be, is her little one more prone to wriggling late at night or early in the morning? How do they respond to music or their mother's mood, to coffee or to cake?

For a first-time mum the initial feelings of a baby moving typically occur between weeks 16 and 20 of pregnancy. Second-time mums tend to notice these movements several weeks earlier because their uterus walls are thinner, but foetuses are moving long before the mother notices. The first movements happen between four and eight weeks after conception, although there is no way a mother will notice these, as the foetus is still the size of a lentil.

Even before the introduction of hormonal pregnancy tests in the 1970s, few women failed to notice the massive changes that sweep through the body after a fertilised egg implants in the womb. The process is started by a flood of human chorionic gonadotropin (hCG to its friends) that gets released when the placenta first forms. This tells the ovaries a pregnancy is taking place and prompts them to keep producing progesterone while the placenta takes over producing oestrogen. The levels of both these two main female hormones will keep increasing throughout pregnancy. A third important hormone, oxytocin, makes its appearance later at the time of the birth.

Progesterone increases the mother's body temperature and metabolism, requiring extra energy, which is one reason she feels tired all the time. Progesterone also relaxes muscle tone, which is useful in later stages of pregnancy but early on affects the stomach and intestine, causing heartburn via acid reflux. Oestrogen changes her senses of smell and taste and is thought to cause the nausea, vomiting and stomach cramps of morning sickness. On top of all that, she has also just found out she is pregnant. It is not unreasonable for her to be feeling a bit fragile and largely in the dark, so that first touch of the baby is reassuring.

In the dark we can listen. Eavesdropping on life in the womb has been an important part of obstetrics for nearly 200 years. The humble stethoscope and its modern cousin ultrasound were both invented by maternity doctors. In 1816 René Laennec invented the stethoscope. He used to get embarrassed about having to put his ear to women's chests to listen to their hearts, so he made a listening tube. Laennec and his colleagues realised this new invention would let them listen to an unborn baby's heartbeat too. The first reports of foetal heart rates are from 1821, by Leannec's pupil Jean-Alexandre Le Jumeau de

Kergaradec (Wulf, 1985). The Y-shaped stethoscope appeared in 1851 and hasn't changed much since then. It is good enough to hear a baby's heart beating from the 22nd week of pregnancy, though this can depend on the orientation of the baby in the womb (and how much mummy's stomach is gurgling). It can even confirm if there are going to be twins.

Measuring foetal heart rate, and how much it varies, can tell doctors about the health of the foetus. The heart rate is controlled by two complementary systems, the sympathetic and parasympathetic nervous systems. The sympathetic nervous system causes increases in heart rate and the parasympathetic causes decreases. Normally they are in balance with each other and the heart rate gradually cycles up and down. A very fast or very slow heart rate, or even a lack of variability, can be a warning sign for doctors.

Medical ultrasound was invented by Ian Donald, an obstetrician working at the Glasgow Royal Maternity Hospital. He knew high-frequency soundwaves were being used in industry to detected flaws in welds and joints, and wondered if they would work on tissue. In 1955 he visited Glasgow engineering firm Babcock & Wilcox. Donald turned up with two carloads of medical specimens and found the industrial ultrasound device could detect the anomalous signals coming from tumours and cysts in the samples. Donald and colleagues built their own version and started using it in their diagnostic work. They wrote up their findings for the medical journal *The Lancet* in 1958 (Donald, Macvicar & Brown, 1958) kick-starting a revolution in medical diagnostics.

Ultrasound and heart-rate monitoring are the backbone of medical monitoring of foetal development. They have also been used by developmental scientists like myself to uncover what babies experience in the womb. Measuring changes in foetal heart rate allows us to determine when a foetus is surprised by something. Ultrasound lets us see how a foetus moves in response to sounds, movements and other stimuli. Coupled with what is known about the biology of the growing foetus, this lets us build a picture of what a foetus can learn in the womb.

Ultrasound shows that the clump of cells that becomes the heart is already beating by the sixth week after conception. At this point the embryo is the size of lentil, but already the ears, mouth and nose are visible. The eyes and nostrils are two little black dots, and arms and legs are still little stubs, the fingers and toes webbed. A six-week-old embryo will already move in response to touches around the mouth and nose area. These are simple reflexive actions but show that the nervous system is already beginning to arrange itself. This also gives a hint as to why mouthing is such an important exploratory skill for babies.

Fruit of the Womb

Over the next two weeks, the embryo doubles to blueberry-sized and then doubles again to the size of a raspberry (according to the fruit-and-veg-based measurement system that seems to be standard in all baby books ever written). At around 10 or 11 weeks the little strawberry has sleep and wake cycles. Mostly, the womb is a bedroom. Throughout the pregnancy a foetus spends over 90% of its time asleep. Sleep cycles are about 40 minutes at a time, punctuated by a few minutes of activity, the amount of activity increasing as time goes by. When it's strawberry-sized, movements are minimal but clearly exhausting, as in-utero yawns have been seen as early as week 11 (Joseph, 2000).

Week 13 is peachy. This is the end of the first trimester, one third of the way through the pregnancy, and the embryo has developed sufficiently for us to start calling it a foetus. The first voluntary movements start to happen around 16 weeks, when the foetus is about 4.5 inches long (11.5 cm) and the size of an avocado. Periods of activity are accompanied by foetal callisthenics. The foetus is recognisably human by now, with a big round head and teeny-tiny fingers and toes.

Foetal development is not simply a process of growth from blueberry-sized blob to bouncing baby. Throughout this time the constant metamorphosis is no less dramatic than from caterpillar to butterfly. Cells are not only dividing and their numbers multiplying, but their functions change and they migrate within the body to different goals and different roles. That blueberry still has gill-like structures which become the jawbone and a tail which becomes the coccyx. Most internal organs are only fully formed by week 20, and neurons keep moving and connecting beyond birth.

As I've already mentioned, the expectant mother will feel the first tickles of movement somewhere between weeks 16 and 20 (avocado to small banana). This is typically when the midterm ultrasound takes place. The foetus is carefully examined to check everything is developing as expected. On modern ultrasounds the sex of the baby can be seen if you know what you are looking for. Chances are the foetus will be asleep during this exam, but if it is moving, you might be in for a nice surprise. In March 2015, Jen Hazel and her husband went for their 14-week ultrasound scan with their doctor in Olympia, Washington. During the scan the foetus clapped her hands together. As Jen describes it:

> We went in for an ultrasound and the baby clapped three times on screen. Not to the music, just clapped three times. So my doctor, he said, 'Well, let's sing a song.' My husband grabbed his video and the doctor reran the ultrasound and played the claps and I sang and he sang with me 'If you're happy and you know it [clap your hands]'.

Their singing isn't great – Jen is laughing too much and her husband doesn't seem to know all the words – but it's a delightful video. And when it was uploaded to YouTube it understandably went viral. At the time of writing it has nearly 12 million views.

So could a 14-week-old foetus be happy? Here we get to the heart of this chapter. Is there a time before smiles? When does happiness and contentment begin? Are they present from the very start or do emotions only turn on sometime after birth? Jen's daughter, Pip, was born safe and healthy. She is a happy, playful baby and she still likes music. But what about when Pip was still a lemon-sized foetus of 14 weeks? Was she happy and did she know it? Could she know it? A single fertilised egg, a zygote, cannot know or show happiness. Nor can the little ball of cells in the blastocyst or even the yawning strawberry-sized embryo. From the many parental reports in my baby laughter survey, I am confident a baby of just a few weeks old can show genuine contentment. So when do the lights come on? When can a smile really be a smile?

No research exists on foetal pleasure. Indeed, it would be hard to know where to start. But foetal pain is a good guide to pleasure. Pleasure and pain are supported by similar circuits and evidence is accumulating that by end of the second trimester, at around 24 to 25 weeks post-conception, a foetus can feel rudimentary pain. The Royal College of Obstetricians and Gynaecologists (RCOG) published a detailed report in 2010 that reviewed the available evidence. They concluded that foetal awareness of pain is not possible before 24 weeks (RCOG, 2010).

For anyone to experience pain, nerve signals from the unpleasant stimulus must reach a cortex capable of processing them. If the signal from some part of the body doesn't reach the brain, we will only experience numbness. This is how a local anaesthetic works: by blocking the nerve signals at source. If the signals reach the brainstem and thalamus but aren't passed upwards to the cortex, we won't feel anything. This is how general anaesthetic works: by blocking all signals from the brainstem to the cortex.

Before 24 weeks a foetus cannot experience pain because the brain is not fully connected. In particular, the thalamus, which is a kind of junction box between brain and body, is not properly wired to the cortex (the wrinkly thinking bit). This is not too surprising when you appreciate how complicated the brain is, and how tangled the wiring. Every part needs to talk to every other part and those wires are long trailing tails of brain cells called axons. To connect one place to another, the cells must be born in one area and migrate to the other, trailing the tail behind them.

As you can imagine, this is complicated and the wiring cannot happen until there is somewhere to connect to. The thalamus and the cortex, initially known as the cortical plate, grow separately. A further group of cells develops in a 'subplate zone' beneath the cortex. From 12 to 18 weeks connections from the thalamus arrive in the subplate zone and then wait as the cortical plate matures. At around 24 weeks they recommence their journey to connect to all areas of the cortex, a process that continues to week 32. Also at 24 weeks, the neurons of the subplate themselves migrate into different areas of the cortex, effectively wiring these areas together. Both these processes are important to an awareness of pain. An 18-week-old foetus moves away from a needle prick and even releases stress hormones, but it doesn't feel the pain. The signals can reach the thalamus and potentially the subplate zone, but they can't ascend any higher. The withdrawal of the limb and the hormone release are reflexes that come from the brainstem.

By 24 weeks nerve signals start to get through the cortex. Brainwave recordings performed with very premature infants show coordinated neural activity in response to a heel prick from 24 weeks of pregnancy. This sets the lower limit recommended by the RCOG. But, as they observe in their report, although this is the theoretical minimum age that pain can be felt, awareness might come later. Electroencephalogram (EEG) activity is not continuous at this point, as it would be in an adult or a newborn. It is not clear whether the pain is being perceived or if the experience requires an experiencer who has yet to arrive.

From the 24th week the brain begins connecting itself up in earnest. The sensory inputs from hearing, vision and touch pass through to the relevant areas of the cortex. Reciprocal connections downward from cortex to brainstem begin by week 26. Feedback loops start to form and the foetus can begin to exert voluntary control over their tiny womb-world. They are starting to hear, feel and even see things, and starting to learn.

It is unlikely the foetus has any kind of experience before this. But in the third trimester they can absorb a surprising amount. Studies looking for changes in foetal heart rate have found that from 26 weeks onwards the foetus can respond to and learn to ignore repetitive vibrations. They can respond to changes in levels of external illumination, to hearing their mother's voice and to feeling her touch through the walls of the womb (Marx & Nagy, 2015).

My favourite study of this kind was done by Peter Hepper of Queen's University Belfast (Hepper, 1991). He tested newborn infants of just two to four days old to see how they responded to music they had heard in the womb. To do this he took advantage of the fact that many mothers watched soap operas.

Half of his sample were fans of the show *Neighbours* and half were not. This meant that half the babies had heard its catchy theme tune many times while in the womb. When he played it to the two groups in the maternity ward, the movements and heart rates of the *Neighbours* babies dropped relative to the control group, as they seemed to enter an alert listening state. To double-check they were not just more likely to respond to music, he tried the *Coronation Street* theme and got no response. A second experiment got similar results, but this time playing the theme tunes to babies still in the womb through headphones on the mummies' tummies. Hepper argues that the babies were learning not just the music, but were associating it with the calm and relaxed state the mother went into as she sat down to enjoy the soap.

One curious feature of most of these studies is that it doesn't seem to matter if the foetus is active or 'asleep'. Recall that foetuses are only active about 10% of the time and the periods of activity in the womb are a dreamlike state not easily comparable to the wakeful attention of a newborn baby. In fact, some researchers go further and say the whole pregnancy is spent with the foetus in a deep sleep. Consciousness expert Christof Koch wrote for *Scientific American Mind*:

> I wager that the foetus experiences nothing in utero; that it feels the way we do when we are in a deep, dreamless sleep. The dramatic events attending delivery by natural (vaginal) means cause the brain to abruptly wake up, however. The foetus is forced from its paradisic existence in the protected, aqueous and

> warm womb into a hostile, aerial and cold world that assaults its senses with utterly foreign sounds, smells and sights, a highly stressful event. (Koch, 2009)

It is a vivid image, but I disagree that life in the womb is spent in such a sedated state. The changes in infant heart rate in various studies suggest they are responsive to events around them and I think some experiences can even be pleasant for the foetus. Anecdotal reports of babies pictured smiling in ultrasounds have been around since 2000, when the resolution of scans became good enough to show facial expressions. Looking at this evidence systematically, the psychologist Nadja Reissland at the University of Durham and colleagues have identified seven foetal facial expressions and confirmed that both crying and laughing are 'practised' in the womb (Reissland, Francis, Mason & Lincoln, 2011).

Using modern '4D' ultrasound, which has good spatial and depth resolution in real time, Reissland's team scanned two foetuses on multiple occasions between 24 and 35 weeks. They recorded 10 minutes of facial expressions on each occasion and used a standard coding scheme to objectively classify what they saw. Facial expressions can be broken down into their component micro-expressions (pursed lips or raised cheeks). The coding scheme designed for very young babies was adapted to define sets of expressions that went together to form a 'cry face' and a 'laughter face'. Some, like a wrinkling of the nose, were common to both. Others defined just laughter (tongue sticking out and lips pulling back) or crying (pulled down lower lip and furrowed brow). Combining data on both foetuses (both girls), they found that the crying expression increased from 0% to 42% occurrence while laughing faces increased from 0% to 35% between the 24th and 35th week respectively. Pleasant expressions were as common as expressions of distress, and both gradually appear as the foetus itself gradually gains awareness. From the baby's personal point of view, there is no time before smiles.

Therefore, when asked, I say the grimaces and smiles of infants in utero reflect something genuine from around week 25. I believe this is the start of foetal awareness of pleasure and pain. This is not too different from the 24-week mark suggested in the RCOG report. But, for idiosyncratic reasons, I prefer week 25, when the universal fruit-and-veg scale says the foetus has reached the size of an aubergine.

A former girlfriend of mine, Belinda, always used to say that the springy tactile pleasures of aubergines reminded her of the chubby arms, legs and tummies of young babies. In the supermarket she couldn't resist giving the aubergines a playful squeeze. When I started to work with babies, she would often ask me, 'How are the aubergines?' It became our secret synonym. And then, a few years ago, while Belinda was pregnant with her daughter Rose, I got a delighted text message letting me know the pregnancy app on her phone had informed her that, after 25 weeks, her blueberry had graduated, and she was now the proud possessor of a little aubergine of her own.

Chapter Two: Happy Birthday

The first thing newborn babies do is cry because their parents haven't bothered to sing 'Happy Birthday' to them.

— Someone on the internet

You don't remember your zeroth birthday, but your mother certainly does. For the last few months of pregnancy she didn't require a smartphone app to tell her that you were swelling up from cute little aubergine through honeydew and cantaloupe to goddamn watermelon. For nine months she had been imagining this moment. The party bag had been packed for weeks waiting for the day. There may have even been a few false alarms. But then the time finally arrived.

Well, almost: babies don't like to rush their grand entrance; nor does the mother's body. The average length of normal labour for a first-time mother is about eight hours and it is largely controlled by automatic processes. The main feature of labour is the regular coordinated contractions of the muscles of the uterus, which are controlled by pacemaker cells, like in the heart. The contractions grow in frequency and intensity, starting 10 minutes apart and increasing to two minutes apart near the end.

Assuming no medical complications, nature then takes its course. But nature can be terrifying and deadly. Historical novelist Philippa Gregory memorably observed that it used to be that 'men die in battle; women die in childbirth'. Historically, mothers had a one in 100 chance of dying as a result of giving birth. It is still that bad, or worse, in some parts of the world. A World Health Organisation (WHO) report from 2015 says the lifetime chance for 15-year-old girl in Africa dying from a cause related to maternity was one in 37. In Europe that number is one in 3,400.

Babies fare even worse. Across the world one in every 45 births is a stillbirth. And of the babies that do survive, 49 out of every 1,000 don't make it to their first birthday. As health statistician Hans Rosling pointed out, mothers and young infants are the most vulnerable and invisible victims of wars, famines and other humanitarian crises. The biggest win one can make for human health is to improve the care of new mothers and their babies.

In Vienna General Hospital in the 1840s there were two maternity wards, Clinic 1 and Clinic 2, which admitted women on alternating days. The first clinic was attended by medical students, the second clinic by midwives. Pregnant women admitted on Clinic 1 days begged to be admitted to Clinic 2, as it seemed to be common knowledge that Clinic 1 was cursed. Data collected from 1842 to 1846 were incontrovertible: maternal death rates were 60% lower in Clinic 2, the midwives' clinic. A junior doctor, Ignaz Semmelweis, was tasked with investigating this. He found no differences in the clinics themselves, nor the delivery procedures. He made the suggestion, unusual for the time, that the medical students wash their hands with strongly chlorinated water. When they did, death rates dropped to levels found in Clinic 2. The medical students had come often from dissecting cadavers in anatomy classes. They didn't wash their hands because, well, why would they? There was no reason. This was decades before the germ theory of disease was proved by Louis Pasteur and Joseph Lister.

Semmelweis presented his findings to his superiors. He could not explain why the washing of hands helped, so they did not adopt his suggestions. Shortly afterwards he was fired and he returned to his native Hungary. Hospitals where he worked showed similar improvements, but his new colleagues would not permanently adopt handwashing either. He spent 20 years in increasingly angry correspondence with the European medical establishment. He was largely ignored. He died in an asylum in 1865, a broken and defeated man. In psychology, the Semmelweis Reflex is a cognitive bias where we reject new evidence when it contradicts existing beliefs or established paradigms.

Curiously, right now in the Western world, with universal access to advanced medical services, the answer to healthier births might also be more midwives and fewer doctors. This was the recommendation of an influential report in the British Medical Journal by Mary Newburn, Director of Policy for the National Childbirth Trust, and colleagues (Johanson, Newburn & Macfarlane, 2002). They recommended that the whole culture around birth needed to change to one 'of birth as a normal physiological process, and having a commitment to one-to-one supportive care during active labour'. Having medical staff on standby during birth is important, but medical staff tend to medicalise everything. In Finland, where birth is treated as a physiological process, 11% of births are by caesarean section. In the United Kingdom it is 25% and in the United States it is 35%. The estimated medically necessary level is thought to be 5% to 10%. At risk of lawsuits, and operating on a precautionary principle, doctors will run tests and even perform operations that are not needed. But there is more to it than that.

When birth is presented to mothers as a medical condition to be treated, then, not unreasonably, they seek more treatment. They have more fear of the act of giving birth itself. They seek more epidurals and pain management. In a medical setting, midwives defer to clinicians. Even maternity doctors themselves feel that they rely too much on medical procedures. When birth is viewed as a natural, physiological process, outcomes are better for mother and baby, and mothers have a better birth experience. The report recommended that, as far as possible, midwives not doctors should direct the childbirth process. It should take place in a non-medical setting and mothers should get to know and trust their midwives.

I spoke to two midwife friends of mine to understand what their role is and to get a better perspective on childbirth. Corinne is energetic and irreverent rather than medical and matronly. She seems more likely to be found marching against injustice than patrolling the wards of a hospital. In fact, that might be where we first met. Corinne has 10 years' experience as a 'baby catcher'. Natalie is small, sparkly and still slightly Dutch despite nearly two decades in London. We met 19 years ago on the very first day of our psychology degree. I remember she was always the first to finish any piece of coursework and she did all the practice essays that I never quite found time for. Natalie used to run marathons for fun, a hobby I didn't understand at the time, but one that probably prepares you quite well for being a midwife.

The word midwife is from the old German '*mit* (with) *weib* (woman)', meaning someone who is with the mother. As Corinne points out, it is a role as old as humanity. For at least as long as we have been walking upright we've needed midwives. The transition to walking changed the shape of our pelvises, narrowing the passage. Combine that with our ballooning brains, and our big-headed babies need help into the world. Fortunately, the reason we grew so brainy was because we are a sociable species. So social support was there for labouring mothers.

When I ask Corinne and Natalie what the main role of a midwife is, their answers are very similar: midwives support mothers to have the birth they want. Modern midwifery is built on three key principles: informed choice, choice of birthplace and continuity of care. The most important of these is informed choice, which is something more than informed consent; it is empowerment as opposed to acquiescence. Midwives want the mother to feel in control. Natalie explains that having a birth plan is very helpful here; the important decisions have been made in advance. The last thing a woman in labour needs is to be asked a lot of questions. She can be directed along the path she has already chosen and the midwife will help smooth the way. If her own midwife is not available at the crucial moment, another midwife can consult the plan.

Corinne explains that for most of labour, 'Our job is to watch and wait. To observe. Sit on your hands. Be responsive to the woman's needs.' Some need a reassuring hand, some need to be left alone. Some need ice cubes to crunch or something sugary to keep them going. As labour progresses, midwives give the mother options to choose, not decisions to make. When there are complications the midwife is the calming voice who makes sure the mother knows what is happening and why.

If anything disrupts the calmness, it can delay labour. Ina May Gaskin, the pioneering American midwife who is credited with reintroducing natural childbirth to the United States, observed:

> The presence of even one person who is not exquisitely attuned to the mother's feelings can stop some women's labors. All women are sensitive. Some women are extraordinarily so. We learned this truth by observing many labors stop or slow down when someone entered the birth room who was not intimate with the laboring mother's feelings. If that person then left the room, labor usually returned to its former pace or intensity. (p.138, Gaskin 2010)

This is also the principle behind hypnobirthing. In the last months of pregnancy some mothers learn relaxation and breathing techniques that they can apply when in labour. They are learning to hypnotise themselves, but this is not to achieve some numbing trance. It worked for my sister Ishbel, who was so calm for her first birth that she had trouble getting admitted to the hospital. They didn't believe she was so advanced with labour and wanted to turn her away. On her recommendation, my aubergine friend Belinda tried it too, with similar success. The idea is not block out the anxieties or the pain, but to make you more aware of the present so you can relax into the actual experience rather than worrying about what it might turn out to be. Starting labour calm and confident helps the natural physiological processes carry you as far as they can. Drugs can always come later. The most important drug is one your body makes itself – oxytocin.

Oxytocin

Oxytocin is the unquestioned chemical queen of childbirth. 'Good old oxytocin', as Natalie calls it. In the last decade oxytocin has also developed an overhyped reputation as the 'love drug', 'hug hormone' and 'cuddle chemical'. It is supposedly present in large quantities when people fall in love and in smaller amounts when they have sex or even hug. Participants in psychology studies have had oxytocin squirted up their noses before having their brains scanned. These studies have claimed it increases empathy, reduces introversion and could even treat autism. The science behind most of these claims is at best 'unproven'. Early studies didn't have enough participants to be sure, or haven't been replicated. It is not even clear whether nasal oxytocin can make it into the brain.

Levels of maternal oxytocin gradually rise in the late stages of pregnancy, when it increases feelings of contentment, calmness and security around a partner. Labour releases it in even greater quantities, increasing contractions. More is produced when the descending baby stimulates the cervix and vagina, creating a positive feedback loop. If labour is not progressing quickly, mothers may be put on an oxytocin drip.

Oxytocin is not the only chemical involved in natural childbirth. As labour reaches its crescendo, a complex network of hormones and chemicals work in concert in mother and baby. Relaxin relaxes the mother's ligaments, and in the baby a protein called noggin makes the head squidgy and deformable to help it squeeze out. Early on, fast-acting stress hormones epinephrine and norepinephrine can slow down or suspend labour if danger is perceived. At the very end of labour a surge of these same chemicals makes sure both mother and baby are alert after the birth.

The slower-responding stress hormone cortisol also builds to 10 times its normal level during birth. This seems to promote the formation of receptors for prolactin, the breastfeeding hormone. Endorphins are released, which aid a mother's ability to cope with stress and pain, and induce a slightly altered state of consciousness. This rises to a kind of euphoria at birth. Endorphins also seem to serve a second role in priming the reward centres in the mother's and baby's brains, preparing them both to imprint, bond and learn how to breastfeed. Maternal endorphins also directly stimulate the release of prolactin. Prolactin is the hormone of breast-milk synthesis but has around 300 other effects on the body, one of which is to stimulate oxytocin synthesis.

This complex web of individual effects and self-regulating cycles is often disrupted in delivery interventions. For example, one issue with epidural pain relief is that the lack of pain prevents the epinephrine-norepinephrine surge. There is less of these hormones in the mother's blood and less is passed to the baby, leaving him or her underprepared for delivery. Similar effects are found with caesarean sections, where caesarean-born babies have much lower stress at the time of birth but much higher one hour later. Caesareans seem to slow the bonding process, but this is partly because the mother is in recovery. Childbirth is a very complicated system and most of the mechanisms still aren't fully understood. These last few paragraphs have attempted to summarise Sarah Buckley's monumental 248-page report on the topic, which itself summaries research from 1,141 other papers (Buckley, 2015).

Corinne tells me that babies are born in a kind of stasis. They do not begin to wake up until after the umbilical cord is cut and they have filled their lungs with oxygen. 'Before that happens they are different. Their colour is different. They are not looking outwards.' Where possible, midwives leave the umbilical cord to pulsate for three minutes to push all the blood stored in the placenta into the baby. The first breath closes holes in the heart, changing the baby's circulation so that blood starts to go through the lungs, not the placenta.

Corinne busts a myth I was not sure about. Doctors don't dangle newborn babies upside down to drain their lungs.

Nor do they spank them to make them cry and start their breathing.

> No! That would be cruel. The action of being squeezed out of a woman is usually enough. If not, rubbing the baby with a rough NHS towel or tickling their feet will stimulate breathing. Just as how, in other mammals, a mother licks her newborn pups to stimulate them to take their first breaths.

Human mothers aren't expected to lick their babies, but since 2014 most childbirth organisations, including the American Academy of Pediatrics (AAP) and the WHO, have encouraged early skin-to-skin contact. Babies used to get whisked away straight after birth to be weighed and measured. Newborns were kept in nurseries and only brought to mothers for feeding. This was supposed to aid mothers' recovery. But the importance of the transition time has been rediscovered. The WHO says that 'the process of childbirth is not finished until the baby has safely transferred from placental to mammary nutrition'.

As Corinne vividly explains, 'Now, where possible, babies are born out of the mother, onto the mother.' A mother's body temperature will increase by a degree or two to keep the baby warm enough and babies have an instinct to crawl towards the breast and seek out the nipple. They work by touch and smell, and they may need a bit of time to get started – they need to wake up enough first. This is also an opportunity for baby to be colonised by the mother's bacteria and it helps the mother start to acclimatise. In Natalie's experience, no one is ever prepared to see their baby for the first time. It takes time to sink in and that is just the beginning of the bonding process.

When it comes to childbirth, experiences can be very varied. Some women do have a wonderful experience, but others experience a nightmare. I haven't yet encountered anyone who would call it 'fun'. 'The joy comes when you have the baby in your arms, which colours everything with joy. But I have never seen anyone enjoying it as it happens,' Corinne reports. Like running a marathon, the joy of childbirth happens after it is complete

For fathers or partners, that time immediately after the baby is born is where the greatest changes take place. During pregnancy, the baby has been somewhat abstract, but now they can hold the baby and interact with it. A partner's oxytocin and prolactin levels rise dramatically at this point. Remarkably, by the end of the first week a father's oxytocin levels can be as high as the mother's.

The emotional and hormonal high the partner feels can often contrast with an equivalent slump for the mother. The first week can be a very difficult time. There is a huge hormonal crash after birth. The placenta is no longer signalling production of pregnancy hormones and the body starts trying to undo nine months of being pregnant. During the first week at home the mother's body is trying to recover, but she's not getting much rest or relaxation with a new baby to care for and worry about.

Utterly exhausted and at the end of a nine-month odyssey, the return home can also feel anticlimactic for the mother. Mothers who had a difficult delivery often feel particularly isolated. The focus is on the baby and she is expected to be grateful for everything, while her own identity fades and there isn't much opportunity to deal with her own needs. It is totally normal to feel overwhelmed or even depressed straight after birth. A recent study found that 81% of women experience a mental health issue during or after their pregnancy (Royal College of Obstetricians and Gynaecologists, 2017). The deep love for the baby doesn't always come straight away, but mothers cannot easily talk about this.

On top of this, a new mother is usually the only one responsible for that baby 24/7. If anything happens she will never not blame herself. Asked about this time, Corinne tells me, 'In my ten years as a midwife, visiting them at home in the first week, I've never seen new parents who didn't look shell-shocked.' Everyone will be overwhelmed by some aspect of first-time parenting, but it gets easier and it is OK to ask for help.

One of the weirdest things about newborn babies is the raw fact of their existence. Here is a whole new person suddenly central to their parents' lives. When my nephew Tycho was born, my sister had some trouble leaving the room he was in. It was hard to process that he had an independent existence, and she had to keep checking. Birth is the opposite of death, but some of the feelings it creates are not so dissimilar to grief. Adjusting to the presence or absence of a significant other is a process. For mothers, a second child can bring even more ambiguous feelings. It changes the relationship with the first child; mother and baby number one are no longer that indivisible pair. Mothers can feel resentment for what has been lost. Again, this is a completely normal, but can be hard to talk about.

Babies recover fast from birth. 'Babies are resilient,' Corinne says. 'I have seen babies go through really traumatic births and they heal up pretty quickly. Heads getting squished looks very traumatic. The first time I saw that as a student midwife I ran off and cried in the toilets for twenty minutes.'

The idea that the trauma of birth can follow you through life has no scientific support. Except for the rare cases with clear medical complications, a traumatic birth is only a small setback. Labour and birth are just one event in the development of a baby. No single moment defines this time; all are important. And although it feels like a rollercoaster, the overall direction of travel is upwards.

Hello, Little Monkey

Some babies are born with a fine black hair on their body. This disappears quite quickly. When I was born, I was my mother's first child of three and she was well pleased with her achievement (as indeed am I). But I was a little furry. Sitting up in her hospital bed, she delighted in scandalising the nurses by asking them to bring her 'her monkey'.

'Mrs Addyman, you can't say that! He's your little baby!'

'Yes, but he looks like a monkey!'

'He's a beautiful baby.'

'A beautiful monkey! Give me my monkey!'

My ears were all curled up too. When the nurses explained that they would unfurl as they filled with blood, my mother nodded calmly and said, 'Ah yes, just like a butterfly's wings.' I think perhaps they'd given her too much laughing gas.

Giving birth is painful and dangerous, and the baby can be unexpectedly early or frustratingly late. There may be false alarms and it is almost always slow. The good news is it could have been a lot worse. Compared to our cousins the great apes, human babies (280 days gestation) are born before they are ready. If we compare the level of brain development of a newborn chimpanzee (253 days gestation), gorilla (270 days), or orangutan (275 days), then one researcher calculated that human babies ought to be born after 625 days in the womb. For any mum who feels ready to burst at nine months, this is a terrifying prospect. It would be deadly for mothers (and would play havoc with our fruit-based measurement system).

Getting born is a big deal too. But, if you think about it, the transition from inside to outside world is about as gradual as we could manage. You've got to come out some time, and humans leave it as late as we safely can for mothers. You've got to give up the secure permanent hug of the womb and its five-star, full-board accommodation with perfectly regulated temperature and muffled insulation from the abruptness of the changing word outside. The 24-hour room service, which is so luxurious that even your breathing is done for you, has to come to an end.

Our nine-month pregnancy is a compromise. A baby would remain resident within if it could, but it needs to escape before it gets trapped: what is known as the obstetrical dilemma. The price is that the first three months on the outside aren't much different from life on the inside. The baby continues their in-utero routine of sleeping, eating and growing.

One reason babies arrive early is the incompetence of nature. American comedian Penn Jillette is more forthright: 'Nobody that has seen a baby born can believe in God for a second … Nature is trying to kill us.' Evolution must work with what it is given, building on what came before, and this leads to numerous kludges and compromises. No intelligent designer would make birth so hazardous and attempt to pass big-headed babies through the fixed girdle of the pelvis. Evolution made that choice for us many millions of years ago and we must live with it. It worked well for little-headed quadrupeds. Even our closest relatives, the chimpanzees, manage fairly easily.

The energy demands of pregnancy on the mother are another restriction. Growing bigger and operating a big brain are both energy-hungry activities. A recent theory proposes that if foetuses got any bigger and pregnancy lasted any longer, a mother would not be able to provide enough energy for herself and her baby (Dunsworth, Warrener, Deacon, Ellison & Pontzer, 2012). Breastfeeding is a much more efficient way of transferring energy than via the placenta, as the calories get passed directly to the child. It makes sense to give birth when we do.

Social from the Start?

Helpless and too early in the world, newborns depend on their parents like no other species, but they do have quite a few tricks up their teeny-tiny sleeves to help with bonding. In the hours immediately after birth, babies are quite alert and can communicate. They like to be held and to be cooed at. They also seem to be able to track your face as you hold them. This is remarkable for two reasons. Firstly, their vision at birth is so blurry that your face will not be much more than a triangle of three dark blobs where your eyes and nose are. Secondly, they have never seen a face before, yet they seem to prefer this over other stimuli.

This was first demonstrated scientifically in the 1970s (Goren, Sarty & Wu, 1975), but was largely overlooked until 1991, when two British researchers revisited the experiment. Mark Johnson and his collaborator John Morton replicated the original finding and gave an explanation for what might be going on (Johnson, Dziurawiec, Ellis & Morton, 1991; Johnson & Morton, 1991). They believe this happens thanks to the interaction of two brain systems, one for recognition and one for learning.

They had conducted the study because Mark Johnson wanted to know if human babies were anything like freshly hatched chickens. Johnson started his career as a biologist working with Professor Gabriel Horn at Cambridge University. Together they studied the brain mechanisms behind imprinting, the process by which little birds learn to bond with mummy birds. Little chickens will follow their mother or anything that vaguely looks like her. This is familiar to anyone who has seen a queue of ducklings following mother duck. But it was first investigated by Konrad Lorenz in the 1930s. He got baby geese to follow him in his wellingtons. He won a Nobel Prize for it. I believe you can visit the Nobel Prize-winning wellingtons at the museum at his old house in Altenberg, Austria. Just like Ivan Pavlov and his Nobel Prize for feeding dogs, there was more to Lorenz's research than meets the eye.

Lorenz shared the 1973 Nobel Prize in Physiology or Medicine with Niko Tinbergen and Karl von Frisch. The prize recognised their roles in founding the field of ethology, which is the study of animal behaviour. Von Frisch is famous as the discoverer of the waggle dance in bees. Tinbergen, like Lorenz, looked at instinctive behaviours and critical periods in animal development. The chicks learning to follow their mother demonstrate how certain survival mechanisms are built in by nature, but the fact they would also follow a pair of wellingtons shows that the mechanism is adaptable. The profound thing about this work was how it gave evolutionary explanations for animal behaviour based on their survival value.

At various points in this book you will read about 'nature versus nurture', the idea that some skills are built in by evolution (nature) while others are learned (nurture). Everyone in developmental psychology acknowledges that both play a part, but there is nonetheless a divide between those that think genes do most of the work and those that think it mostly down to learning. Johnson and Morton's work was an important effort to demonstrate that we always ought to be talking about 'nature plus nurture'.

For the case of newborns' ability to follow faces, nature specified the two brain systems required: a circuit deep in the brain that quickly orients to patterns that resemble faces, and the more general, higher-level cortex that learns from whatever it sees. This learning is nurture. Because the baby sees lots of faces, she becomes a face expert. She learns to tell one person from another, male faces from female. Because she sees her parents more than anyone else, she learns to recognise them fastest. This is due to a combination of genetics, environment and behaviour. Johnson and Morton's theory provided a mechanistic account of how these different elements interact. Johnson calls this process 'interactive specialisation' and he developed the theory further with colleagues in a highly influential book called *Rethinking Innateness* (Elman et al., 1996).

This experiment was also directly responsible for my career in baby science. Thanks to this research, Birkbeck recruited Mark Johnson as a professor in 1998 and invited him to set up the Centre for Brain and Cognitive Development, also known as Birkbeck Babylab. One of the first people he recruited was my Ph.D. supervisor Denis Mareschal, whose lectures to undergraduates on infant development first inspired me. Reading *Rethinking Innateness* on Denis's advice convinced me that I wanted to be a baby scientist too.

The Joke Is on Scientists

My favourite study from when I was a Ph.D. student looked at a similar early ability of newborn babies. In 1977 Andrew Meltzoff and Keith Moore (Meltzoff & Moore, 1977) published a remarkable short paper that appeared to show that newborn babies are little jokers. The paper contained a wonderful set of pictures that captured the essence of the experiment. On the top row were three pictures of Meltzoff sticking out his tongue, opening his mouth wide and pursing his lips. Below this were three pictures of three tiny infants copying him. The infants were between 14 and 17 days old, and all seemed to have a twinkle in their eye. I had that image as my computer desktop wallpaper for a long time. It never failed to cheer me up. Unfortunately, the study has not fared well in the test of time.

Going further than Johnson and Morton's study, here we seemed to see babies doing something even more amazing than turning their heads towards a face. The babies in Meltzoff and Moore's study were imitating an adult. They could copy facial expressions without ever having seen their own faces and long before they could have learned from positive feedback. The original study also used unusual hand gestures. Like tiny wannabe rappers throwing gang signs, the babies appeared to imitate the gestures.

It was always a controversial finding, because the tasks are a lot more challenging than simply recognising faces. Rather than a simple face-detector circuit, being able to imitate in this way would require a brain area that recognised several different facial expressions or bodily gestures. And this would all have to be encoded genetically. Explanations along this line were given, invoking 'mirror neurons' or a special social-imitation module in the brain.

Some experiments seem to have confirmed the finding, including one with newborn chimpanzees. Others couldn't reproduce the effects. A recent review of all the published studies on the topic (Oostenbroek, Slaughter, Nielsen & Suddendorf, 2013) concluded that only tongue protrusion seemed to be consistently reproduced. This need not be imitation; it could be that babies stick their tongues out a lot when excited, or it could be a simple reflex that disappears with age. This last explanation seems the most parsimonious.

Newborn babies have a range of simple reflexes. We've already encountered the rooting and breast-crawl reflexes that let them find the nipple for their first feed. They also have a walking reflex. Hold them over a flat surface and their little legs will make a sequence of tiny steps in a fair imitation of walking. Newborns also have a grasp reflex. They hold on and do not let go. The ability to cling to mum's fur is important to a newborn primate so that they don't fall out of the tree. All monkey and ape species have this ability and baby humans retain it. I vividly remember being taught in Denis Mareschal's undergraduate class that you could leave a newborn baby dangling by its own grip from a washing line if you wanted. I have yet to meet anyone who has tried this and I don't recommend it. When babies do feel like they are falling they throw their arms wide and then draw them closely in again, decreasing the chance of falling and then getting a better grip. This Moro reflex doesn't benefit human babies, but is an inbuilt reflex left over from our primate past.

Following their critical review, Oostenbroek and colleagues decided to conduct a definitive study of infant imitation to see if this was also a reflex. Newborn infants were shown 11 different gestures at several different points between one and nine weeks of age (Oostenbroek et al., 2016). The expressions included the mouth opening, tongue protrusion, happy and sad faces, some finger movements and some simple sounds. The babies did not imitate. They were just as likely to show matching as non-matching gestures. The study did find that tongue protrusion, mouth opening, happy faces (smiles) and 'mmm' sounds were all commonly produced. Analysis showed that the patterns of previous experiments could be reproduced if not all possible alternatives were included. But this was not a sign of imitation. For example, the best way to make the babies smile wasn't to smile at them but to make an 'mmm' sound.

In fact, the one big giveaway as to why such an early ability to imitate might not have been a real thing was the lack of strong effect for smiles. After all, if you were Mother Nature building in a set of endearing imitations for a brand new baby to show off, what would be the most obvious one to include? A smile would have had babies winning friends and influencing people from day one. Yet these studies didn't find that. Babies did smile and stick their tongues out from a very young age, but it was not in response to someone else doing the same thing.

I find this very interesting because it suggests those first smiles are not signs of politeness. They are signs of pleasure. Babies might smile early on, but only if they mean it. Besides which, babies' genuine smiles are recognisable as such. In adult research there is a well-established difference between pleasure smiles and social smiles. The genuine smile of pleasure is known to psychologists as the Duchenne smile after the person who described it, Guillaume Duchenne. Non-Duchenne social smiles have the grin, but the smile stops at our eyes. Duchenne smiles light up a whole face. Not only is there a big grin, but additional muscles around the eye socket called the orbicularis oculi cause the crinkles at the sides of our eyes. This can even be seen in the puffy, bewildered faces of newborn babies and in Nadja Reissland's ultrasound scans.

Just google 'smiling newborn baby' for some endearing examples. There is one famous picture on the internet of a smiling mother holding her smiling newborn. The caption says that the baby is just seven seconds old. I use it a lot in my talks. I have never found the original source, but the smile is unmistakable. I was also lucky to hear from my fellow infant-laughter researcher, Francesca Cornwall, who researches how laughter might help in nursery education. She knows the difference between real and social smiles. Naturally, she paid close attention when her son first smiled at three weeks old. It was a broad grin with full activation of the orbicularis oculi. Being a conscientious scientist, she even took a photo.

Although it takes 12 muscles to create a real smile and only 10 muscles for a social smile, a real smile is easier and earlier. A real smile is spontaneous and involuntary, signalling genuine pleasure or satisfaction. A social smile is harder because it is a voluntary action, something we must choose do. And the failure of imitation studies suggests that brand-new babies don't have a way to do this.

This underlines the ultimate importance of smiles and laughter. They are not there for social niceties. Babies are social beings from the start, but it is a slow start and begins with authenticity. The smiles seen in the womb are real. The first smile you see will be real, an indication that the baby is happy. But if newborn babies smile when they are happy, the next question is: what makes them happy?

Chapter Three: The Simple Pleasures

I am besotted by a being who is, at this stage, just a set of emotions arranged around a gut.

— Anne Enright, *Making Babies,* 2005

Milk Drunk

If you want a picture of pure pleasure, you can't do much better than a milk-drunk baby leaning on mummy for support. And if you want to find such picture, just head over to Instagram and scroll through the #MilkDrunk hashtag. According to the Milk Drunk Diaries blog, there are nearly 100,000 of them, every one showing that unmistakeable state of sleepy, blissed-out satisfaction tiny babies get when they are warm and full to bursting with fresh milk.

The founder of that blog, Sophia Walker, was largely responsible for popularising the tag. But its success is because this is something any new parent can recognise – once you realise what it is you are seeing. This was Walker's own experience. As she describes in one of her columns, the first week back home was rather nerve-racking. She and her husband were googling every twitch, gulp and squeak that their newborn son made to check it was as expected. Then, 'One night mid-feed, my baby passed out and went limp on me. So alarmed was my husband that he went to dial NHS Direct, but Dr Google came to the rescue just in time and enlightened me that my baby was in fact… milk drunk!'

It is a label that nicely captures a recognisable state of being in very young babies. They can be happy drunk, daft drunk, dribbly drunk, passed-out drunk, wobbly drunk or even angry drunk. As Sophia explained to the press when she got swept up in this latest viral baby phenomenon, 'There's nothing more adorable than a woozy baby contented with a full tummy and milky moustache! It's such a hit because it's something every parent knows and loves. It's a bit like being part of a special club!'

Sophia's story captures a lot of the ups and downs of those first few weeks home from the hospital. For parents, their lives are never the same again. Even if you've read all the manuals, you aren't prepared for parenting. Like learning to swim, reading about it in a book doesn't prepare you for the actual practicalities or the shock of the first time your head dips beneath the surface. Now just keep going for another 18 years.

For babies, the first few months of life outside the womb aren't so different from life inside. To settle a baby in this stage we swaddle her or rock her gently, both attempts to recreate the familiarity of the womb. This is the 'fourth trimester'. Mostly this time is about sleep, food and growing. But it comes with raw emotion and building intimacy with caregivers. The umbilical cord has been cut and in its place is a new dependency and a new sense of agency. These two facts are related and essential to understanding the first few months. Now that babies are not receiving a steady supply of nutrients, there is far greater variety to their experience. They get hungry. They get thirsty. They get angry. They get upset. They also learn they can do something about it. With the support of their caregivers, this is the beginning of their emotional life and their sense of self, and the start of happiness.

The World Health Organisation (WHO) recommends breastfeeding within one hour of birth and keeping going if you can. A massive review entitled 'Breastfeeding in the 21st century' published in the medical journal *The Lancet* in 2016 concluded that breastfeeding is better for mother and baby. It protects infants against infections, diabetes and obesity. In mothers it protects against breast cancer and may reduce the risk of diabetes and ovarian cancer. It reduces the risk of infant death but does not seem to help with allergies or asthma (Victora et al., 2016).

The benefits have long been recognised in lower-income countries. In 1982, Cesar Victora and Fernando Barros started following the fates over 4,500 babies born in their home city of Pelotas in the south of Brazil. They found differences between breast- and formula-fed babies that were detectable 30 years later, including higher IQs and incomes (Victora et al., 2015). Their study found many benefits to breastfeeding and helped change attitudes to it in Brazil and elsewhere. However, in richer countries the benefits may be more marginal. A study of a large British sample by my colleague Sophie von Stumm concluded that 'breastfeeding has little benefit for early-life intelligence and cognitive growth from toddlerhood through adolescence' (Stumm & Plomin, 2015).

The Lancet study, a summary of 28 other summary studies, each looking at a different aspect of breastfeeding, was huge. Victora, the lead author, argues strongly that breastfeeding is beneficial in rich and poor countries alike. His co-author, British paediatrician Simon Murch, is quoted as saying, 'Breast milk is the ultimate personalised medicine for infants.'

Sucking Equals Milk Equals Comfort

However, the most important thing about feeding time is not the food. It extends to comfort and security. Baby bliss starts in the land of milk and mummy.

Especially at the start. In their first few weeks babies need to learn that 'sucking equals milk equals comfort'. This is the mantra of Penelope Leach in her book *Your Baby and Child*, a modern classic in parenting that has sold over 3 million copies. If you want a practical guide to parenting from someone who also understands the science, it is my top recommendation. Originally published in 1977 and revised many times since, it is a worthy successor to Dr Benjamin Spock's hugely influential *Baby and Child Care*, first published in 1946. Leach's book carries forward the same idea that relaxed, confident parents have an easier time and raise happy babies. The emotional experience of the child is always at the forefront of her advice.

One reason that mothers give up on breastfeeding is that it takes time for the baby to understand the situation. A hungry baby does not know he is hungry or dehydrated. He can be uncomfortable and listless or furious and uncooperative. This is understandable – even as adults we often get cranky with the world when all we need is a cup of tea and a biscuit. Breast milk can do the same job for a baby. Foremilk, which comes first during a feed, is more watery. This quickly stops the baby feeling thirsty. Hindmilk, the latter part, is richer in fat. This will make the baby feel full and content, although it is not always that easy. A very upset baby cannot feed. This also upsets mum and the stress hormones can affect milk production. Both need to be calm and connected before feeding will be effective. This is what Dr Leach wanted her readers to realise: that for babies, eating is emotion. Infant emotions are complex, so mealtimes can be complicated.

Feeding is the beginning of bonding. Bonding is more than just a parent's growing love for a baby; it flows both ways. Professor Ruth Feldman from Bar-Ilan University, Israel has been studying the parent–infant bond since the early 1990s. She says that the heart of the relationship in the first few months is how parents' mature physiological systems help regulate their infants' immature systems. And in Professor Feldman's opinion it all comes back to oxytocin.

Oxytocin is old. It is found in a huge range of species who last shared a common ancestor about 600 million years ago. Oxytocin has been around since then and has remained unchanged. This tells us that it is massively important. In humans, it helps coordinate the wiring of the brain early on and is both a hormone and a neurotransmitter. As a hormone, it is part of the endocrine system, having a general effect on many organs and brain areas. As a neurotransmitter it interacts with dopamine in our reward system and plays a central role in the amygdala, the emotional 'heart in our head'.

In mothers, oxytocin not only sends signals to the breast to release milk (the let-down reflex), it changes the brain. Immediately after a baby is born, mothers' brains are at their most plastic and adaptable in their adult lives. 'Baby brain' is real and useful. A new mother might feel more forgetful and unfocused, but is becoming more empathic, better at mirroring and at emotional regulation. Oxytocin acts on fathers too. The more they are involved in childcare, the more their behaviour changes (Feldman, 2012). Increases in parental oxytocin lead to increases in infant levels, although the effects in babies are harder to measure, as there is no non-invasive test for oxytocin levels. But we know that premature birth and environmental stress reduce oxytocin, while sensitive caregiving increases it. Synchrony is central to that sensitivity. Professor Feldman has looked at how parents and babies respond to each other through touch, eye contact, shared emotions and the sounds they each make. These connections are all at their strongest when a baby is feeding. And the connections are there whether feeding via bottle or breast.

A feeding newborn is held closely, at just the right distance to feel your heartbeat and see your face clearly. The synchrony between parent and baby is a feedback loop. The more in sync a parent and baby are early on, the better the baby's ability to regulate her side of the interaction. This improves the quality of the interaction and so parent and child can be even more in tune. Emotional stability helps the baby interact with the world, and the effects are long-lasting.

Professor Feldman has followed many babies from three months old all the way through adolescence. Some of the children in her studies are now turning 20. She finds that parental attentiveness in infancy sets children on a path to greater sociability and greater empathy into their teens and beyond (Feldman, 2007, 2015). Of course, the opposite could happen too: a bad beginning could make everything more difficult. But the hopeful message here is that these systems are not fixed and gradual improvements accumulate. Paying more attention today makes things easier tomorrow, and so on.

Good Breast, Bad Breast

One curious thing about Professor Feldman's research is that it lets us reinterpret ideas first stated in the object relations school of psychoanalysis. In the 1930s Melanie Klein proposed that a baby's response to early feeding patterns could determine their future happiness and ability to form relationships. When a hungry baby is fed, the mother becomes the 'good breast'. When feeding is withheld, she is the 'bad breast'. Klein thought that long-lasting problems occur if the baby fails to realise that good breast and bad breast co-exist in the same person.

I must admit, the first time I encountered these ideas I found them absurd, and the florid language of psychoanalysis doesn't help. In 'A contribution to the psychogenesis of manic-depressive states', Klein says that:

> From the beginning the ego introjects objects 'good' and 'bad' for both of which the mother's breast is the prototype – for good objects when the child obtains it, for bad ones when it fails him. But it is because the baby projects its own aggression onto these objects that it feels them to be 'bad' and not only that they frustrate his desires: the child conceives of them as actually dangerous – persecutors who it fears will devour it, scoop out the inside of its body, cut it to pieces, poison it – in short compassing its destruction by all means which sadism can devise. (p.145, Klein, 1935)

This is, of course, ridiculous. Babies do get distressed but fear none of the horrors Klein imagines. They are not capable of this kind of catastrophising. Their problems are more immediate. If they are hungry or uncomfortable they want that to stop. Once they are fed they are happy. Ruth Feldman's research shows that their early interactions have long-lasting consequences, though not in the way Klein would have it.

Even many psychoanalysts were shocked by Klein's lurid imagery. Yet they welcomed her ideas as an improvement on those of Sigmund Freud. Freud was never too bothered with babies as babies. Freudian psychoanalysis is a form of talking therapy for adults that relies on stories, archetypes and mythologies. Stories are more human and more relatable in therapy, but for Freud the stories had to be interesting. Therefore, he often paints a picture of our deeply complex subconscious as full of primitive emotions and unresolved conflicts. He imagines we are born flawed, full of love, hate, envy, fear and guilt. Actual infancy is not like this, but he did not let that get in the way of a good story. For Freud, babies were there to blame for the faults of the adults they become.

Freud's youngest daughter Anna and fellow analyst Melanie Klein did put children first. They both worked directly with children and took children's emotional lives very seriously. Anna Freud published *Introduction to the Technique of Child Analysis* in 1927. Her work perpetuated her father's beliefs that our minds are compartmentalised into ego, id and superego, and that we progress through a series of clearly defined stages of psychosexual development. Klein published *The Psychoanalysis of Children* in 1932. She rightly saw that emotional development was much messier than Freud's neat stages. But she went much further in exaggerating the anger and anxiety of infancy.

After Freud's death in 1939, Anna Freud and Melanie Klein fought over Freud's legacy. In 1944, they agreed to disagree, and psychoanalysis divided into Freudian and Kleinian schools, and an independent group which disagreed with both of them. The Anna Freud National Centre for Children and Families in London has been carrying out important research on child mental health for over six decades, and Kleinian ideas are still very influential in Britain and Latin America. Arguably Klein's most important legacy was through two of her pupils, Donald Winnicott and John Bowlby. Both were trained as medical doctors and qualified as psychiatrists, and both already worked extensively with children before undertaking psychoanalytic training with Klein. Ultimately, they both rejected her dark and turbulent prototype of the mother–infant relationship.

No Such Thing as a Baby

There is no such thing as a baby, meaning that if you set out to describe a baby you will find you are describing a baby and someone. A baby cannot exist alone but is essentially part of a relationship.

— Donald Winnicott, *The Child, the Family and the Outside World*, 1964

Winnicott had a much more positive message for mothers than Klein: by and large, mothers will take naturally to mothering and will have unconscious knowledge of how to look after their babies, having been babies themselves. In 1943 he gave a series of talks on BBC radio entitled 'Happy Children' and discovered a talent for expressing himself in simple language. He was invited back to present many other programmes including 'Getting to Know Your Baby' in 1945, where he addressed himself directly to new mothers. He reassured mothers that they would be 'good enough' for their babies. In the first few months of holding, feeding, attending and attuning to the new baby, he said, the mother is the baby's world.

In his view, an attentive mother empowers her baby. She notices the baby is hungry and by feeding him quickly makes the baby feel powerful, calm and confident. The mother holds the world for the infant. Attention may seem a small thing, yet it makes a huge difference in the world of the baby. One other thing Winnicott got exactly right was his dislike for 'people who are always jogging babies up and down on their knees trying to produce a giggle'. He saw this as a selfish act, seeking entertainment from the baby rather than tuning in to the baby's own needs at that moment.

John Bowlby's work was similar but complementary to that of Winnicott. Whereas Winnicott remained within the object relations tradition, Bowlby was more influenced by biology, psychology and other sciences. He was inspired by and corresponded with Konrad Lorenz and other ethologists. He attributed much of the mother's caregiving skill and connection to her infant to evolutionary instincts rather than unconscious memories of her own infancy. From the perspective of the infant, he felt that real experiences and relationships were more important than thoughts and fantasies.

Bowlby worked at the Tavistock Clinic, a centre for the study and treatment of mental health problems in London. It is telling that when he took over the department for children, at the end of the Second World War, he renamed it the department for children and parents. During the war Bowlby had studied troubled children and childhood evacuees from London. He identified a common theme of extended separation from the primary caregiver as the cause of many problems. A few years later he would team up with Canadian Mary Ainsworth. They worked directly with babies and mothers and developed the hugely influential idea of 'attachment'.

> Intimate attachments to other human beings are the hub around which a person's life revolves, not only when he is an infant or a toddler or a schoolchild but through his adolescence and his years of maturity and on into old age. (p.442, Bowlby, 1969)

I will revisit this in more detail in later chapters. For now, it is worth appreciating Bowlby's and Winnicott's work for what it achieved. Not only did they make it possible for theories of child development to trace a sensible path from the dark psychoanalytic fantasies of Melanie Klein towards Ruth Feldman's neurobiology of love, they also had a very large impact on the lives of many families. This included those they helped directly in their clinical work but many others too, in the way their work changed social perceptions of what constituted good parenting in postwar Britain. They helped parents move beyond the idea that harsh authoritarianism and cold aloofness were necessary to build character and prevent clinginess, and they spelled out very clearly the value of closeness, love and empathy. They empowered mothers to trust their own instincts over those of authority figures. Bowlby and Winnicott would both have been quick to say that all mothers can discover most of this for themselves.

In her memoir *Making Babies*, Irish novelist Anne Enright recounts her first feeds. Sitting up in the dark in her hospital bed, she wonders at her recently arrived daughter, a 'White Dracula' always hungry for milk, an intense look in her eye and complex emotions playing across her face. She is as amazed by her own ability to produce milk as by her daughter's ability to consume it. As the first few months unfurl, she keeps being surprised by the mysteries of motherhood. It is only much later that she decides:

> Motherhood is, for me, a simple thing. This is an achieved simplicity, and I'm quite proud of it.

What Is Pleasure?

One mystery attached to the milk-drunk baby is that we don't completely understand what is so enjoyable for her. We know she is eating to grow and that as she eats she is growing emotionally too. We know that a full tummy stimulates the vagus nerve to set off a cascade of chemical messengers, changing levels of insulin, ghrelin, leptin and others. We know these chemical changes will prompt her body to digest dinner and send the baby off into happy milk-drunk sleep. But we still don't know what pleasure is.

Ask a brain scientist and the answer is sometimes 'dopamine-based reward circuits'. As an answer this is mostly useless. Ask a psychoanalyst and they might say that pleasure is fulfilled desire. This is mostly useless too. Individually these answers are not wrong, but they don't add much to our understanding. Why do we enjoy what we enjoy? Why does this baby laugh when being carried downstairs, while this one is inseparable from Sophie the Giraffe? Why do I like Iron Maiden while you like Madonna? Why does anyone like opera?

Does it even matter? Writing in the 1890s, philosopher and

psychologist William James remarked that it was odd to even need to ask questions like 'Why do we smile when pleased and not scowl?' Most people would not think to ask this question. Maybe we like the things we do because they are intrinsically likeable. To paraphrase James, a mother hen would think it monstrous if any creature did not find a nest of eggs utterly fascinating and precious.

Economists and philosophers do get very excited about pleasure but I suspect this is mostly a reflection of how dull it must be to be an economist or a philosopher. Contemporary economists translate most things first into money and then into incomprehensible equations. It is not for nothing that they call it the dismal science. And if you want the opposite of a pleasant experience, I suggest you try reading the *Stanford Encyclopaedia of Philosophy*'s entry on pleasure (Katz, 2016).

To be fair to modern philosophers and economists, their ideas probably became so obscure because all the simple suggestions had already been made. You cannot make a career out of saying 'I agree with Aristotle' or copying and pasting John Maynard Keynes. Philosophically, the ancient Greeks covered most of the angles. Plato shared our common-sense notion that pleasure was the satisfaction of biological appetites and needs. A hungry baby stops being hungry. An overheating adult moves out of the sun.

Aristotle was dismissive of such animal pleasures and thought pleasure came from achieving a sense of mastery over the world. The fed baby is pleased with her own success in getting food. An adult enjoys art because they appreciate what it takes to make 'good' art. Epicurus, whose name has become synonymous with pleasure-seeking, took a simpler view that pleasure is freedom from pain, stress and 'trouble in the soul'. A warm, well-fed baby is happy because they're not unhappy, like a cat lounging in the sun. Epicurus said that pleasure is found in experiences, not thoughts. His ideas are often thought to advocate mindless hedonism, but his philosophy is more subtle: he urges us to cultivate immediate pleasures because the greatest destroyer of pleasure is anxiety about the past or future.

Adam Smith, the founder of modern economics, also had some wise things to say about pleasure. Smith's ideas on free trade and the market economy grew out of his concerns for people and society. In his view, Epicurean pleasure was too simplistic and self-centred. The opening sentence of his 1851 book *The Theory of Moral Sentiments* explains his whole philosophy:

> How selfish soever man may be supposed, there are evidently some principles in his nature, which interest him in the fortune of others, and render their happiness necessary to him, though he derives nothing from it except the pleasure of seeing it.

In other words, we take pleasure in a feeling for the well-being of others. By this principle of 'mutual sympathy', Smith explains pleasure, pain, anger and grief. Early in the book he contrasts a poorly infant who can feel 'only the unpleasantness of the present instant' with the distress of the infant's mother.

Her own sorrow grows out of her imagining of her infant's helplessness and suffering.

Today the science of happiness is still in its own infancy, trying to get to grips with our simple pleasures, and this puts babies back on centre stage. When trying to understand happiness, neuroscientists are happy to agree with Aristotle that it can be divided into two parts, momentary pleasures and deeper satisfaction, or *hedonia* and *eudaimonia*, as the ancient Greeks would have it. Most research has focused on hedonic pleasure rather than eudaimonic life satisfaction, because meaningfulness and satisfaction are very hard to pin down. We know from our own experience that satisfaction is hard to find and harder to hold on to. Not only is it elusive, it is enigmatic, completely different from one person to the next. It also spreads out in time. Something might only be satisfying in retrospect. Not surprisingly, therefore, it has been almost impossible to localise in the brain.

Pleasure itself is more than just some nice sensation. Neuroscientists Kent Berridge and Morten Kringelbach call it a 'hedonic gloss' that overlays particular experiences, marking them out as different. Furthermore, they believe pleasure consists of three components: wanting, liking and learning. Liking is the experience of pleasure itself while wanting and learning are what happen before and after respectively, the anticipation and the afterglow (Berridge & Kringelbach, 2011).

Most of the research into pleasure is done on the pleasures of food, not least because food rewards work superbly in animal experiments. It's hard to ask a mouse or a monkey about their favourite song but they are very forthcoming about their food preferences. The same is true for babies. Once a baby graduates to solid foods, parents can expect many years of tantrums and stand-offs when their child is given food they do not like. Or do normally like, but do not want today, thank you, Mummy. For every face of food disgust there's another display of delight. Those vegetable rebellions contrast with the ice-cream smiles.

Amazingly, the faces pulled to convey these preferences are universal across our wider monkey family. We know this thanks to an unusual experiment performed by Berridge and colleagues back in 2001 (Steiner, Glaser, Hawilo & Berridge, 2001). First they gave sweetened water (with sucrose) and bitter water (with quinine) to newborn babies and filmed the faces they pulled. Then they did the same with a barrel-load of our monkey cousins. They tested 11 other species, including all the great apes (gorillas, orangutans and chimpanzees) and many fantastically named monkeys, including the red-capped mangabey and Humboldt's night monkey. They even threw in a mongoose lemur for good measure.

The basic finding was not too surprising: all 11 other species preferred sweet to bitter. The remarkable thing was that the facial expressions they made were almost identical. Baby humans and baby monkeys would all squinch their eyes and wrinkle their noses at the bitter tonic and they would stick their tongue out when given what was effectively lemonade. And when the videos were carefully analysed in slow motion, the expressions spread at similar rate across their faces once you adjusted for their size. The grimace spread more slowly for the gorilla than the golden-handed tamarind, but it was the same grimace. Interestingly, when expressing pleasure, only humans and the other great apes smiled.

The conclusion from this study is not only that all monkey babies love lemonade but that our hedonic responses are millions of years old. It is not surprising that fruit-loving members of the primate family all like sweet things. But our most recent shared ancestor with the monkeys of South America is 30–65 million years ago. The lemurs are even more distant relatives. The expressions on all our monkey faces are not identical, but they are close enough that we confidently say the reactions are the same.

An obvious retort to this is, 'So what? The simple pleasures of babies and monkeys are one thing, but surely this doesn't tell us very much about the refined pleasures of adults?' Actually, it might. Even the most sophisticated adult tastes for fine food, expensive wine or abstract art represent the same essential pleasure seen on the face of that happy baby marmoset.

This is the view of Paul Bloom. Bloom is a Canadian psychologist working at Yale. He is an expert on babies. He has written three books about them and what we can learn from them. But he has also written extensively on many other topics including morality, empathy and pleasure. In his book *How Pleasure Works* (Bloom, 2011) he puts forward an 'essentialist' position that all pleasurable things share an essence that makes them pleasurable. So, for example, artworks attributed to great artists widely enjoyed by connoisseurs suddenly lose value and appeal when revealed to be ingenious fakes, as they now lack the essence of the master.

Bloom does not talk much about babies, but their pleasures and preferences are the genesis of our own. One of my favourite sweets as a child was cherry lips, the hard, floral sweet that got stuck to your teeth and had a texture and flavour reminiscent of plastic. My mother ate them a lot when I was in the womb. That is very likely where my preference came from. (Where her craving came from, we don't know.)

Julie Mennella has investigated how flavour preferences are passed from mothers to babies. Working at Monell Chemical Senses Center in Philadelphia, her earliest work showed that when mothers drank a lot of carrot juice during pregnancy or while breastfeeding, their babies liked carrot-flavoured cereal when they started on solids (Mennella, Jagnow & Beauchamp, 2001). Appropriately enough, this was inspired by earlier work with rabbits. In 1994, Agnes Bilko and colleagues had found that baby rabbits would develop a strong preference for juniper berries if this was what their mothers had been fed. In the rabbits the preference was passed on even if the babies were only exposed to juniper in the droppings of nest mates. Naturally this was not tried with human babies, but the research shows that preferences can come from exposure in the womb or through milk.

Mennella's research team has tested vanilla, aniseed, mint and garlic, and all these can be passed from mother to baby. Our national food preferences could be passed on with mother's milk. Mennella, who is Italian American, likes this as an explanation of her own preference for garlic-heavy cooking. However, these preferences can only go so far. A lot of green vegetables are quite bitter and young children are more sensitive to this. Getting children to eat their greens is still beyond the reach of science.

Shits and Giggles

Lifted off the potty,
Infants from their mothers,
Hear their first impartial
Words of worldly praise:
Hence, to start the morning
With a satisfactory
Dump is a good omen
All our adult days.

— W. H. Auden, 'The Geography of the House' in *About the House*, 1965

In his book *About the House*, poet W. H. Auden set himself the task of reflection on life from the perspective of each room. The poem composed on the lavatory is a particular highlight. Talking about the primal pleasures of pooping, he delights in combining toilet humour with intellectual reflection on Luther, Freud and St Augustine. He recognises the delight we all experience in a satisfactory dump and links this back to those earliest of days when we get praise for this act of self-control. He even goes as far as to suggest that 'All the Arts derive from/ This ur-act of making'. Paraphrasing slightly, he means that all acts of artistic creativity are but examples of their authors trying to reproduce the pleasure of a good poo.

Never having been a parent himself, Auden underestimates the amount of praise parents have heaped on babies for 'good pooping' from far before you can get them on the potty. Straight from birth, well-timed poos draw approving coos from proud parents, which is just as well, because parents quickly learn that newborn babies create joy and shit in large quantities.

Not surprisingly, nappy manufacturers encourage this celebratory approach. Mamia and Pampers have both produced 'poo face' adverts. Each is filled with a montage of babies making unmistakeable faces as they happily fill their nappies. Filmed in glorious slow motion and set to stirring classical music, both the adverts won industry awards. Which is completely reasonable, once you stop to wonder how they captured these emotion-laden bowel movements.

When faced with poo, parents are well advised to take the same cheerful attitude. There is no escape. A typical Western baby gets six to twelve nappy changes a day, which could add up to 3,000 in the first year alone. That's a lot of poo and pee, and not all of it will end up in the nappy. Poo magically gets everywhere – on baby, on baby's clothes, in the bath, on furniture, on pets, on everything and everyone. And even if poo is not in evidence, a fair amount of time gets devoted to assessing and evaluating the consistency of it and sniffing baby to see if it is time for yet another change.

It is amazing how often boy babies spray wee everywhere when you lay them out naked for a change. My parents' nickname for me when I was brand new was 'Fountains Addy', as my display of waterworks when being changed could rival the famous local tourist attraction of Fountains Abbey. One gleeful six-year-old once told me, 'I've got a new baby brother and the only time he smiles is when he pees.' The delight on his face suggested that this might be the best bit about having a new brother.

In *Making Babies*, Anne Enright observes that: 'Babies need you to smile at them when they are feeding and also – and more urgently – when it is coming out the other end.' Freud thought something similar. One famous aspect of his theory of psychosexual development was the concept of the anal-retentive personality. Freud believed that babies moved from a stage of oral fixation in the first year, which was all about the breast and eating, to an anal stage from 18 to 36 months, which was focused on bowels and pooing. He worried that if parents were overly demanding during toilet training, a baby would grow up to be inflexible and too focused on cleanliness or following rules.

Freud was both right and wrong. His description of the anal-retentive personality type would become the basis what psychologists now call obsessive-compulsive personality disorder (OCPD), a real disorder affecting 2% of the population. But neither OCPD or the closely related anxiety disorder obsessive-compulsive disorder (OCD) have any basis in toilet training. I will not delve much further into Freud's theories because they are not scientific and they are not informative about babies. Whenever Freud was talking about early childhood, it was to illustrate some idea he had about adulthood. The terminology and mythology of psychoanalysis is an attempt to grapple with the complexity of a whole human. Psychoanalysis is trying to find a story that patient and therapist can use to improve the patient's outlook on the present. The underlying truth of the theory is a secondary consideration.

Curiously, Freud viewed laughter, like pooing, as a 'discharge phenomena'. Far be it from me to say Freud was full of shit, but perhaps this was the start of his problems. The idea goes back to an essay on the physiology of laughter by Herbert Spencer in 1859. Spencer was a philosopher, anthropologist, sociologist and political theorist. He's relatively obscure now, but in the 19th century he was a philosophical superstar. A prolific author and the most famous intellectual in Europe, he was the Bertrand Russell or Stephen Hawking of his day.

Spencer was a major influence on Freud. Spencer's theory of laughter is neatly summed up in the phrase 'laughter is a smile that burst'. He believed that feelings that pass a certain pitch need to vent themselves bodily. This hydraulic model of emotions building up and having to be discharged became central to Freud's theories. But while this makes sense for accumulating poo satisfyingly dumped, it is a broken metaphor for our emotions.

Chapter Four: SLEEP!?

The smile that flickers on baby's lips when he sleeps – does anybody know where it was born? Yes, there is a rumour that a young pale beam of a crescent moon touched the edge of a vanishing autumn cloud, and there the smile was first born in the dreams of a dew-washed morning – the smile that flickers on baby's lips when he sleeps.

— Rabindranath Tagore, 'The Source' from *The Crescent Moon*, 1913

One early surprise for new parents is that babies will often smile, and even laugh, in their sleep. The Bengali poet and polymath Rabindranath Tagore clearly encountered this, as his poem 'The Source' describes. It occurs early in *The Crescent Moon*, his sequence of poems on children and childhood, published in English translation in 1913, the same year he won the Nobel Prize for Literature. In typically lyrical fashion, Tagore identifies the magical moments in everyday life that others overlook. Another poem, 'Baby's World', marvels at how different the world appears for babies. In 'The Source' Tagore pauses only briefly to wonder if babies' sleeping smiles are a signifier of infant dreams before chasing away after other ideas with a childlike exuberance of his own.

A similar scene occurs a few pages later in a poem called 'Sleep-Stealer'. Tagore describes a mother who puts her baby down for an afternoon nap and gets on with some chores. Not long after, she returns to find her baby wide awake and crawling across the room. 'Who stole sleep from our baby's eyes?' she asks as she laments another visit of the sleep-stealer. For what other explanation could there for this baby who ought to be tired but is resolutely wide awake? The poem entertains a brief fantasy of finding the sleep-stealer's nest and stealing back all the missing sleep.

One gets the sense that, even though Tagore had five children, someone else was usually left holding the baby. Unlike most parents, Tagore is rather amused by the wide-awake baby. He finds it rather funny and there is little sense of frustration. Or exhaustion: there is no mention of the mother's own stolen sleep, let alone his own.

To be honest, I used to be a lot like Tagore. I find babies enthralling and constantly wonder what is going on in their little minds. I spend a lot of time observing them closely. Not being a parent myself, it has often been quite an intellectual engagement, especially when it comes to sleep. I wonder about babies' dreams. I know that they wake up quite a lot and I wonder why. But all of the babies that come to our labs are wide awake or just finishing a nap. We specifically schedule them that way. We want babies at their most alert when they come to see us so that they do their best on our tests; because we are not usually studying sleep, the topic doesn't always come up. Their parents often look tired, but they're too polite to make a fuss.

It was not until I went to Brazil that I appreciated just how important babies' sleep patterns are to parents. I was sitting in the compact living room of Ana Luiza, a 40-year-old mother of three. We were on the 10th floor of a well-kept high-rise building in the Vila Moraes district of São Paulo. The apartment was small, simple and immaculate, but it still felt homely. The elder two daughters, eight and four, shared a bedroom that just about fitted their two small beds. The youngest, another girl, aged one, slept in the cot at the foot of her parents' bed. For an hour I had been listening to Ana Luiza talking about her youngest daughter's sleep. Not speaking very much Portuguese at the time, I only understood about a fifth of what was being said. But the overall message came over loud and clear. Babies' sleep is a huge preoccupation for parents. This was why I was in Brazil.

I was there with Cinthia Oliveira from Pampers and Luciana Martins from Ketchum, Pampers' PR consultants. Ana Luiza was the sixth mother we had visited. We met Yasmin and baby Felipe, who slept in a cot covered in hundreds of tiny skull-and-crossbones stickers. We met Gabriella and baby Giovanna, who both wore lots of pink. We met super-talkative Helena and her super-smiley baby João. At each visit, the mothers easily filled the hour we had to spend with them talking about sleep, bedtime routines and nappies.

One nice thing about being a baby-laughter researcher is the charming and surprising directions it takes you in. Two months living and working in São Paulo is certainly a highlight in that respect, although when I first heard about the project I thought it might be a joke. In February 2015, out of the blue, I had received a call from Luciana. She introduced herself and said that Pampers Brazil was interested in using science to prove that babies wake up laughing. At first, I laughed myself, as this is not normally how science happens. But it turns out she was quite serious.

Across the world, Pampers already had some adverts on the theme of 'giggly mornings'. These featured happy babies bouncing up and down in their cots. The adverts proclaimed that babies waking up in Pampers nappies wouldn't be unhappy because they would not be uncomfortable or wet. The Pampers team in Brazil wanted to go a bit further than this. They wanted to work with me to test this claim scientifically.

As someone who had left the corporate world behind to hang out with babies, I readily admit I was dubious. However, I watched a few more of Pampers' short information films for new mums. I was impressed. They were very clear and scientifically sound. I then went to speak my colleague, Professor Annette Karmiloff-Smith, who had worked with Pampers in the past. Annette is a legend in our field. She was the last Ph.D. student of Jean Piaget, the founding genius of developmental psychology, and she herself was the author of numerous incredibly influential books and papers. At the time of our conversation she was 76 and still working hard, although sadly she died a year later.

Annette told me she had worked successfully with Pampers on several baby sleep projects. She put me in touch with Dr Frank Wiesemann, the head of the Procter & Gamble baby care research team. Chatting on the phone with Frank, I was greatly reassured about prospects for the project. Frank is cheerful, pragmatic and direct with a typically dry German sense of humour. He too laughed at the overenthusiasm of his Brazilian colleagues to prove 'with science' that babies wake up laughing. But as we discussed it, we realised that very little research looks at how babies' sleep quality affects their morning mood. So I booked my flight to Brazil.

The 'Experts'?

Preparing for our study, I began to consider infant sleep properly for the first time. It turns out that parents, experts and scientists see sleep quite differently. Parents, like other victims of sleep deprivation, will agree to anything that gets them a good night's sleep. The experts cater to this desperation, promising the magic formula for a 'clockwork baby' or otherwise failsafe sleep training. Meanwhile, the scientists are still trying to discover why we sleep at all. All the purposes of sleep are still something of a mystery to us.

Here in the UK, Gina Ford is the most infamous of baby experts. A former nurse, she has sold countless books promising a Contented Little Baby to any parents who adhere to her strictly timed routine of feedings and bedtimes. A typical entry in her guide requires that a three-month-old baby 'must be awake two and a quarter hours from the time he went down, regardless of how long he slept' (Ford, 2004). This doctrinaire approach strongly divides parents. Many swear that the techniques work miracles. For others G**a F**d is worse provocation than any four-letter word. Her name was banned on the website Mumsnet after angry outbursts from opponents of her approach brought legal threats from the woman herself. These commenters were repelled by requirements like leaving babies to cry themselves to sleep.

There is something monomaniacal about Ford's insistence that everything must obey a schedule. In her book, parents of a freshly hatched six-to-eight-week-old are confronted with a schedule of 52 bullet-pointed instructions for each 24 hours. And it seems like neither they nor the baby are allowed a single lie-in during the first year. Not even on weekends. Every day at every age the timetable begins, 'Baby should be awake, nappy changed and feeding no later than 7 a.m.' For many parents with babies that seem never to sleep there is plenty to cling to in the confident predictions of Ford's books. But her advice appears not to be based on any research beyond her personal experience advising parents. It says something that 12 out of the 21 titles suggested in 'Further Reading' in *The New Contented Little Baby Book* are other books by Gina Ford.

The strict routine from the very beginning of life even contradicts the views of Dr Richard Ferber, the man whose name has become synonymous with this approach to sleep training. For better or worse, American readers will recognise this 'cry it out' method as 'Ferberisation', although Ferber never uses the term himself and does not require parents to enforce a routine as rigid as Ford's.

Dr Ferber founded the Pediatric Sleep Disorders Center at Boston Children's Hospital in 1979. His 1985 book *Solve Your Child's Sleep Problems* was the first to suggest a routine of putting babies to bed while still awake and leaving them to cry in their cots for longer and longer each night. The theory is that they will not rely on closeness to a parent to get to sleep and will get progressively better at sending themselves back to sleep. Critics say this method does not stop babies feeling distress, but merely teaches them not to manifest it.

Over the years, Ferber has been misquoted by fans and critics alike. Firstly, he introduced his method only for parents confronted by big problems with infants settling. If your baby is mostly sleeping fine, he sees no upside to sleep training. Secondly, it will not work for babies under six months. These babies need to wake up in the night to feed and Ferber does not recommend sleep training under this age. Nor does he insist on a strict routine for the rest of the day.

My own favourite expert is Dr Harvey Karp. Dr Karp would agree with Ferber's claim that 'a baby's needs are best met when everyone is getting good sleep'. His book *The Happiest Baby on the Block* (Karp, 2002) is all about good sleep for the baby. But it takes the exact opposite approach to Ford and Ferber. In his view the key is to attend to the baby and soothe him or her quickly.

Dr Karp has a sequence of five 'S's to be deployed in turn to soothe a baby who will not go back to sleep. First there is swaddling the baby. By stopping the baby from flailing, you give her one less thing to worry about. Second you could try putting the baby on her side or stomach for a while. Third, you can literally shush the baby with a continual white-noise 'shhhhhh' sound. In some ways, this is the aural equivalent of swaddling. Fourth, you can swing the baby. Starting out by jiggling them quickly but gently and moving into a swing to rock-a-bye baby. The fifth S is sucking – on breast, finger or dummy.

The good news is that most methods seem to work to some degree. A big review of 52 different sleep interventions, by Jodi Mindell and colleagues (Mindell et al., 2006), found that sleep training led to improved sleep. It also worked if parents stayed in the room but ignored the baby. So did having a standard bedtime routine that involved target bedtimes and putting babies to down to sleep while drowsy. There was even success with a bizarre technique of 'scheduled awakenings', where parents work out the times the baby was likely to wake up crying and deliberately wake them up 20 minutes before this to pre-emptively console them. The 'awakenings' are then gradually removed.

All of these studies used parental reports, which are subjective. It is arguable that they are just training parents to perceive fewer problems. Two more recent studies looked at Ferber-style controlled crying using actigraphy, which uses a special Fitbit-like device to record babies' movements throughout the night. In both studies, parents in the controlled-crying group reported more improvements. But, crucially, the objective actigraphy data showed sleep was no better with sleep training than in the control group, which was not subjected to sleep training (Gradisar et al., 2016; Hall et al., 2015).

We do know that crying increases babies' heart rates, blood pressure and cortisol levels, which, arguably, are not going to help him or her sleep well. We do not know what, if any, long-term effects there might be to leaving babies to fend for themselves. No well-controlled studies of the long-term effects of sleep training have ever been done. In the absence of strong evidence in favour of controlled crying, Dr Tracy Cassels, author of the Evolutionary Parenting blog, argues that sleep training should be avoided. I agree that the attentive caring approach is better.

Why Sleep Anyway?

Parents wondering why their baby will not sleep can take dubious satisfaction from the fact that the world's best sleep experts do not fully understand why any of us need to sleep in the first place. Despite our best efforts, we have no comprehensive theory of sleep. We do not entirely understand what sleep does in adults, let alone in babies. One reason most psychologists have stayed aloof from these discussions is because we know that sleep-deprived parents do not want to hear, 'It's complicated.'

Sleep is not my main topic of research, so to learn more I strolled down the corridor to speak to Goldsmiths sleep expert Professor Alice Gregory. On first impressions Alice seems too young and too impish to be a professor. But as you look down the forbidding titles on her list of over 100 scientific papers on sleep, you realise that that Alice is a world expert and that sleep is, indeed, complicated.

As luck would have it, Alice had just finished writing *Nodding Off*, a popular science book about sleep. The subtitle is 'Understanding sleep from cradle to grave', which makes her the perfect person to explain sleep to me. I started her off with the BIG question. What is the purpose of sleep? And the answer was that this is the wrong question. 'Some scientists say to ask why we sleep is as ludicrous as to ask why we wake. Researchers no longer talk about the function of sleep. They now agree that it has multiple functions,' she said. The big four are restoration, metabolism, learning and what, for the lack of a better term, might be called therapy.

The restoration hypothesis was championed in the 1960s and 1970s by husband and wife sleep researchers Ian Oswald and Kristine Adam at Edinburgh University (Adam & Oswald, 1983). In its original form, it was pretty simple. It said that that deep sleep restores you physically and dreaming restores you mentally. Restoration is not simple 'rest'. Sleep is not that restful. In fact, you burn 12% more calories while asleep than you do sitting watching television. It is an active time. Sleep is not about saving energy through inactivity and does not seem to be about simple physical recovery. Go out and run a double marathon (I will wait right here). For a couple of days afterwards you will sleep a bit sounder and a bit longer and then your sleep will be back to normal (Shapiro et al., 1981).

Central to the restoration hypothesis are the distinctions between different types of sleep. Sleep happens in 90-minute cycles: first we descend through four stages of deeper and deeper sleep, then transition into a period of dream sleep. Then we repeat the cycle over and again until morning. Dream sleep is also known as rapid eye movement (REM) or paradoxical sleep. It is REM because under the eyelids the eyes appear to dart about. It is paradoxical because the brain is just as active as if you were awake. I will come to dreaming presently, but first let us examine deep sleep more deeply.

Only birds and mammals dream, but all animals need to sleep. Reptiles, amphibians, fish, insects and even tiny nematode worms all sleep. Sleep seems to be standard for all animal life and yet this is strange, because sleep is such a vulnerable state to be in. From evolution's perspective, surely it would be better to simply rest and recover while remaining alert? This is not what happens and so there must be very good evolutionary reasons why not.

One clue comes from the fact that without sleep you will eventually die. Some gruesome studies in the 1980s by Allan Rechtschaffen and Bernard Bergmann at the University of Chicago proved this, at least in rats. In one elegantly sadistic experiment researchers built a circular chamber with a horizontal rotating disc at its centre suspended over shallow water. The chamber was divided into two rooms by a vertical wall down the middle. A single rat sat on each semicircular half of the platform. The brainwaves of one rat were recorded and whenever that rat entered a sleep state the platform started to rotate. This required both rats to keep moving or fall in the water. Thus the monitored rat could never get properly to sleep. The other rat had to move at this point too, but it could sleep whenever the first rat was awake and active. Both rats experienced the same environment but only one was being deliberately deprived of all its sleep. Guess which rat died? In the words of the original study: 'Experimental rats suffered severe pathology and death; control rats did not.' (p.182, Rechtschaffen et al., 1983)

Eight out of eight actively deprived rats died or had to be euthanised after between five and 33 days of sleep deprivation. In their last hours the sleep-deprived rats had skin lesions, swollen paws, balance problems, muscle problems and weakened brainwaves. After death they showed ulcers, haemorrhages and lung problems. Control rats were a little frazzled but otherwise fine. Although unluckily for them, they were also killed when their partner died so comparative autopsies could be performed. (It never ends well for lab rats, whichever experimental condition they are in.)

Undoubtedly, similar effects would happen in humans, although there is only one recorded fatality that I am aware of. In 2012, Chinese football fan Jiang Xiaoshan died after reportedly staying awake 11 nights in a row to watch Championship football broadcast from Europe. In 1964, 15-year-old Randy Gardner stayed awake for a world record 11 days and 25 minutes. Randy did not seem to suffer many ill effects, but others who have attempted similar feats have become angry and delirious. Guinness stopped listing the record shortly after because attempts to beat it could be dangerous.

A scientific consensus is emerging that certain physiological processes need us to be asleep. Interrupting sleep stops these happening, with disastrous consequences, and the reasons have deep evolutionary roots. We do not know how or when life started, but for as long as there has been complex life there have been cycles of night and day and this baked sleep deep into our metabolism.

Biology is all about metabolic cycles and they always have two halves. Anabolism, where bigger molecules are constructed out of smaller ones, which usually consumes energy, and catabolism, where big molecules are broken down into smaller ones, which usually releases energy. Basically, this is all life is, an unending battle to keep the cycle turning. The metabolic theory of sleep says that the most efficient way to achieve this is to divide catabolism and anabolism into two separate activities: wakeful activity and sleeping reconstruction. What theorist Markus Schmidt calls 'running the machine' and 'maintaining the machine' (p.126, Schmidt, 2014).

Of course, that alone does not explain sleep. But the cycle of night and day has been lining up the chemistry of life into circadian rhythms for a very long time. Some of the earliest forms of life, ancient plants and algae, were already doing it: photosynthesis does not work at night. Animals are not constrained in this way, but it makes a lot of sense to specialise as a nocturnal or diurnal animal. Otherwise you are at an evolutionary disadvantage to other species which are nocturnal or diurnal specialists. The original land animals were probably all diurnal: awake in the day and asleep at night. They would have been cold-blooded and, like modern reptiles, they needed the sun to warm them up to a working temperature. They had no choice but to sleep at night. But this left a night-time niche to be exploited. Our ancient ancestors may well have become warm-blooded to turn nocturnal. (Once you are warm-blooded you can take your pick.)

Markus Schmidt's metabolic hypothesis can also explain why our sleep comes in cycles. He agrees with Oswald and Adams that deep sleep restores you physically while REM sleep restores you mentally. The surprising thing is that REM sleep requires even more energy. While dreaming, warm-blooded animals turn off their thermoregulation to devote even more energy to rebuilding the brain, so our core temperature rises during our dreams. If they went on too long, we would overheat, so we switch back into deep sleep, where we cool down again. The smaller mammals gain and lose heat quicker and so must go through their cycles faster. Mice have more sleep cycles than elephants and they dream less. Humans will have longer cycles it if is cold. A study in 1983 found that we average 109 minutes per cycle if the ambient temperature is 13°C compared to 85 minutes at 25°C. You sleep better in a cool bedroom.

Another role of our nocturnal downtime seems to be some neural housekeeping. Biochemist Robert Cantor sees sleep as an 'inevitable consequence' of how our brains use neurotransmitters (Cantor, 2015). Each firing of a brain cell sends a splash of neurotransmitter chemicals across the synaptic gap between two cells. Most are absorbed on the other side but, over time, concentrations build up in the brain fluids and fat layers surrounding the cells. This stops the cells functioning efficiently and so the brain needs to shut down to sluice the excess chemicals away. Amazingly, the network that does this, called the glymphatic system, was only discovered in 2013 (Xie et al., 2013).

The synapses themselves need some attention too. Synapses are what make our memories and represent our experience. They are the junctions between brain cells and all through the day we are forming new ones. Researchers Giulio Tononi and Chiara Cirelli (2014) have proposed that sleep prunes back these synapses, supporting their idea with a massive study of mice brains. Tononi explains that, at a functional level, 'Sleep is the price we pay for learning.' Probably this couldn't easily happen while those circuits were being used, but the details are still a something of a mystery. How does the brain know which connections to prune and which to keep? Part of the answer lies in dreams.

Live Your Dreams

Did you ever play Tetris? Really play it? For hours at a time? Giving in to its frustrating addictiveness and keeping going for 'just one more game', again and again? And then did you dream of falling oblongs and angular Ss and Zs? What about your dreams while learning to ski, surf or salsa dance? Or during your first week in a new job, new city or new country? Dreams are always more vivid in novel situations.

Scientists have always known that dreams are a replay of your day. But their exact purpose is still mystery. When I ask

Alice Gregory about dreams, she shakes her head sadly. 'I've always avoided dream research. Dreams are really hard to study scientifically.' This is understandable, as how do you objectively investigate this most subjective of experiences?

Take one simple example, the rapid eye movements that give REM sleep its name. Researchers suspect that our eye movements correspond to what we are seeing in our dreams, but they have never been able to prove this. The closest was a team from Paris who studied people with a sleep disorder that means they are not fully paralysed during REM. Their muscles partially act out their dreams. There were strong correlations between their actions with their eye movements. For example, their eyes would 'look' towards their hand if they grabbed for something or scan up and down if they appeared to be climbing (Leclair-Visonneau et al., 2010). But as proof of dream content, this is tenuous at best, as other researchers have pointed out.

Nevertheless, scientists are still keen to unlock the secret of dreams. If sleep is as old as life, dreaming might have started a mere 220 million years ago. All warm-blooded creatures dream, except whales and dolphins, which sleep with half their brain at a time to avoid drowning. The body is paralysed during REM sleep, making the dreamer extremely vulnerable. This is why predators sleep more than prey and why many large quadrupeds get by on just a few hours a night. Horses, which spend 98% of their time standing, sleep very little and giraffes can go up to a week without any sleep at all.

Amongst primates, humans are unusual in that our sleep is shorter, deeper and with more dreams. Humans in hunter-gatherer societies seem to average about six and a half hours a night. Compare this to chimpanzees, which get 11 hours a night, or our old friend Humboldt's night monkey, which sleeps for 17 hours every day. Human adults spend 25% of their sleep time in REM sleep. This compares to around 10% for other primates, and 18% for chimps (Samson & Nunn, 2015). For human babies, REM sleep takes up 45% of their sleep time, and given that they sleep 18 hours a day, that's eight hours of dreaming. From this perspective, dreaming is important to all animals, but most of all for human babies.

The two benefits of dreaming seem to be learning and happiness. There is lots of evidence that sleep consolidates learning and memory, and helps regulate our emotions. Dreaming seems to be the trick to integrating new experiences into our model of the world, preparing us for an unknown future. It also helps deal with how scary that can be. Countless studies with adults, animals and babies have shown that sleep improves learning. But learning is a much misunderstood concept. Most learning is nothing like school. It is not a parade of prepared facts packaged up to be swallowed whole. Learning is more like a rat running around a maze or a teenager playing video games or a baby just being a baby. There is no teacher and at first you have no idea what you are supposed to do. But by exploration and trial and error, you get better.

One of the biggest problems with the world is that mostly it does not make a lot of sense. This is true for rats, babies and even adults. Most things we encounter are irrelevant, incomprehensible or maybe just uninteresting. We will see in later chapters how much of a challenge this is for babies and how they solve these problems while they are awake. But here we are interested in what sleep and dreams add to this process.

Memory and learning are about survival: we remember the past to help us in the future. Learning is the ability to generalise; to know how to apply past experience to present problems. This cannot happen while we are awake, as we have already got enough stuff going on, like finding food, avoiding predators, playing with our toys, learning to stand, learning to talk. But in sleep old and new can come to an accommodation. This is where dreams come in. They mix yesterday with everything that went before and try to make it all fit together.

The brain area called the hippocampus coordinates the process. The hippocampus seems to be the seat of memory, acting as librarian in indexing the episodes of our lives. Memories are spread out across the brain and the hippocampus knows where to find them – often quite literally, because the hippcampus is also the home of our mental maps. It is active when we move around, and highly active when we dream. This may be why such a lot of our dream imagery is so geographical and so episodic.

Why are dreams so crazy? Primarily because they are not supposed to make sense. Dreams are about trying things on for size. Our psyche is involved in non-judgemental brainstorming, just in case some interesting connections are made. These flights of fancy attempt to connect the new to the old in ways that might turn out to be useful. Clinical psychologist Magdalena Fosse and colleagues asked 29 people to keep detailed logs of their daily activities and dream diaries for two weeks. They found that 65% of the dreams reflected activity but only 1% replayed actual events (Fosse et al., 2003). The details of your day do not matter, but concepts do.

A recent study illustrated this by showing that sleep enhances memories that the brain expects to be of future use. Ines Wilhelm and colleagues (2011) asked participants to learn words, learn a finger-tapping task or memorise locations of objects. Sleeping after the task improved their performance, but only if participants thought they would have to remember things. If they did not know they would be tested, sleeping on things was no better than staying awake.

The lesson here is if you want to learn something, sleep on it. While writing this chapter I was on a road trip through California. The first day on American roads, with the country's unfamiliar customs and a strange left-hand-drive car, was terrifying. Every lane change felt like a near miss, every junction a strange dilemma. I slept quite fitfully, with vivid dreams. The next day was not nearly as bad. The day after was almost fun. My driving had improved overnight.

In this context, nightmares make a lot more sense. They are a form of disaster planning, a whole set of worst-case scenarios, training us for situations that may help us outwit predators and rivals. There is nothing deliberate or rational about this. Your brain goes into overdrive and recombines the events in new and interesting ways that might kill you so that hopefully, in the daytime, they do not. No wonder dreams are so emotional. They would not be nearly as much use if they were not. As we grow, our genuine fears of the unknown are reduced, but with a good imagination you will still be having nightmares into your old age. I would wager that even tigers have nightmares. We dream up ghosts, aliens, zombies and vampires because you just never know what might kill you. Even falling blocks. And not only are nightmares good for our survival, they are good for our sanity.

Overnight Therapy

Sleep is the best meditation.

— Tenzin Gyatso, His Holiness the 14th Dalai Lama (b. 1935)

The Dalai Lama is a big fan of neuroscience. He attends neuroscience conferences and encourages his monks to lie in brain scanners to help study the minds of expert meditators. Even so, he was wiser than he realised when he said that sleep is the best meditation. The Dalai Lama gets up at 3 a.m. and spends about seven hours every day meditating. But he still appreciates the benefits of a good night's sleep and heads off to bed around 7 p.m. to make sure he gets almost eight hours a night. The goals of meditation are to know your own mind with clarity and to face the world with equanimity. You probably cannot find time for seven hours of daily meditation, but your night's sleep is serving a similar purpose.

According to Alice Gregory, while sleep researchers continue to argue about what the most important function of sleep is, more and more of them are happy to agree with the description of sleep as overnight therapy. The phrase originates with

Matthew Walker, a sleep researcher from the University of California in Berkeley, who thinks that this is one important role of dream sleep. It helps us learn from our terror without being paralysed by it. Right now this is mostly theory, but Walker and his colleagues have assembled a range of evidence that supports the idea.

Just next door to the hippocampus is a brain structure called the amygdala. It deals in emotion and, especially, in fear. Using brain scans and electroencephalogram (EEG) recordings, which track brainwave patterns, Walker has discovered that during REM sleep the circuits connecting the amygdala to the hippocampus are active, but the amygdala's ability to respond is suppressed. This weakens the emotional salience of our experiences. To test this, he showed people scary pictures (such as sharks, snakes or angry faces). After a night's sleep, one group rated pictures less scary with fewer rated at the most extreme intensity. For another group, which stayed awake, the pictures were still perceived as scary (Van Der Helm et al., 2011).

In the 1980s, American sleep researcher Rosalind Cartwright tracked the nightmares of people with depression. Amazingly, those with the worst dreams were the ones who recovered best. Walker believes that a breakdown in this process could be responsible for post-traumatic stress disorder (PTSD). Soldiers and victims of violent crime or disaster all suffer repeated nightmares, and the emotional aspect of the original events never weakens. Giving these patients drugs that suppress the amygdala function seems to help them sleep better and start to heal.

Disrupted sleep is a common feature of mental illness. Much

of Alice Gregory's own research has been trying to understand if bad sleep is a symptom, side effect or cause of mental illness. At the moment, Alice tells me, we do not have a good answer. But this can be a good place to start a clinical interview.

'We know that sleep is associated with all sorts of elements of psychopathology,' she says. 'Sometimes in a clinical setting it can be useful to start by talking about sleep. If you have a patient in your office and start asking them about their depression or their family, it can be difficult for them. But talking about sleep is a good way to build rapport. Because who minds talking about their sleep? It that sense, it's useful. But poor sleep can be a predictor for the onset of some other difficulty you are interested in.'

This all suggests that Freud had it completely backwards. Freud thought dreams were about wish fulfilment. He believed that they were a 'royal road to the unconscious'. He encouraged his patients to recount their dreams, which he would then interpret with lurid symbolism. But the lesson is that you should not be trying to remember your dreams or interpret them. You should let them go. If you do want to interpret your dreams, you should ignore the narrative, be thankful for the drama and try to hold on to the originality.

Happy Brazilian Babies

Back in São Paulo, we decided we use a sleep diary to understand what makes a good night's sleep. We recruited the parents of 117 babies, who told us a range of basic information about their family and their baby, including how old the baby was, where they slept, what nappy they wore and so on. Every morning for 10 days the parents filled in a set of questions about their babies' sleep the night before. They told us what time they went to bed and woke up, how many times the baby woke up or was changed in the night, and in what state their nappy was in the morning. We also asked parents to rate how happy and how energetic their baby was in the morning and what was the first thing to make them laugh.

Our study included babies from two months to two years old. The first thing we noticed was that they all slept similar amounts of time during the night. Babies averaged just under 10 hours a night. The difference between younger and older babies is the amount they sleep during the day. Typically, newborn babies sleep an average of 16 to 18 hours each day. This gradually drops to 12 to 14 hours for two-year-olds, which is still 50% more than adults.

Of course, there was a lot of variation. Some nights for some babies it was only five hours; some nights were over 13 hours. Sometimes the data showed babies sleeping a negative number of hours per night. Maybe it felt that way to the parents. But we attributed this to a sleep-deprived parent putting the times in the wrong columns. We corrected the mistakes where we could. The clearest pattern we found was that the earlier the baby went to bed, the more they slept. Bedtimes could vary a lot, but the babies would always wake up at a similar time. This makes sense, as there is less leeway in a family's morning routine. But we found parents rarely had to wake their babies up.

An interesting comparison arose when we repeated our survey with 142 British babies, all aged between seven and thirteen months. There were lots of nights where parents reported no wakings but, overall, the average number of wakings reported was higher than in the Brazilian study. In Britain there were more nights with many wakings, including one poor mother who reported 15 wakings in one night. British babies averaged 11 hours' sleep per night, over an hour more than the Brazilian babies. There's nothing magic or lethargic about British babies, but they get put to bed several hours earlier than in Brazil and are out of bed an hour earlier.

In the British survey we also asked the mothers about their own sleep quality and found that it depended very heavily on the number of wakings and barely at all on the total length of sleep. Parents do not suffer too much if bedtime is a bit late or waking too early. They do suffer with every extra disturbance in the night.

Science can explain the apparent paradox of why babies can get lots of sleep while managing to keep their parents awake all night. The short answer is that babies sleep differently. This is to do with sleep cycles. Babies are small mammals and in line with the theory that smaller mammals have shorter sleep cycles, their sleep cycles are 50 to 60 minutes compared to adults' 90 to 100. This means they not in sync with their parents, and will often come out of their sleep cycle as their parents are sleeping more deeply. This totally sabotages the restfulness of parents' sleep.

It can also take a surprising amount of time to get babies settled again. Their sleep cycle is back to front. Adults drop quickly into deep sleep and move into REM sleep at the end of their cycle. Babies start with the lighter REM sleep (called active sleep in babies) and move into deep sleep 20 to 25 minutes later, which means it can take that long before they are settled. This all makes babies' sleep seem more problematic for us than it is for them.

Speaking to Alice about this, she tells me, 'The way we define sleep problems depends upon our expectations. I might want to put my child in the cot and have it sleep through until morning. In that context, if it cries, I might see that as a problem. But if I want to cuddle my baby and if it wakes up I put it in a sling and carry it around, I might say my baby sleeps like a log.'

Given this variability, our next result was remarkable. We found Brazilian babies almost always wake up very happy. Across all the babies and all the nights, we found that parents rated morning happiness at eight, nine or 10 out of 10 in 80% of cases. Which is certainly not what my mornings are like. Is this true? It certainly seems that way. An unrelated study by Jodi Mindell found something similar. In a survey of 1,300 Brazilian families, she found that 77% of the babies were waking up happy (Mindell & Lee, 2015).

Interestingly for Pampers, we found some curious effects of nappies on sleep. Generally, babies were full of energy in the mornings, with 60% of babies rated an energetic eight, nine or 10 in the morning. There were some babies on some mornings who were more sluggish, being scored at two or three out of 10. When I peered into their nappies (so to speak) I discovered that these babies had the driest, unsoiled nappies. It seemed as though these babies were the most comfortable and so had still been sleeping, only to be woken by their parents. They didn't seem any less happy, though. Generally, the more sleep a baby got the more energetic they were in the morning.

Morning happiness could also depend on the type of nappy. When we divided the group into those in more absorbent nappies and those in the cheaper ones, we found extra sleep made babies happier in good nappies but not in bad ones. Babies benefit from extra sleep if they are comfortable. Although there was a caveat to this. Recall that our British babies slept a whole extra hour. Overall they were not as happy as the Brazilian babies and their nappies did not affect their happiness as much. Are Brazilian babies just more happy? Are they more sensitive because it is warmer in Brazil, leading to lighter sleep? As we say in so many studies, more research is needed.

Was Pampers right to think that babies start the day laughing? Laughter is spontaneous and fleeting, so it is difficult to capture in numerical data. Therefore, every day we asked parents to answer the open-ended question: 'What was the first thing to make your baby laugh this morning?' We had 1,157 individual answers from the Brazilian parents, which seems like a lot of giggly mornings. Seeing their mother for the first time that day or playing games were the most likely things to make the babies laugh. Surprisingly, the moment of changing nappies was the next most popular response, making that even more popular than seeing their daddy. This fits with the theory that infants laugh most in social situations. When a mother is changing a baby's nappy, it is one of the few times when the baby has her undivided attention, and this is probably why the babies enjoy it so much.

To finish my visit to Brazil, Pampers arranged an event with many local 'mummy bloggers' and their babies. We gathered in a wonderfully vibrant play centre and I talked them through our results (with the help of a translator – my Portuguese was still in its own infancy). The overall story was very positive. These babies were benefiting from their sleep more than we normally give them credit. Whatever their night was like, they usually woke up happy and refreshed. This was unaffected by their personality. If you want a baby to sleep more, just put them to bed earlier. Brazilian babies seemed remarkably happy and did indeed wake up laughing. I was happy too because Cinthia, my host from Pampers, showed me how to pour blue liquid into a nappy, just like in the commercials.

Sleep Like a Baby?

People who say they sleep like a baby usually don't have one.

— Leo J. Burke, clinical psychologist

There is a reason we put babies to bed in cages: they wake up a lot. So do you. But when you wake up in the middle of the night you go back to sleep. You've had a lifetime of practice at this. Most of the time you do not even notice that you have woken up. Babies and children have yet to learn this particular skill. This can be frustrating and exhausting for parents but, as Dr Ferber himself says, the majority of babies are doing just fine and do not need any special coaching.

Yet if you visit the parenting shelves of your local bookstore you will find almost half the baby section taken up with books on sleep. These books are incredibly repetitive and incredibly popular. *Healthy Sleep Habits, Healthy Child* by Marc Weissbluth, MD runs to 660 pages but it has sold over a million copies.

Providing parents with routines to follow at bedtime does make them more aware of their own bad habits. This gets away from the situation where babies are training their parents to always come running. But there is no magic formula that will provide you with a 'clockwork baby'. It would be a miracle if there was. Each baby is different and so is each night. However hard you try to enforce a routine, life does not work that way. Equally important are the ebbs and flows of baby development, which mean that what worked last week might not be applicable this week. Parents will often be kept guessing and there will always be some sleepless nights.

Very rarely do baby sleep manuals say why sleep is good for us or what it achieves. They miss the big picture of just how deeply sleep is ingrained in our biological inheritance, and do little to reassure parents that except in very exceptional circumstances babies' sleep will run itself, rebuilding and repairing the body and brain. These books certainly never celebrate those night-time wakings for what they are: the sign of another successful sleep cycle completed.

Babies and children need a lot of sleep and they will get it. They sleep a lot because they are doing a lot of all the things that sleep is good for. They are growing physically. They are building their brains, creating and connecting synapses. They need their sleep to process everything they have taken in. Every new day is a new adventure in an alien land, a new level of their challenging and immersive video game to master. They are integrating vast amounts of new information and so they need lots of REM sleep. Perhaps most importantly of all, sleep is the therapy they need to cope with all the intense emotions they feel. It is often a scary business being a baby, but sleep seems to work, because they wake up laughing, ready for another wild ride.

At the end of our conversation, I ask Alice if being a sleep researcher helped with her own children's sleep. She said: 'When my first son was born, I'd been studying sleep scientifically for around ten years. However, just like many other parents, I wasn't prepared for just how difficult the marathon of night wakings can be. Being a parent also reinforced to me the idea that a child's sleep always needs to be considered in the family context. One of my sons occasionally had seizures during the night. That meant that my ideal of letting him self-soothe at night was sometimes replaced with me lying on the floor of his room holding his tiny hand and anxiously watching his every breath. As long as safety is put first, family preferences should be respected.'

In 2011 another poem about wakeful babies caused a big splash. Author Adam Mansbach was struggling with his toddler's bedtimes. He jokingly suggested to fellow parents among his Facebook friends that someone ought to write a storybook with the title *Go the Fuck to Sleep*. They readily agreed and pointed out he was the perfect person to do it. He teamed up with illustrator Ricardo Cortés to create a very sweary storybook for parents. Each page featured a sweetly illustrated verse ending with an increasingly desperate plea to his daughter to please go the fuck to sleep.

Even before it was published, the book was a huge viral hit after a PDF version was leaked online. Millions of people shared the text, and hilarious audio versions were recorded by surprising celebrities, including Morgan Freeman and Werner Herzog. The official audiobook was read by Samuel L. Jackson. Mansbach's book struck a chord with frustrated parents everywhere and was a common joke gift for sleep-deprived friends and relatives.

The theme is not that different from Tagore's 'Sleep-Stealer'. A young child wide awake when by rights they should be sound asleep, and the adults are at a total loss. The subtle amusement of Tagore may have been replaced 100 years later with the incongruous comedy of Samuel L. Jackson in full four-letter flow. But the sense of humour is not too different. We know babies need sleep. We know they will not be persuaded by reasoning. The evidence is that sleep training will only help up to a point. Sometimes, seeing the funny side might be the only solution.

Chapter Five: First Touch

A Newborn Baby's Most Important Sense

Never miss an opportunity to hold a baby.

— Mary Ainsworth, pioneer in the study of infant bonding, 1978

This chapter shows how important touch and close human contact are to the health and well-being of very young babies. Touch is a baby's first and most important sense. Operating from before birth, and well before sight, sound and smell, touch is our most ancient sense. Most mammals are born blind and helpless and depend heavily on a mother's touch at birth. Humans aren't much different. It might seem obvious, but science has taken a long time to catch up. Only thanks to a truly transformative discovery in 2005 are we beginning to appreciate the importance of this ancient mechanism and the reason why a mother's hug lasts long after she lets go.

It is a remarkable story but, be warned, it contains a lot of rodents! At first, this won't seem to have too much to do with laughter, but be patient. Our ability to thrive on surprise and to share a joke both build from our sense of security.

As adults in the Western world, we live in a sedentary, visual culture. We underestimate the power of touch and movement. For babies, touch is their first and most immediate contact with the world, and movement is their first means of exploring. Together they let babies establish their sense of self and build their knowledge of their own body. At the start of life, touch and holding are as almost as important as mothers' milk. Overwhelmed by the confusing sights and sounds of their new world, very young babies rely heavily on the simpler signals of touch and smell. Light touches on their cheek provoke them to turn their heads, rooting out a nipple. Sucking on the fingers can soothe them when not nursing. Mouthing at objects remains the favoured method of exploration for most of the first six months.

Perhaps most important of all, human touch of all kinds has a vital role in starting your child's social development. That was the message of Mary Ainsworth. Working in the 1960s and 1970s, Ainsworth was a Canadian researcher who was interested in the attachment a baby has to his mother. She was trained in London by John Bowlby, who first put forward the idea of attachment theory. Attachment, in Bowlby's words, is 'lasting psychological connectedness between human beings'. It starts in infancy but crucially, according to Bowlby, it has evolutionary origins and is not learned. The idea is that infants have an inbuilt need for parental reassurance when stressed or fearful. In simple language, when babies get scared, they want their mummy.

This contrasted to the prevailing theory at the time. Behaviourists who worked with rats learning to press levers for food rewards saw babies' connections to the mothers through the same lens. Their theory was that because the mother fed the baby, the baby became attached to the mother. In the early 1950s Bowlby had observed that babies and young children became very distressed when separated from their mothers and could only be soothed by their return. Reassurance from a stranger would not help, much less a 'food reward'.

Behaviourism may seem absurd from our perspective. Its attraction was that it was 'scientific'. Behaviourists could carefully control all the parameters of their experiments. Hungry rats and pigeons would be placed inside mechanical contraptions that would carefully dispense individual food pellets whenever they pressed the right lever. The scientists could plot pretty graphs of how quickly the animals learned. You don't have to be a scientific genius to know that this wouldn't work with young children. To be fair to the behaviourists, people playing fruit machines and one-armed bandits behave almost identically to rats receiving randomised rewards. But it wouldn't tell you anything about a baby's relationship with his mother.

Mary Ainsworth's contribution was to come up with a way to study this relationship. In the late 1960s she invented the 'Strange Situation', a procedure for assessing how a baby copes with separation from his mother. It is still used today, but only with infants over 12 months old, so it is a little early in our story to talk about it. Suffice to say, if Mary Ainsworth offers you advice on bonding with infant, it's a bit like Gary Kasparov offering you advice on how to play chess. You should listen.

Whenever Ainsworth was interviewed towards the end of her long and groundbreaking career, she always offered the same advice. If you get the chance to hold a baby, you should take it. You shouldn't just say hello and pull a few faces, you should pick the baby up and make a proper connection. Once you are holding a baby it is harder to ignore it. You must give it your attention. You must tune in to it in a way you don't have to when the baby is in a seat or otherwise at a distance. You also make it easier for the baby to tune in to you. The baby benefits from a better quality of interaction.

Obviously, for the nine months before birth mothers have no choice but to carry their babies around 24/7. The passenger is far from passive; pregnancy is an active time for the baby. It's dark and muffled in the womb but babies can still go exploring. By only the eighth week of pregnancy foetuses can move around and have a sense of touch. Their skin sends them signals as they move, and they start to touch their faces and suck their thumbs. The foetus is curled up like a prawn, so her hands are naturally near to her face. This provides an excellent opportunity for her to learn. Coordinated signals from the nerves in the hand and from the face provide feedback on the location of various features and how they are arranged. This is one of the reasons why even very young babies start putting things in their mouths – they've already had lots of practice.

Kangaroo Care

When we appreciate how much an unborn baby is learning, we get a greater sense of how much of a change it must be to be born. During pregnancy mother and baby are in incredible symbiosis. Foetuses are sensitive to mothers' hormones and stress. Mothers respond to unborn babies' activity levels. For most newborn babies this partnership continues in a new and different way. Full-term infants have become very familiar with this environment but they're ready to cope with life outside the womb and a parent who is there for them 24 hours a day.

For premature babies the story can be quite different. On top of the trauma of losing the perfect incubator of the womb, the infant faces physiological and psychological challenges caused by being whisked away from their mother and kept in a noisy and brightly lit plastic box surrounded by strangers. For all the advanced care and monitoring of a state-of-the-art intensive care unit, it seems that a cuddle from mother can do it better. That is the wonderfully simple idea behind kangaroo care.

Kangaroo care was originally developed by Professor Edgar Rey Sanabria in 1978. He worked on the newborn intensive care unit at the Instituto Materno Infantil in Bogotá, Colombia. It was an invention born out of necessity. A shortage of equipment and personnel meant that there were not enough incubators for all the premature and low-birth-weight babies being born in the hospital. Professor Sanabria suggested that if the babies were able to breathe on their own then they should be given to their mothers to be cared for. He recommended direct skin-on-skin contact to keep the infants warm in the absence of incubators and to allow mothers to breastfeed at will. Amazingly, this worked better incubators alone.

Absolutely central to its success is the skin-to-skin contact between mother and infant. This is better for regulating infants' body temperature but also reconnects the infant to the rhythms of its months in the womb. Mothers experience a closer bond with their infant, have more success with breastfeeding and establish a better milk supply. They are also better able to cope with their situation, showing increased resilience and feelings of competence and confidence. Infants receiving kangaroo care sleep longer, cry less and are more alert. They grow faster, gain more weight and so can go home earlier. They also have increased survival rates and lower risk of respiratory disease, infections and other illnesses (Conde-Agudelo, Diaz-Rossello & Belizan, 2003).

These benefits are long-lasting. A recent study followed up a group of children 10 years after receiving kangaroo care (Feldman, Rosenthal & Eidelman, 2014). The researchers found that the mothers were more sensitive to their children, showing more maternal behaviour and lower anxiety. The children also showed lower stress responses and slept better. They did better on measures of thought and attention.

The overwhelming benefits of this simple physical reconnection between mother and baby has seen kangaroo care spread widely. It is now used in the majority of US neonatal intensive care units and it has also changed attitudes to the immediate postnatal care of babies in general. It is not only premature babies who can benefit. Extended skin-on-skin contact with mother and father is good for all babies and all parents. It is perhaps obvious with hindsight that this would be the case. But touch is invisible and its benefits are surprisingly, well, intangible. In our verbal, visual culture we often forget that we're merely mammals.

It leads to another question…

Is Caressing a Baby Like Stroking a Cat?

Babies don't purr. They would if they could. Caressing a baby has a lot in common with stroking a cat or dog. This may seem self-evident. Or perhaps it doesn't. Perhaps it seems offensive to compare your cute little angel to domestic animals. Until very recently science was silent on the subject but, in just the last few years, research has revealed that a human caress is paradoxical mixture of simple and sophisticated. After 30 years of searching, scientists have finally found nerve cells that respond to specifically to stroking. They found them in mice, but it was quickly confirmed that humans have similar receptors. Separate research has looked at so-called 'affective touch' and found that as far as the brain is concerned there is no such thing as a simple touch; the identity and relation of the person touching you always matter. Every touch is laden with emotion.

Your skin is rather remarkable: a flexible and stretchy waterproof coating that helps keep your insides in and bugs and parasites out. It helps with temperature regulation, aiding both insulation and heat dissipation. The skin is also your largest sensory organ. It has a wide range of specialist receptors for touch, pressure, pain, heat, cold, itch and injury. Most of these have been known about for years and years and are named for their discoverer. There are Ruffini corpuscles, discovered by Angelo Ruffini in the 1890s, which respond to sustained pressure. Meissner corpuscles (Georg Meissner, 1852) respond to light touch and texture. Merkel's discs are for sustained touch (Freidrich Merkel, 1870) and Pacinan corpuscles for vibrations (Filippo Pacini, 1831). And my favourite are the cold sensors discovered by Wilhelm Krause in 1860, which are known as the end-bulbs of Krause.

Imagine, therefore, everyone's surprise when in 2013 researchers discovered a new type of receptor cell in the skin that responded exclusively to stroking (Vrontou, Wong, Rau, Koerber & Anderson, 2013). The new neuron goes by the name of MRGPRB4+. The less-than-catchy name is not a result of all the good names being taken but a consequence of the fact that when it was originally discovered no one knew what it did.

The MRGPRB4+ neuron was associated with hair follicles but it did not seem to do anything. When tested in a test-tube the neuron did not respond to any type of stimulus. It was only when researchers labelled it with florescent markers to observe its action in real live mice did they discover that MRGPRB4+ responded exclusively to stroking. If they stroked the mice, the cells would light up; if they poked them, nothing happened. What's more, the mice preferred a chemical that stimulated this nerve to one that did nothing, proving that the sensation was pleasurable for them. They were measurably less stressed afterwards, showing it had a calming influence. All mammals have a version of MRGPRB4+, so stroking a baby makes them as happy as a tabby.

This probably goes back to the days when all mummy mammals licked their pups. Immediately after birth they had to lick away the amniotic sack to clear the mouth and nose to allow breathing. Licking can also start other bodily functions and can be a means of monitoring which pups are still alive. (Some carnivores will eat the babies that don't appear to be responding.) Licking also helps a mother know that her babies are her babies, helping her learn their scent and marking them with her own. Research has found that for baby rats, the amount of licking they receive can make a dramatic difference to their later life. This series of surprising findings has revolutionised our understanding of an age-old debate about nature versus nurture.

A Tale of Two Orphans

The experiment itself sounds like something from a story by Charles Dickens or Hans Christian Andersen. It involves identical twin orphans separated at birth and raised by good and bad foster parents. In this case the orphans were rats. And, not surprisingly, so were the stepmothers. There are two types of rat mothers. Some rats are neglectful and do not lick their pups very much. These rats are themselves high in anxiety. Other rats are nurturing and attentive, licking their pups often and carefully. These rats are calmer. These traits appeared to be passed on to their offspring. The goal of this experiment was to find out how.

The experiment was conducted by Dr Michael Meaney (which is a very Dickensian name). Dr Meaney and his colleagues at McGill University in Montreal took rat pups from their birth mothers and cross-fostered them. His initial sample were half good mothers and half poor mothers. Within an hour of birth pups were swapped from good mothers to bad and vice versa. The results were clear cut: good step-parents raised good children who went on to be good parents who also coped better with stress. The babies with anxious stepmothers became anxious mothers themselves. The differences in early experience were passed down the generations and they were passed on as a result of upbringing.

The key to the outcome was the mechanism by which those babies coped with stress. By regulating their babies' stress when they are young, the nurturing rats help set up the systems to allow the young rats to regulate their own stress. More dependence early on produces greater independence later. Firstly, protecting the pups from stress in the first few weeks gives their own stress-regulating system the opportunity to mature. Secondly, the type of care may cause differences that get wired into the baby rats' brains. In neglected rats the hippocampus becomes less sensitive to cortisol levels, which in turns makes the hippocampus worse at passing on messages to the adrenal glands to control the production of stress hormones.

Dr Meaney and his colleague Moshe Szyf believe this happens when a gene in cells in the hippocampus is turned off. Without the gene turned on, the hippocampus cannot send signals to the adrenal glands to halt the production of cortisol. In effect, the rat cannot calm itself. This does not change which genes you have, but can change which ones are active, by a process called methylation. All cells in an organism have the same DNA coding, with a complete set of all your genes. But different genes can be switched on or off in different cells. So, for example, some become brain cells while others become liver cells. Or in the case of the rat hippocampus cells, some can become good at managing hormones while some become bad.

There are numerous mechanisms by which information encoded in genes comes to be used or not. Methylation is just one of these. In fact, there is a whole subfield of biology dedicated to the study of these mechanisms, called epigenetics. Your epidermis is the top layer of your skin; an epicentre is the point on the surface immediately above an earthquake. Epigenetics concerns changes that happen on top of your genes.

These findings were the result of many years of careful research by Dr Meaney and his colleagues. But the proposal that a mother licking her pups causes methylation was not without controversy. It was popular with psychiatrists, as the idea that early experience has a profound impact on later life is a cornerstone of their field. It appears to connect to extensive research indicating that children who are abused go on to be abusers themselves. However, for the biologists who know a great deal about epigenetics, methylation is a very delicate mechanism that is difficult to study. They are used to studying it in single-celled organisms, like yeast living on petri dishes. They believed that it would be almost impossible to detect such changes in just a single area of the brains of rats. Moshe Szyf, himself a molecular biologist, describes the contrasting reactions:

> 'The psychiatry field is glad to have this mechanism they were missing,' he says. 'It was the thing that bothered them and now it's like, "Oh wow, this makes so much sense." But then the epigeneticists say, "Oh come on, that's just magic."' (p.148, Buchen, 2010)

In case it wasn't clear to you, in the world of science 'magic' is used as an insult. But whether by magic or not, the evidence is clear that wicked stepmothers are very bad for you. The paper was turned down by the two highest-profile science journals, *Nature* and *Science*. It was eventually accepted by *Nature Neuroscience* and published in 2004 (Weaver et al., 2004). It has since gone on to become the most highly cited paper ever published in that journal. It finally provided a biological explanation of how childhood environment can have long-lasting consequences for the future.

Recently, researchers have found direct evidence that touch will reduce a baby's reactivity to stress too (Feldman, Singer & Zagoory, 2010). There has even been a human version of the Michael Meaney study. Well, kind of: no baby scientists would be that wicked. Sarah Moore and colleagues from the University of British Columbia used data from thousands of baby diaries to find mothers who had either very large or very small amounts of physical contact with their five-week-old babies. Several years later these children were tested for gene expression and methylation. They did not find differences in the target genes but did find significant differences elsewhere in the genome and the high-maternal contact babies were epigenetically younger, which is a good thing (Moore et al., 2017).

Hugs are good, but before you rush off to lick a baby, it is worth remembering that our most recent common ancestor with rats and mice is a small, furry creature called *Protungulatum donnae*. Mr and Mrs P. Donnae lived about 63 million years ago at the end of the Cretaceous period. Quite a bit of evolution has happened since we were small, furry rodents hiding from dinosaurs and dodging comets. In fact, when it comes to babies, the story is less to do with licking baby rats and more like picking nits off a fellow Cro-Magnon. Perhaps that doesn't seem like much of an improvement. But touch for babies is the beginning of life as their social primate

Infant Massage

Use an oil to massage your baby that you would eat on a salad.

— The International Association of Infant Massage

Infants spend the first nine months of their existence in a perpetual cuddle, so it isn't surprising that they appreciate a good massage. A lot of research suggests that mother and infant both benefit from infant massage, and there's no reason why fathers and grandparents can't get involved too. It doesn't have to be official infant massage, either – any extended physical interaction with your baby is beneficial. Research shows that mothers who are most in tune with their babies are those who score highest for the amount of affectionate touches they give their little ones (Ferber, Feldman & Makhoul, 2008).

Massage has been tried with premature infants. But, unlike kangaroo care, the evidence for genuine benefits is mild. There is some evidence that massage helps babies gain weight and reduces the time they spend in hospital. One study followed up two groups of premature babies after leaving hospital and found that the group who received massage still showed better weight and better cognitive scores one full year later.

The researcher running that project was Tiffany Field. She is the world's leading researcher of infant massage. Her interest began in 1982 after noticing that massage calmed her own daughter, who was born prematurely. At the time she was a professor of paediatrics and psychiatry, but in 1992 she founded the Touch Research Institute (TRI) at the University of Miami Miller School of Medicine to focus entirely on research into touch and massage. In the three decades since it was founded the TRI has conducted research showing massage produces a wide range of benefits at all ages. It boosts the body's immune response, helps manage pain and increases alertness while decreasing stress. The benefits for babies and parents are particularly great – although Professor Field sometimes got carried away, once claiming: 'My daughter is taller and smarter than I am because we gave her touch therapy.' (p.3, Field, 2003)

In one study a course of infant massage helped depressed mothers improve depression scores and increased their sensitivity to their babies' needs during normal interaction

(O'Higgins, James, Glover, Roberts & Glover, 2008). When fathers massage their babies they become more expressive and warm towards their babies, and get more enjoyment out of physical games with them. Babies sleep longer and better if they get massages. They get to sleep more easily and wake up less. A group of 18-month-olds with problems getting to sleep received a month of daily massage 15 minutes before bedtime. When compared to a similar group who were read bedtime stories, they went to sleep more quickly and were less resistant to bedtime. When assessed by independent observers during the daytime, the massaged children were more alert, more active and happier.

No doubt there are many direct benefits for the baby that seem to arise from the physical stimulation of massage. The chances are that babies' brains are responding to touch in a similar way to those of rat pups, with gentle, soothing touch improving their ability to regulate their stress and their alertness. We cannot easily measure this in babies, but the underlying biological mechanisms are likely to be similar. Massage researchers think that an equally important feature is the two-way, non-verbal communication that takes place during massage. The parent must tune in to the baby, and babies are signalling and responding too. You cannot touch without being touched.

Babies react to their parents' stress too. When mothers were put in a stressful situation by being made to give a short presentation, their babies' own stress levels changed to mirror those of their mothers (Waters, West & Mendez, 2014). Every time you pick up a baby to soothe it, there are clear patterns of touch and movement associated with your calming voice. The baby learns to associate all these physical sensations with the reassurance they receive.

Once again, as body language is something invisible to us, we underestimate its importance. But it is particularly vital to very young babies. The first two years of life are a state of helplessness. Knowing that parents and caregivers are there to depend on is a crucial scaffolding for babies to build their understanding of the world, which is a mysterious and sometimes scary place. Having a familiar and reassuring starting point helps babies make sense of their environment. But we also forget that people are part of that. Understanding other people is the biggest mystery we face – and one we never completely solve. Massage and other soothing touch makes that interaction with others a little less confusing. We will see in later chapters the remarkable importance of having conversations with your baby. Massage is a conversation before words.

Chapter Six: Tickling, Tumbling and Toe-Nibbling

Round and round the garden
Like a teddy bear.
One step, two step,
Tickle you under there.
— Traditional English nursery rhyme, 1940s

At first glance, tickling is a whole bunch of paradoxes. Traditional theories of ticklishness suggest it is a defence mechanism against creepy-crawlies. But why would something so gruesome in origin be such fun? Why does a light touch feel ticklish but a slightly firmer one not? And if so, why is it that a poking, prodding tickle draws the most laughter? Why do you have ticklish toes while I have a ticklish chin? Why can't I tickle myself? Why do all babies seem to love it when lots of adults absolutely hate it?

Tickling babies has caused some surprisingly highbrow speculation on the nature of comedy. It also throws up some interesting philosophical conundrums about minds, bodies and our sense of the self. Tickling and other very physical games played with babies are qualitatively different from the soothing, social touch we encountered in the previous chapter. Touch, cuddles and caresses regulate emotions, while tickling and rough-and-tumble games accentuate them. These physical games tap into babies' awareness of their own bodies and, ultimately, their identity. These are things that are invisible to us. We have lived with our bodies so long it is almost impossible to imagine our bodies and ourselves not being identical. Trying to imagine not being me is even harder. But watching young babies start to grapple with these challenges reveals them to be things we learn.

The delight babies find in tickling and other simple physical activities, like splashing in the bath, is intrinsic to them becoming aware of their bodies and of how this makes them part of a wider world. Well before they try to sit up or start moving around, babies have a lot to learn about how they control their own movements. This important process of embodiment is a key principle of developmental psychology and we will see it is helping overturn four centuries of Cartesian mind-body dualism. Nice work, babies.

Medical researcher Thomas Mintz evocatively described a tickle as 'the itch that moves'. But if we were being precise, then any ticklish sensation that is like an insect skittering across your skin is an example of knismesis (pronounced nis-me-sis), while gargalesis is the word for the ticklishness of being poked in the ribs or grabbed on the knee. These were the two distinct types of tickle decided on by Stanley Hall and Arthur Allin in 1897, and researchers have been happy to go along with that classification ever since. Likewise, it is generally agreed that although knismesis is pleasant, only gargalesis leads to inescapable laughter. Mind you, it is only a handful of academics who ever use the terms. My spellchecker and the Merriam-Webster dictionary do not recognise them as real words.

When I ran my global survey of baby laughter I asked parents, 'What one thing is guaranteed to make your baby laugh?' The results could not have been clearer: tickling came out top, with more votes than the next four items combined (peekaboo, funny noises, funny faces and other people laughing). If parents want to make their babies laugh, tickles are the way to go.

Many of the first-ever laughs parents hear from their babies are a result of tickling. A parent of baby boy in the UK told me, 'His first laugh was in his sleep at about two weeks old; his first awake laughs were for tickles.' Another parent of a boy aged two months said, 'It was after I changed and fed him. I was talking to him and smiling at him. I tickled the sides of his face, telling him he was cheeky and very cute.' Several mothers reported that a dad's 'tickly whiskers' or bushy beard provoked the first ever laughs. One of my favourite quotes came from the mother of a three-month-old from the USA, who said, 'I was doing "chipmunks" on his stomach (rapid tickles with fingertips) and working my way up to his cheeks and he just went ballistic. It was the cutest thing I have ever seen.'

This simple joy in such tiny babies makes it seem that tickling is a primal force of nature. But how can we be sure this is something we are born with, not something we learn? Perhaps tickled babies laugh because their parent is laughing? In the 1940s, sceptical psychologist Clarence Leuba decided to test this possibility with his own two babies. From the babies' births, Leuba and his wife avoided tickling them during normal play. All tickling was under 'laboratory conditions'; Leuba wore a mask to hide his facial expression so the babies would not be laughing in response to his smiles. Tickling was a serious business and yet tickling provoked laughter in both babies at about six months old. This is older than most of the babies in my survey, but in the normal range. Although, let's be honest, Dr and Mrs Leuba were clearly not the most normal of parents.

Natural history suggests tickling is in our genes. Plenty of other animals love it too. Our pet cats and dogs, obviously. Shakespeare noted that trout like being tickled and some foolhardy soul discovered that sharks like it too. A video of Cookie the penguin from Cincinnati Zoo chasing his keeper's hand for more and more tickles has 14 million views. Meanwhile, tickling even provokes laughter in chimps, bonobos, gorillas and orangutans (Davila Ross, Owren & Zimmermann, 2009).

In the 1970s baby chimpanzees were observed making tickle requests. Usually it would be infants requesting tickles from their mothers, but tickle play was also common in juveniles (Plooji, 1978). These are some of the earliest communicative signals we see in chimpanzees. Mother chimpanzees tickle their very young babies on their necks and the babies smile and raise their arms defensively. One-year-old chimpanzees make the same smile and raised arm gesture before being tickled as an invitation to play. Amazingly, this might be true of all mammals.

Ticklish Rodents

Let's go tickle some rats.

— Professor Jaak Panksepp to his colleague Dr Jeff Burgdorf, spring 1997

I often think my job is weird: trying to figure out what babies are thinking and then trying to make them laugh. Brian Knutson's job was weirder. In 1994 he worked in a lab studying social interaction in young rodents. More specifically, his job involved him eavesdropping on baby rats as they played games. He discovered, to his and everyone else's surprise, that they appeared to be giggling.

Rats are intelligent, social creatures and like all mammals they are playful, especially when young. Play is such a universal feature of mammalian life that it must serve an important function. Scientists were not sure what that function was, so Knutson's job was to find out just what baby rats got up to in their spare time. He was observing some juvenile rats in rough-and-tumble play. One young rat would play-attack the nape of the neck of another and place its paws on the first rat's back. The attacked rat typically rolled away onto its belly to get away, whereupon the attacker playfully held the other rat down for an instant or two before the game moved on to other rat high jinks. Previous research had found that deaf rats played less, so he wondered whether their squeaks might be part of the game.

Rodents' vocalisations are ultrasonic, far beyond the range humans can hear. But sensitive microphones (and cats) can hear them. Knutson recorded his playful rats with a 'bat detector', which slows down ultrasound to our audible range. The slowed-down squeaks sounded a lot like human laughter. Knutson took his findings to the head of his lab. It was one of those classic moments in science that could have gone either way. The senior scientist could have dismissed the unusual finding. It is a big no-no in the study of animal behaviour to anthropomorphise our furry friends, attributing human qualities to them that might be instinct or learning. The head of the lab could well have laughed at his junior colleague and his laughing rats. But Brian was lucky. His boss was Jaak Panksepp, who takes animal emotions very seriously.

One could even say he wrote the book on the topic. Panksepp's book, *Affective Neuroscience*, has become the standard reference work in the field (Panksepp, 1998). It has been cited in over 8,000 other scientific publications and the title has become the accepted name for the study of the neural mechanisms of emotion. Panksepp's work is often compared to Charles Darwin's overlooked masterpiece of 1872, *The Expression of the Emotions in Man and Animals*. It is similarly wide-ranging and emphasises the continuity between human emotions and the fear reactions of animals. Panksepp and Darwin are kindred spirits in the tremendous respect and empathy they show for the animal kingdom.

So Brian Knutson was in the right place to discover laughing rats. Panksepp believed him, but still it was necessary to be sure. Together they ran experiments to rule out less interesting explanations (Knutson, Burgdorf & Panksepp, 1998). They found rats would made the ultrasonic 'giggling' noise when they played together but not alone, and it happened more when they were playfully bitten on the back of the neck. Rats who had been deprived of company made the noises more than those who hadn't. The giggling seemed to be a social signal that said: 'Keep playing with me – I like it.' (But in a squeaky voice only other rats could hear.)

Despite Panksepp's involvement, it was very difficult to get the work published. Emotion researchers were very resistant to the idea that animals have feelings. Panksepp had previously encountered this resistance when trying to argue that distress vocalisations in puppies, chicks and guinea pigs have a lot in common with childhood crying. When you are up against people who aren't moved by crying puppies, you know you have an uphill battle.

This resistance goes back to British psychologist C. Lloyd Morgan in 1894. Morgan's canon is the most widely quoted statement in psychology. There's no need to repeat the long-winded original here. To paraphrase, he says you should always explain animal behaviour in the simplest possible terms. This might seem an overly Victorian attitude of not attributing emotions where they're not wanted. But it's a useful rule of thumb, a version of the famous Occam's razor, perhaps more commonly known these days by the acronym KISS: Keep It Simple, Stupid.

Morgan claims we cannot know that Pavlov's dogs expected food when they heard the bell, so we should only talk about their behaviour. This led to a school of psychology called behaviourism, which ignored all internal mental attributes in animals and even in humans. Clearly behaviourists went too far, because humans undoubtedly do have internal mental states and humans aren't so different from our animal cousins. So maybe dogs act hungry because they feel hungry?

Maybe rats laugh when they feel happy? That's what Panksepp and Jeff Burgdorf tried to prove next. They showed that baby rats laugh when playing together and in anticipation of play. They laughed more after being kept alone without a chance to play. The real fun began on that spring morning in 1997 when Professor Panksepp decided it was time to tickle some rats. To be certain that the high-pitched chirps were laughs, Panksepp needed to be able to provoke them in controlled conditions. He reasoned that since tickling makes human babies laugh, it might work on baby rats too.

Initial fun and games showed rats chirped most when they were tickled on the nape of the neck. Just like Pavlov's dogs salivating at the sound of dinner bell, Panksepp's rats laughed when the tickling hand was present. Curiously, young rats laughed or chirped more than older rats and male rats laughed more than female rats, both patterns we see with laughing babies. The chirping shared other features with laughter. It was only present when rats were in a good mood. They did not laugh when stressed by very bright lights or by the smell of a nearby cat (Burgdorf & Panksepp, 2001). Later experiments found laughter to be as rewarding as food: the rats would run around mazes or press levers in order to be tickled. Finally, rats chirped when given drugs (amphetamines) or when happy signals were zapped into their brains.

Intriguingly, Panksepp and Burgdorf also bred rats with a greater or lesser tendency to laugh. The jolly rats were stress-resilient, less aggressive and showed signs of positive mood in their brain chemistry. The straight-faced rats were less sociable and more stressed. Other researchers do not like to interpret the chirps as laughter. But no one has come up with a better explanation. As Panksepp and Burgdorf concluded in one of their papers, 'We would be surprised if rats have a sense of humor; they certainly do appear to have a sense of fun.' (p.368, Panksepp & Burgdorf, 1999).

Humans and rats diverged as species about 60 million years ago. Either tickling babies is a very, very old pastime or evolution has discovered its delights more than once. Burgdorf and Panksepp would answer that ticklishness and laughter are a key part of mammalian play. They are part of a reward system that promotes juvenile play for the tickler and the ticklee. Parents undoubtedly love being the tickler. Baby humans seem to love being the ticklee, probably even more than baby rats. But, in the fiercely sceptical tradition of Dr Leuba, it might be worth asking…

Do Babies Like to be Tickled?

A young child, if tickled by a strange man, would scream from fear.

— Charles Darwin, *The Expression of the Emotions in Man and Animals*, 1872

I have run my baby laughter website (laughingbaby.info) for eight years now and in all that time the most popular post has been one entitled 'Should we tickle babies?' Every month it seems to generate more hits than anything else – a sign that people are typing the phrase into Google. There are sceptics out there. My post was written in response to an email I received from Johan in South Africa. He wrote:

> I grew up in a boarding school and I can remember what a dreadful experience it was to be pinned down by bigger kids and them tickling you until you are silly. Sadly, it happened to many smaller kids, who had no defence against this.
>
> My question: Babies have no way of defending themselves against tickling, whether they like it or not. They also cannot protest. Isn't it quite a bad idea to tickle the small ones?

Johan raised an interesting point. How do we know for sure? Tickling can provoke laughter even when we are not enjoying it.

Charles Darwin was interested in how tickling and laughter were related. He wondered if they always came together and as the quote at the beginning of the section shows, he found that this was not necessarily the case. Darwin was famously hands-on in his research. He bred pigeons and cultivated flowers to understand inheritance. He dug up thousands of earthworms and observed them carefully to write a whole book about their importance in the ecosystem. He tested the appetites of his carnivorous plants by feeding them his toenail clippings. I can guarantee he discovered for himself how young children react to being tickled by strange men. It tickles me that big hairy Darwin looming over those Victorian prams discovered babies have very effective ways of letting you know if they do not like something.

Johan was right that tickling can be traumatic; the Romans and the ancient Chinese both used tickling as a form of torture. I have a friend who is a professional dominatrix. Alongside such simple pleasures as beating, bondage and verbal humiliation, a lot of her clients like to be tied up and tickled. She says this is her favourite part of the job. I am very ticklish, so I let her tickle me once. It was fun at first, but she is quite merciless. If I had not been able to wriggle away it would have stopped being pleasurable. There may even be a 'sport' of competitive endurance tickling, although, as the 2016 documentary movie *Tickled* revealed, this seems even stranger than the consensual tickling torture beloved of my friend and her clients.

Tickling someone who cannot escape and ignoring their protests certainly crosses the boundaries of consent. It is not enough to assume just because child is laughing while being tickled they are enjoying it or they do not mean it when they say 'stop'. Jennifer Lehr, in an article in the *Huffington Post*, documents cases of children like Johan tickled by someone more powerful than them, despite their obvious protests (Lehr, 2017). She considers this a form of abuse and I would agree. She goes on to quote an evolutionary biologist, Richard Alexander, who says tickling 'does not create a pleasurable feeling – just the outward appearance of one'. She concludes: 'If a child is too young to talk, don't tickle them. Better safe than sorry.'

I disagree with both these statements. It simply is not true that the pleasure we can get from tickling is somehow not genuine. The long evolutionary history of the sensation suggests the exact opposite, and I find it bizarre that a biologist would think this. The pleasure is real, but it can be overwhelmed by other feelings. But context matters, as Darwin found. Consent matters too, and that is what was lacking for Johan and others.

Having said that, there is evidence showing why tickling might be painful. Back in the 1920s and 1930s, physiologists Edgar Adrian and Yngve Zotterman discovered how nerves signalled touch and pain. Tickle, itch and pain are all carried by the same Group C nerve fibres, although the signals are different from each other, so the brain can tell the difference. When the signals reach the brain, tickle sensations light up the anterior cingulate cortex (ACC). The ACC is involved in the processing of pain, reward, emotion and even consciousness. It also interacts with the hypothalamus to enable a range of functions of the autonomous nervous system (ANS).

The hypothalamus and the ANS control all kinds of important automatic processes like body-temperature regulation, hunger and thirst management, sexual arousal and sleep cycles. By acting on the hypothalamus, the ACC can help prepare the body for highly stressful situations – the so-called fight-or-flight response. Tickling seems to cause a cascade of arousing hormones that puts the body on high alert. It seems tickling games are a form of mock attack and laughter is an important part of the game. Laughter acts as a feedback mechanism that regulates the interaction. Interestingly, hearing the sound of someone else laughing from being tickled seems to activate the same brain areas in our own brain (Wildgruber et al., 2013). The tickler can share the feelings of the ticklee.

The Most Ancient Joke

I forge recklessly into the paleohumorology fray, proposing my candidate for the most ancient joke – the feigned tickle.

— Robert Provine, *Curious Behavior: Yawning, laughing, hiccupping, and beyond*, 2014

The anterior cingulate cortex is also heavily involved in anticipating future rewards. It helps us spot mistakes and learn from rewarding situations. It is therefore not surprising that babies rapidly realise what is coming next when we approach to tickle them and start to laugh in anticipation. Once that happens, the game gets much more interesting and suddenly lots of philosophers get very excited too – the baby has made a leap from reflexive laughter to protean humour. Their laughter is no longer happening as a direct physical response to tickling. It is now cognitive. It is a laugh about an idea. Their very first joke.

Aristotle decided that humans are the only animals that are ticklish, attributing it to the fineness of our skin and being the only creatures who laugh. He was wrong on both counts. He never knew the great apes like being tickled, let alone that rats do too. His idea of comedy is also somewhat different from ours. Aristotle's *Poetics*, written around 335 BC, was about drama and epic poetry. It contained a book on comedy and another on tragedy. Tragically, his book on comedy has been lost, so we don't know exactly what it said. But comedy and tragedy were defined in dramatic terms: very simply, comedy ends well and tragedy ends badly. Elsewhere in *Poetics*, Aristotle's definition of funny is: 'The ridiculous is a mistake or unseemliness that is not painful or destructive.'

Others have seen this idea of harmlessness as key to part of what transforms the tickle game into the birth of comedy. In his final treatise, *Passions of the Soul*, seventeenth-century philosopher René Descartes argued that tickling is pleasing because we recognise that although it is very close to pain, it falls short of harming us. Amusing things share a similar quality – they resemble the strong passions but turn out to be harmless.

Twentieth-century polymath Arthur Koestler examined humour in great detail in his book *The Act of Creation*. He speculates that babies 'must perceive the tickling as a mock attack', and thinks this anticipation marks the first joke:

> It is probably the first situation encountered in life which makes the infant live on two planes at once, the first delectable experience in bisociation – a foretaste of pleasures to come at the pantomime show, of becoming a willing victim to the illusions of the stage, of being tickled by the horror-thriller.
>
> — Arthur Koestler, *The Act of Creation*, 1964

Like Darwin, Koestler seems to have done his research because his description fits nicely with many of the stories I have received from parents about their games of tickle, chase and 'eat the baby'.

> Just today, at just over five months old, I realised that I can make her laugh now with just eye contact. It all still revolves around tickling her or 'threatening' to tickle her. Initially, she'd only laugh when tickled. Next, she'd laugh when I pretended to come close and tickle her, holding my hands above her belly or going towards her with my face pretending to tickle her. Now, just the 'roaring' sound I usually make with it or a mischievous look from me will set off a giggling fit.
>
> — Mother of baby girl, five months old, UK

Robert Provine goes even further and thinks a baby's first joke is also humanity's first joke. Being aware that tickling-chase is a popular game among chimpanzees and other great apes, he decided that the feigned or threatened tickle is 'the only joke that can be told equally well to a baby human and a chimpanzee'. In fact, it is the beginning of all jokes, the first idea that ever made a primate laugh. He is the first to admit he will never be able to prove this. It is a reckless hypothesis, but I am willing to give him credit. I cannot think of an older joke. Can you?

Elmo, Tickle Thyself

Tickle Me Elmo was the toy craze of 1996 in the United States. The animatronic version of the endearing, bright red *Sesame Street* character would shake with laughter if you poked his belly and declare, 'That tickles!' Toy company Tyco initially made 400,000 of them, and with demand strong and steady they ordered a further 600,000 for Christmas. Suddenly, around Thanksgiving, at the end of November, demand went crazy. In the run-up to Christmas 1996, newspapers reported fights breaking out over the last Elmo in the store, and black-market prices apparently reached $7,000. As Neil Friedman, the head of Tyco, recalled, 'When you played with [him] for the first time, it brought a smile to everyone's face. It was a magical surprise.' (Greenwood, 1999).

Tickle Me Elmo has entered popular culture, becoming the punchline of many jokes and cropping up in some freaky viral YouTube videos. New versions were released in 2006 and 2017 with upgraded animatronics. Other *Sesame Street* characters were released but none were as popular as Elmo. His childlike qualities made him more of a natural ticklee than Tickle Me Big Bird or Tickle Me Ernie. They even made a Tickle Me Cookie Monster, which makes no sense whatsoever, as baked goods are his hedonic soft spot. But that aside, why does Elmo need you to tickle him? Why can't he tickle himself?

Elmo can't help it: he's made that way. But why can't we tickle ourselves? For once, the common-sense answer is largely the right one. You were expecting it. You could no more tickle yourself than you could surprise yourself by saying, 'Boo!' But the mechanics of your programming reveal some rather subtle points about our sense of self.

Touch your own face or body with your hand and you get simultaneous sensations in your hand and the skin you are touching. The two are perfectly correlated. This delights your brain. The brain is a pattern-recognition device par excellence. Its job is to notice coincidences. It has long been known that a baby starts to learn the rhythms and cadences of a mother's voice and accent in the womb. We are just beginning to appreciate that a foetus learns a surprising amount about its own body too.

Minoru Asada from Osaka University in Japan builds robots that learn like babies. He does this for two reasons. He wants to understand how babies learn and, since babies are the most impressive learners on the planet, he hopes that copying babies will teach his robots a thing or two. It is a strategy that seems to be working. In one remarkable study he programmed a virtual robot foetus to wriggle around at random like a baby in the womb (Asada et al., 2009). He found this activity allowed the robot to learn many useful things about itself. As its hand brushed randomly across its face, its brain would get perfectly correlated signals from nerves in the fingers and different parts of the face. Coincidences mean something. They tell the brain these two parts are connected. In effect, they are both bits of the baby robot.

Furthermore, the hands would move across the face in a systematic way. Brush your hand across your own face. Your right hand naturally moves from bottom left to upper right and your left hand does the opposite. The same was true for the baby robot. Starting out knowing nothing, the robot learned where its eyes, ears and mouth were in relation to each other. Effectively it worked out what a face looked like by touch alone. The baby robot was building up an internal representation of itself. The fact we are not ticklish shows we have done something similar.

In the late 1990s, Sarah-Jayne Blakemore and colleagues used a brain-imaging machine and tickle machine to understand how this works (Blakemore, Wolpert & Frith, 1998). A brain-imaging machine is a giant super-conducting magnet and highly sensitive radio antennae that costs about £1.5 million. A tickle machine is a length of plastic dowel, a hinge and a finger of foam rubber. It costs about £10.

Volunteers would lie down with their head nestled in the middle of the large doughnut-shaped magnet. The tickle machine was placed so that the foam rubber finger could rest lightly against their left palm. Participants tickled themselves by wiggling the rod with their other hand. The study compared this to same action by performed by an experimenter. Self-tickle produced less activity in several crucial brain areas. There was less activity in the ACC, which we previously saw to be associated with the pleasurable sensation of tickling. Self-tickle feels less fun. Self-generated movements had less activity in the secondary somatosensory cortex, an area associated with bodily sensations. Self-tickle feels less noticeable. Finally, there was reduced activity in the cerebellum, the motor-planning area that predicts 'the sensory consequences of motor commands' (Blakemore et al., 1998).

The situation was a bit more complex than found in Asada's robots. In humans the action of the cerebellum meant the self-tickle was actively cancelled by the brain. But it gets weirder than that. One of Blakemore's co-authors, Chris Frith, is a world authority on schizophrenia. He knew that often schizophrenics can tickle themselves. He speculated that schizophrenics would have problems with this forward prediction. A tickle activates something essential to our sense of self and something that is deeper than mere surprise.

Laughter researcher Robert Provine, reflecting on what this means, says, 'Because you cannot tickle yourself, tickle involves a neurological self/non-self discrimination, providing the most primitive social scenario' (p.215, Provine 2004). So not only is the feigned tickle the oldest joke, but tickling games are also conversations. Tickling is entangled with our sense of self and other.

There is good news for the robots too. Roboticists from South Korea set out to build an intelligent robot that could tickle people and make them laugh (Kishi et al., 2016). So the next generation of Tickle Me Elmo might be able to tickle you back.

From Toes To Nose

This little piggy went to market,
This little piggy stayed at home,
This little piggy had roast beef,
This little piggy had none.
And this little piggy went
'Wee, wee, wee' all the way home…

— Traditional English nursery rhyme, *c.*1760

Where are your toes right now? You don't even have to think – you know exactly where they are. You have clear sense of their location in space. You have strong sense of ownership too. They're your toes, the furthest parts of your whole person. They mark the boundary of you. Wriggle the toes on your left foot. Now the right. Again, it was easy and accomplished without much thought. Just as easily you could close your eyes and swing your finger swiftly and precisely to the tip of your nose. We are not born knowing all this. And our lack of knowledge has more profound consequences than it first appears.

I remember being three years old and being quite troubled by the 'little piggy' nursery rhyme as my mother taught me how to play this game with my baby sister. My overactive imagination was concerned with the possibility that my toes might detach themselves and go AWOL. That little piggy was not going anywhere, silly song, but this always disturbed me more than the other apparently removable body part of the 'got your nose' game. The fact that pigs would eat roast beef did not disturb me at all (until now).

At three years old I already had a well-established sense of my body. My sister was about one year old, so she did too. A large part of your idea of your body and your ownership of it happens in the first six months. Long before we can walk we know where to find our toes. Long before we can name the parts or understand a command like 'touch your nose' we can pick up small pieces of food and put them expertly in our mouths.

Taking control of our own bodies is the one of the huge achievements of the first year. Parents watch week by week as their baby progresses from a flopping and flailing newborn into someone who can string several wobbly steps together. Initial reflexes are replaced with purposeful actions. Hands that could only swipe and grasp become delicate pincers that can pick up individual peas.

There is a lot we see but do not appreciate. Most parents will have seen a four-month-old baby transfixed by their own hand. But few of them will have ever watched this carefully. One person who did was the psychologist G. Stanley Hall, who we encountered at the start of the chapter coining obscure words for types of tickle:

> Sometimes the hand would be stared at steadily, perhaps with growing intensity, until interest reached such a pitch that a grasping movement followed as if the infant tried by an automatic action of the motor hand to grasp the visual hand, and it was switched out of the center of vision and lost as if it had magically vanished. (p.352, Hall, 1898)

It is a wonderful image. A baby lunging with her hand to try and grab the same hand. It makes a lot of sense if your body isn't yet quite your own. This is a favourite quote of Professor Andy Bremner from Goldsmiths, University of London. Andy is one of the few researchers who has delved deeply into what is happening here. He is also my boss, so I had better be careful what I say.

Andy has investigated this problem by looking at something called the crossed-hands deficit. I still get left and right confused. Maybe you do too? It is no big deal – they are simply labels (just don't ask me for directions). Once I remember my right hand is called 'right' and my left 'left', I do not get them confused. If psychologists put two buzzers on my hands and buzz them in quick succession, I can tell them which came first. But if they cross my hands I will get worse. You will too.

Andy Bremner played this same trick on babies (Bremner, Mareschal, Lloyd-Fox & Spence, 2008). He put them in cute mittens with buzzers inside. Sitting on a parent's lap, they got little buzzes on either hand. Then their arms were crossed. Sure enough, ten-month-old and six-and-a-half-month-old babies both showed a version of the deficit. The younger babies would wiggle the correct hand more often if it was on the correct side. Already, at this early age, babies had some notion that their right hand was supposed to be on the right, though, curiously, they would not often look in the direction of their hands. Ten-month-old babies both moved the buzzy hand more and looked towards it more if it was on the correct side. They had a mental image of where their hand was located in space and knew where to look for it.

Things got interesting when Andy and his Ph.D. student, J. J. Begum Ali, decided to test four-month-old babies (Begum Ali, Spence & Bremner, 2015). It is quite hard to cross the short, chubby arms of a typical four-month-old baby, so instead they crossed their feet. For comparison they tested some six-month-olds, who performed as predicted. They mostly wiggled the correct foot when their feet were uncrossed but were essentially guessing when their feet were crossed. Four-month-olds wiggled the correct foot in both crossed and uncrossed postures. In other words, they were less confused than six-month-olds.

It is always pleasing for baby scientists when we get a result like this. It is a sign the experimental task taps into something very fundamental. If older babies succeed and younger ones fail in some task one boring explanation is the younger ones did not 'get it'. The task was set up in a way that made them fail for other reasons. Imagine asking three- and five-year-olds to draw you a car. The three-year-old will probably fail but that does not mean they do not know what a car is. You asked the question in the wrong way.

If all Andy and J. J.'s babies had failed completely at the crossed-leg task it might have been because they cannot move as easily when their legs are crossed. The fact that four-month-olds succeeded ruled out this 'boring' explanation. The experiment reveals that young babies are living in a simpler world. Touches on their bodies do not map easily onto the external world because information from different senses is not yet combined. This is something Andy calls 'tactile solipsism' (Bremner, 2016).

All of that staring at their hands has an important function. Babies must map what they see, what they hear and the effects of their own movements into one coherent whole. Incidentally, this helps confirm that Melanie Klein had it exactly backwards on babies' terrible fear of being eaten. 'Eating the baby' is one of the top ways we make little babies laugh. Your baby's toes, naked and wriggly, are a bit like little piglets, all lined up and good enough to eat. Gentle nibbling on toes or the more monstrous 'nom nom nom' is not horrifying to babies. It is delightful and educational. It helps them establish the boundaries of the self.

Upsy-Daisy

Rock-a-bye baby, on the treetop
When the wind blows, the cradle will rock
When the bough breaks, the cradle will fall
And down will come baby, cradle and all.

— Traditional English nursery rhyme, *c.*1765

My partner, Kate, and I were on a long-haul night flight to Singapore. We got lucky and were in the seats at the front of a section with extra legroom. Especially lucky for me, because next to us were three families travelling with babies. The extra space let them set up travelling bassinets for the babies to sleep in. Babies being babies, the four-month-old next to me didn't want to go to bed just yet. Once the seatbelt signs were off, her dad stood in the limited space by the emergency exit to rock the baby to sleep.

He swung the baby around left and right, twisting from the hips, and at first it did not work, so he added a forward and backward rocking from front foot to back foot. It took a while, but it worked, the fidgeting baby relaxed, her eyelids drooped and soon he could transfer her to the cot. All being well, she would now wake up happy and smiling when she met her grandparents for the first time in 10 more hours.

Later in the flight we hit some turbulence. The plane leaped and dropped like a rollercoaster. Kate gripped my hand hard enough to almost start me screaming. I tried to be calming but I was quite excited. I love rollercoasters and it is not like there is anything to crash into at this height. Strangely, Kate was not too comforted by these observations. I pointed hopefully at the aircrew, but they had strapped in and look a little worried too. We were pitching up and down quite heavily. I should have pointed to the sleeping babies. Not one of them was the slightest bit bothered. They all slept straight through.

Maybe they even enjoyed it? In my laughter survey, I was not surprised when many parents reported babies like being dangled upside down. But I was surprised that younger babies seemed to like this the most. I had included the question, picturing the rough and tumble of rambunctious toddlers. Yet parents reported this was popular from as young as two months. Very young babies do seem to love all those games dads play that mums often hate. Throwing the baby in the air, swinging them round and round, dropping them onto the bed.

My old banking colleague, Tom, is a former gymnast and pole-vaulter. On his first days in the office he amazed us all by bending over at the waist, putting his hands on the floor and lifting his legs up slowly and gracefully up into a handstand, still in his full suit. On his Facebook page he has a great video of him balancing his three-month-old baby vertically in his hand. The baby's mother can be heard to complain, 'No, put him down,' and baby gets returned to the sofa, a big smile on his face. The mother was worried, but the baby clearly enjoyed it. Then, with impeccable comic timing, the baby slides slowly over onto his side, still too young even to sit upright on his own.

By the fifth month of pregnancy, a foetus possesses an awareness of movement and a knowledge of up and down. These are both functions of the vestibular system, which is already working by this age. The vestibular system is part of the inner ear and has two types of sensor. Three semicircular canals detect rotation in each of the three dimensions while two otolithic organs sense gravity and movement. When combined with an awareness of where the limbs are in space, these all create our hidden 'sixth sense' of proprioception: being aware of our body and its location in world.

Up and down have little meaning in the womb. There is not much room to stretch out either, so the full range of bodily motion is not explored yet. Only once they are out in the world can babies learn what all these senses mean, and it is not easy. A lot of the comfort for upset babies comes from removing the uncertainties that come from these additional freedoms. Rocking babies to sleep is likely to remind them of the sensations of mummy walking around. As we saw in the sleep chapter, swaddling them recreates some of the cosiness of the womb and removes the signals they get from waving arms and legs. It reduces their world, removing some of the confusion and saving the puzzles for another time.

Those proprioceptive puzzles grab us from birth onwards and we grab back. In doing so we start to solve the problems of action, agency and even identity. In one experiment, neuropsychologist Audrey van der Meer put newborn babies in a darkened crib. She shone a narrow beam of light over their nose and chest, parallel to their body. It was designed in such a way that normally they would not see it. If the baby's flailing arm crossed the beam, they would see it. The babies adjusted the position and acceleration of their arm to keep their hand visible (van der Meer, 1997).

This is an exaggerated version of what happens every time a baby moves a limb, her head, or gets picked up and flung around. A rewarding set of signals arrive from eyes, ears and body, and the baby is faced with making sense of them. Depending on their mood, this can cause laughter, tears or transfixed concentration. The delight at being swung overhead or dangled upside down is one example, and the laughs and smiles of being bounced vigorously up and down is another. Getting your legs bicycled, your arms waved or being balanced on Daddy's hand are not things a new baby can do for themselves, but they are intently aware of what is happening to them.

Proprioception is more than knowing where your body is or where you are in space. It is knowing you are part of the world and that you are you. As researchers Phillippe Rochat and Tricia Striano observe, 'proprioception is indeed the modality of the self par excellence' (Rochat & Striano, 2000). This adds up to a far bigger set of achievements than we give ourselves and our babies credit for. The fault goes back to René Descartes.

Babies Against Descartes

First of all, then, I perceived that I had a head, hands, feet, and all other members of which this body – which I considered as a

part, or possibly even as the whole, of myself – is composed.
— René Descartes, *Meditations on First Philosophy*, 1641

By all accounts, René Descartes was a cold fish. He was a sickly child who became an antisocial adult with very few friends. He avoided social contact and never married, but had a relationship with a servant. Their daughter, Francine, died age five. Renowned in his lifetime as a mathematician, Descartes was also interested in metaphysics and philosophy. He was intensely absorbed in his work but had little tolerance of the ideas of others. He is most famous for the idea that mind and body are different kinds of things and the associated philosophy of rationalism, which theorises that we can work things out by reason alone. All of this is summed up in his famous catchphrase: 'I think, therefore I am.'

It is commonly said that if Descartes had had a pet dog his philosophy would have turned out quite differently. Along with this mind–body separation comes a separation of man from the animals: 'I think, therefore I am. Fido, you don't, so you aren't.' In the Cartesian worldview, animals have no souls. The speculation is that a pet dog would have made Descartes more humane and hesitant to draw his line of separation – or he might have ended up dissecting poor Fido. One of the few things we know about his personal life is that he would invite visitors to his house to see the latest animal he had dissected. Perhaps it was a way of getting rid of them.

As described in his 1641 book *Meditations*, Descartes arrived at his position by a process of radical doubt. He was sceptical of his senses, which sometimes mislead him, and he imagined a malicious demon was trying to deceive him about everything:

> I shall think that the sky, the air, the earth, colours, shapes, sounds and all external things are merely the delusions of dreams which he has devised to ensnare my judgement. I shall consider myself as not having hands or eyes, or flesh, or blood or senses, but as falsely believing that I have all these things. (René Descartes, *Meditations*, 1641)

Descartes thought you could be misled about all these things, but you would still be you; you have a core consciousness that is being misled by the demon, although the demon cannot take away the fact that you think and therefore exist. But for us to have any certainty about the wider world, Descartes concluded, the world would have to be in the hands of a benevolent god.

Without these stark divides between mind and body and between humans and other animals, Western philosophy and psychology might have taken a very different path. Largely because of Descartes there is a big gap between the study of thought and perception, and the study of the body and actions. Perception and action are treated separately. The dominant idea is: 'We see the world. Then we act on it.' Finally, babies are helping to change that.

Obviously, most scientists do not appeal to God or an immaterial soul to explain experience, but the idea that the mind and body are separate kinds of things is still very pervasive. The philosopher and cognitive scientist Daniel Dennett calls this

Cartesian materialism (Dennett, 1991). Materialist philosophy says everything is made of matter. Cartesian materialism says we are our brains, but there is a magic leap from the material of the brain to the experience of consciousness. Dennett criticises all philosophical approaches that draw this line between your thoughts and the world. Wherever the line gets drawn creates a 'Cartesian theatre'. Effectively, it suggests a little person sitting in your head receiving the inputs of your senses and pulling the appropriate levers. 'You' are this puppet master, your body is just the puppet show. What is sometimes called 'the ghost in the machine'.

The alternative is to resist the temptation to draw that line, and instead to see the self as something inextricably entangled with the world – what is sometimes called an 'ecological self'. Most baby scientists and most new parents see the sense of self emerging in this way. It makes no sense to think of babies as rational minds passively observing the world and figuring things out. They are not tentatively pulling a few levers to see what happens. The theory of embodiment says things are more tangled up than this. It is wrong to think of us pulling on our own strings. There are no strings. The boundary between mind and body cannot be drawn.

This is better explained with a concrete example. If you tie a ribbon from a baby's leg to a colourful mobile above their cot, their kicking actions will cause the mobile to move. Very young babies quickly learn this connection and delight in their newfound power over the world. One notable version of this was an experiment by Lewis, Sullivan and Brooks-Gunn (1985).

Babies from as young as 10 weeks old were connected by ribbon to a video player. Pulling on the ribbon, they could make it play videos of children singing taken from *Sesame Street*. Babies smiled and showed pleasure when they succeeded in making the music play. When the ribbon was disconnected, removing the babies' control, they cried and became angry. My own mother used to tie the tin lids from my baby-food jars to my feet and then put a tray at the end of my cot. I would entertain myself for hours with exuberant tap dancing.

It is very tempting to look at this and Audrey van der Meer's experiment with newborn babies as early performances in a Cartesian theatre. They could lead one to imagine that the true essence of the baby is somewhere inside the baby's head, observing her experiences and learning to pull the strings that lead to the most exciting outcomes. It seems like a simple explanation, but it is not. It applies adult standards to the wrong situation. Infancy researchers have our version of Morgan's canon (that you should explain behaviour in the simplest terms): we must continually remind ourselves to 'be careful of anthropomorphising babies'. Babies are not simply adults-in-waiting.

To see this point, it is worth remembering the other half of the Cartesian bargain, the division between man and other animals. This was a huge gulf in Descartes' time, but since Darwin there has been no dividing line. The difference between the consciousness of a dog and a person is a matter of degree, not of kind. Emotion, awareness, ticklishness: all the important bits are there in dogs, chimpanzees and rats.

In future, consciousness may even be there in robots. There is nothing magical about the human brain.

The most promising experimental work to understand consciousness is being conducted with mice. Masanori Murayama from the RIKEN Brain Science Institute in Japan thinks the surface of the skin is a good place to search for answers to the mysteries of consciousness. For him, our interface with the outside world is a very active part of our experience. By blowing gentle puffs of air onto the hind paws of mice and carefully recording the response in the brain, he thinks he is beginning to map out the 'neural correlates of consciousness'. Important to this is an understanding of how inside meets outside. When the skin is touched, it sends nerve signals up to the brain which have to be integrated with what the brain has already experienced of the world. The difference between conscious and unconscious is not a rational mind but a set of expectations.

Comparing awake and anaesthetised animals, Murayama found a crucial difference in the brain's response to the puff of air. In both cases there is a 'bottom up' blip associated with the arriving nerve signal, but only in the awake mouse was there a second 'top down' blip arriving 10 milliseconds later. These two then combine to cause that part of the brain to fire repeatedly, creating a perceptual awareness. This spike of electrical activity is a characteristic feature of an awake and conscious brain (Manita et al., 2015). Consciousness is not a top-down observer watching a bottom-up theatre show. Both matter: we are brains entangled with the world.

Yale developmental psychologist Paul Bloom wrote a whole book against Descartes' dualist philosophy called *Descartes' Baby* (Bloom, 2004). His starting point was an eighteenth-century rumour that Descartes travelled everywhere with a very lifelike mechanical doll, said to remind him of his dead daughter Francine. It was supposed to be so lifelike that it freaked out a sea captain, who threw it overboard. Bloom writes, 'We do not have immaterial souls; we are material beings, no less than the "monstrosity" drowned by the captain. We are Descartes' babies.'

It is a confusing title. As far as I can tell, there was no truth to the rumour, and Descartes would disown any claim that the mechanical doll was his baby. Grieving his lost daughter or not, to him the doll would be nothing but a machine. Bloom's point is that although we know Descartes was wrong, we feel like he was right. Even scientists believe that, deep down, the world divides into mind and matter. Intriguingly, if Descartes was alive today, he would very likely see things differently. As a mathematician he would be well qualified to understand that brains and computers are doing the same thing. Everything can potentially be explained on a material basis. Sadly, Cartesian dualism cast a long shadow over our concept of ourselves.

With a few deft waves of their arms and some exuberant kicks of their feet, tiny babies are challenging nearly 400 years of philosophical status quo. The mind and body are not divided, as centuries of Cartesian bias have insisted. The concept of self is entangled with our bodies from the very beginning.

Chapter Seven: The Joys of Toys

Everyone can play. Play is not a great thing, just a little thing done with great love. Play is nothing less than the creation of the human we are meant to be. To be fully human is to be handmade.

— O. Fred Donaldson, preschool pioneer, 1994

It is 10.30 a.m. on a Saturday morning in June and I am at the Cheltenham Science Festival. I am sitting on an upturned crate in an empty dance studio. Laid out in front of me are 24 matching toyboxes made of fabric and sitting next to me is Dr Nathalia Gjersoe, a fellow development psychologist from the University of Bath. We are both nervous as we await the audience for the world premiere of our show, *The Joys of Toys*.

The show starts at 10.45 and now the audience are arriving. They park their pushchairs and start crawling over to the toyboxes. Some have brought their parents as chaperones, others are here with grandparents. I would guess the average age of the audience is about 11 or 12 months. *The Joys of Toys* is a show about baby science for an audience of babies (and their carers).

We are nervous because we have not had any rehearsal

time, we have never done anything like this before and we are operating without the standard academic safety net of a PowerPoint presentation packed with graphs. We are excited too. The great thing about a show for babies is there will be chaos anyway. If you embrace it, you will be fine. Won't you?

The whole show is a perhaps an act of foolishness. Several months earlier I had received a call from Dr Gina Collins, who heads science programming for Cheltenham Festivals. Dr Collins started out asking us to do a standard talk for adults about how to study babies, with full, glorious PowerPoint. She also challenged us to think of something for an audience of babies. I was excited by the possibility. The summer before I had been scientific adviser on a play for babies about baby science. That show, *Shake, Rattle and Roll* by Sarah Argent, had held audiences of 20 babies in rapt attention for nearly 40 minutes.

Sarah's show had a professional director and a full production team at the Polka Children's Theatre in Wimbledon. Maisey Whitehead, the performer in the show, was a professional actor, singer and acrobat. We had none of these things. I wasn't sure about Nathalia, but I can't sing, I can't act and I only dance a little. I also knew it is lucky for anything to hold a baby's attention for more than five minutes. If we were going to create a show for babies about baby science, we would need a whole bag of tricks to keep them entertained… or a box. We also needed a theme.

The solution, as you might have guessed, was toys. We all know babies love toys. The idea for the show was to give babies toys while explaining the related science to parents. With a box of toys in front of every baby, Nathalia and I would be under less pressure to mesmerise the babies ourselves. Each box would hold an identical set of toys, which would let us perform a range of experiments with the babies. Well, that was the idea.

Dummies

Babies only play in three different ways:
Bash it.
Bite it.
Throw it.
— Matt Coyne, *Dummy*, 2017

The first toy out of the box was a set of interlinked teething rings and the challenge was to see how fast each baby put it in their mouth. Of course, for this to have worked we probably should not have laid the toyboxes out before the audience arrived. We tried to tell the parents to keep the boxes out of reach and await our instructions, but the babies had different ideas. Plenty of them had dived straight in. Even before the show had officially begun the chaos was in full flow.

Nevertheless, when the babies found or were given the teething toys, the 'experiment' mostly worked. Almost all the babies put the rings straight in their mouth, especially the youngest ones. As experiments go, this is hardly groundbreaking: every parent quickly learns to be on guard for this. If an object is small enough to lift, it is headed for the mouth. If it is too big, one can often expect a gummy lunge and an exploratory nibble.

Which all makes perfect sense if you are a baby. Your tongue, mouth and lips are very sensitive with many nerve endings, and this was the first sense you developed, way back in the eighth week of pregnancy. For the next seven months in the womb one of the few ways you had to entertain yourself was sucking your thumb. Using your mouth is also the first skill you need on the outside, as you latch on to a nipple in order to eat.

The oral exploration of objects has some surprising features, and babies can learn a lot from nibbling on things. Meltzoff and Borton (1979) gave one-month-old babies either a knobbly dummy or a smooth dummy to suck on for 90 seconds. The dummy was removed, taking care the baby never saw it. Babies were then shown large styrofoam models of the two dummies. They preferred to look at the one that matched the shape of the dummy they had been sucking. A few years later Eleanor Gibson and Arlene Walker (1984) performed a similar study, also with one-month-olds. This time the babies nibbled on a spongy finger or an acrylic rod and then observed new objects with similar properties. This time they preferred to look at the type they had not seen before. The opposite outcome but the same conclusion, in both cases: the babies are noticing visual and tactile similarities and differences.

One reason babies put things in the mouths is to combine the knowledge they gain from both vision and touch. Remember that in the beginning babies are clumsy fools. Initially all they can do is swipe at an object, occasionally grabbing it by luck. You cannot tell much about something just by holding it; you need to turn it over and move your fingers over the surface.

This ability to manipulate and explore an object with both hands arrives at four to five months (Rochat, 1989). Earlier than this, having a good chew is the best way to learn. We see this in the surprising finding that blind babies are slower to develop manual exploration of objects than babies with sight (Fraiberg, 1977). In the absence of vision, tiny, clumsy hands are no match for sensitive lips and mouth.

Babies will continue to bite things long after they become manually dextrous. Why wouldn't they? It is their first reference and a simple, solid foundation for the bigger challenges of dexterity and vision. Visual understanding of the three-dimensional world is a difficult problem. It helps to suck it and see.

Vision Thing

A recurring theme of this book is that you learn by doing. Nowhere is this truer than for vision and yet nowhere is this harder to visualise. If we imagine a baby learning to see, we think about them learning to recognise things. 'This is Mummy, this is Daddy, this is my favourite toy, this is a cat, this is the room where I go to sleep.' But most of those happen after we have learned to see.

The first flickers of vision must be strange indeed. The brain cannot prepare us for it and infant vision does not work in the way you would imagine. Mark Johnson listed some of the strange ways newborn vision is not like our own (Johnson, 1990). Move something small and brightly coloured slowly backwards and forwards in front of a newborn and their eyes will jump from one place to the next, lagging slightly behind the object itself. They have not yet learned to smoothly track movement, much less predict how it will move. If the object passes behind something, they are truly bamboozled. With non-moving objects the opposite can happen, as babies can get 'sticky fixation'; their gaze locks on to the corner of the room or a bright spot on the wall and they cannot disengage. This can agitate them – a baby who seems to be staring at something deep in thought suddenly crumples into tears. They'd like to look away, but they are mesmerised.

A newborn's vision is blurry and this is something of a blessing. If the world was crystal clear at the start it would be chaos, a hypersaturated nightmare. The soft-focus world of the newborn removes an information overload that would be no use to the baby at this stage. Blurry vision simplifies things and may perhaps be an important evolutionary adaptation.

From the moment we open our eyes there are three big problems to solve with vision. How do I assemble the signals from the cells of my retinas in my brain? How do I do this when my head and my eyes and objects in the world are all constantly moving? And how do I use both eyes together to see in three dimensions?

To solve these problems, vision must be an active process. We know this thanks to some brave little kittens who fell into the clutches of Richard Held and Alan Hein in the early 1960s. Twenty kittens were raised in the dark from birth. From two to 10 weeks old, pairs of kittens were taken for a daily visual adventure. They spent three hours each day in a kitten merry-go-round inside a stripy drum. One kitten was always put in a harness and the other was put in a yoked basket. This let one kitten run around while the other came passively along for the ride.

When Held and Hein tested the kittens' visual abilities, there were big differences. The passive kittens would not blink as objects approached them, couldn't lunge for things and would walk straight over the edge of an apparent visual cliff. After these tests all the kittens spent 48 hours in a brightly lit room, at the end of which both groups were performing normally (Held & Hein, 1963). Kittens needed to actively explore the world for vision to work.

A kitten cannot learn to see by sitting and watching the world go by. Early results with babies, on the other hand, seemed to contradict this. When scientists tried to lure young babies over the edge of a visual cliff, the babies did not fall for it, either literally or metaphorically. They could not literally fall because a visual cliff is just that: a glass platform suspended one metre above a checkerboard floor. And, just like adults refusing to stand on those scary glass-floored observation decks found on some tall buildings, the babies would have been perfectly safe but chose not to venture out into thin air.

This visual-cliff experiment was invented by Eleanor Gibson and Richard Walk in 1960. It became an instant classic. Illustrations of babies refusing to budge appear in hundreds of psychology textbooks. Even with mummy coaxing them to cross the imaginary abyss, they stayed put. It seemed as though babies understood depth. Of course, these babies had to be old enough to crawl for the experiment to work, so they had lots of visual experience. But active exploration matters. Joseph Campos discovered it was only after several weeks' experience of crawling that babies would refuse to move. New crawlers pressed fearlessly ahead, often with a smile on their face (Campos et al., 1978).

Karen Adolph replaced the visual with an actual cliff and the results were even more dramatic. She removed the glass and many babies plunged straight over the edge. Adolph caught them all, discovering that babies need lots of locomotor experience before they correctly judge the difference between a small step and steep drop (Adolph, 2000). It only took psychologists 40 years to discover what parents learn in the first few minutes of having a mobile baby.

The battle over how much of vision is programmed and how much babies must learn continues to rumble. At first glance there seems like a lot could be built in. Newborns are aware that objects get smaller as they move further away (Slater, Mattock & Brown, 1990) and can tell if people are looking directly at them (Farroni, Csibra, Simion & Johnson, 2002). Baby mountain goats are bounding around confidently a few hours after birth, suggesting it is possible to have very good 3D vision from birth. To be fair, they probably need it.

Yet vision remains so complicated that getting computers to understand the visual world is still an unsolved problem. It is unlikely that everything our brains need to know about the visual world can be encoded into our genes and be ready to go from day one. During my Ph.D., one of our professors, Marty Sereno, was fond of saying that half the cortex is involved in vision. He had spent 25 years mapping out the visual pathways of the brain, so he was biased, but his guess is far better than yours or mine. One study run by his student Tessa Dekker showed the visual system is still developing up until we are 10 years old (Dekker, Mareschal, Sereno & Johnson, 2011).

Tessa was my girlfriend at the time, so I helped run the study. Maybe I am biased too, but this is lovely study that gives a big clue as to why babies love toys. Tessa wanted to know which bits of the brain recognised objects and animals. To do this, she put children in the brain scanner and showed them pictures of objects and animals, and the same pictures scrambled like a jigsaw puzzle. Including scrambled images let Tessa find the areas of the brain that were responding to a whole object, not just its features: the whole goldfish, not a patch of orange, or a pair of scissors, not just the blue of their handles. Tessa's study confirmed that by six years old children process animals and objects in different areas of the brain. But development has not stopped.

My role was to help run an unusual perspectives task. Participants would be shown pictures of objects from unusual angles, such as a fork looking down the prongs, a mug from directly above, a pair of glasses edge-onwards. If you know what the object is then you easily recognise it; if not, then it is a lot harder. We had created most of the photos on my kitchen table. When we tested adults they were close to 100%. But the children's ability was correlated with their age. Their brains were becoming more efficient at this task even up to 10 years old. Our understanding of objects increases all through childhood. Toys keep teaching object lessons.

The challenges of visual object recognition have long fascinated philosophers. In 1689, William Molyneux, whose wife was blind, wrote to his friend, the philosopher John Locke, wondering what might happen if by magic a blind person had their sight restored. If they were shown a cube and a sphere, would they know which was which just by looking? Remarkably, technology has now advanced sufficiently that this magic is possible.

Molyneux's experiment was performed for real in 2010 by kitten tormentor Richard Held, who was still going strong at the age of 88. Although the real hero was Pawan Sinha, Held's colleague at the Massachusetts Institute of Technology (MIT) and founder of Project Prakash, a charitable venture restoring sight to children in India with cataract operations. Held and Sinha located five children who had been functionally blind from birth and gave them the cataract operation. A few days later they were given an object-matching task with large Lego-like blocks. They could easily match identical blocks by touch alone and even by newly restored sight, but when given one block to hold and asked to match one of two visual choices, they could not map the object in their hands to the visual image in front of them. This answered Molyneux's question in the negative. You cannot see just by looking: combined visual and tactile experience is necessary.

It is over 320 years since Molyneux's thought experiment and over 50 years since Richard Held and Eleanor Gibson pushed kittens and babies off imaginary cliffs. We still do not fully understand how adult vision works and can only imagine the visual experience of young babies. We do know that toys loom large in this process. Basic depth perception and rudimentary face recognition are present from the start, but it is harder to understand the myriad of different objects we encounter and the myriad of ways the same object can look quite different. It is a problem babies must turn over in their hands and look at from many angles.

How do they even know where to begin? A baby's world is not a single object isolated on a plain white background. Just a few minutes into *The Joys of Toys* and we could easily see this. Two dozen babies had scattered their toys everywhere and over two dozen adults added to the clutter by moving things around and waving rabbits, warthogs and rubber ducks at their darlings. What does that look like from the babies' point of view?

Hanako Yoshida and Linda Smith have an answer. In 2008 they strapped tiny video cameras to the foreheads of 19 toddlers. Four disliked this enough not to take part, but a surprising 15 out of 19 tolerated the camera. Yoshida and Smith were able to record mothers and babies playing with toys from the baby's point of view. They counted the number of toys in the baby's field of view frame by frame. Over half the time there was just one toy in view (Yoshida & Smith, 2008).

We forget, when we hand a baby a toy, that their arms are so short. They hold objects far closer to their face than adults do. Any object appears 10 times bigger to them and fills up their visual field. Yoshida and Smith found this with 18-month-olds and the effect is likely to be even greater for smaller babies.

This helps them focus on just that thing. It helps them learn some of those difficult facts about 3D objects.

I thought I would be clever and try to illustrate this for the audience of *The Joys of Toys*. In their toyboxes every baby had a rubber duck. To give the adults in the room some sense of the babies' perspective, I brought out a huge rubber duck as large as a Christmas turkey. It almost worked. I got a laugh from the adults. But I had forgotten that not all babies in my audience were small and pre-mobile. Some were toddlers and toddlers are no fools. Three or four of them quickly spotted the giant duck and rushed over for a closer look.

Newton's Cradle

The most exciting phrase to hear in science, the one that heralds new discoveries, is not 'Eureka' but 'That's funny…'

— Commonly attributed to Isaac Asimov, scientist and science-fiction author

As a baby scientist, I am fond of saying that babies are little scientists. As we will see in the next chapter, the parallels run deeper than you might think. The job of a scientist is to try and discover laws by which the world works. This is harder than it looks. The starting point is to look at something and have an idea, but often the first impression isn't very reliable. 'Common sense' can't guide you in unknown realms. Where do you think common sense comes from? This is the challenge for babies: to discover for themselves all the things we think are obvious and which are not obvious at all.

In 1666, Isaac Newton fled Cambridge University to avoid the plague. He went to Woolsthorpe Manor, his family home in Lincolnshire. Sitting under an apple tree, he observed a falling apple and discovered the laws of gravity. There is no evidence it hit him on the head. The inspiration was real; as an old man five decades later, Newton would often retell the tale. The apple tree is still there, cared for by the National Trust.

When your baby sits in her high chair and throws her apple to the floor, this helps her realise what Newton realised. It took someone of Newton's genius to get the maths right, but every one of us intuitively knows that falling apples rush to the ground and stop once they get there. We learned this as babies. In fact, we learn many of the laws of physics so well as babies that they become invisible to us.

We learn which stacks of blocks will stand and which will fall. We learn many properties of solid bodies, that our spoon will not go through the table, and the stiffness and bounce of different materials. We learn how size predicts weight and principles of inertia. By waving bigger or smaller toys and tools we learn about levers and angular momentum. We learn how liquids fill their containers or splash around merrily without them. We learn how light and shadow interact with different textures. It is not just gravity and Newton's other laws of motion, it is fluid mechanics, optics, materials science, and amazingly, it's fun. And funny.

We take a lot for granted because we've forgotten we had to learn these things and we cannot imagine it any other way. As an example, let us take Newton, discoverer of the laws of gravity and an archetypal science guy. He didn't discover things fell to the floor but he didn't take it for granted either. His breakthrough was to work out how and why. One starting point was the alternative: what if everything just stayed where it was? Wouldn't that make a lot more sense? And in fact, it happens a lot. Newton discovered the rules behind the principle of inertia and how these could be applied both to orbiting planets or colliding billiard balls.

Newton's cradle is an 'executive toy'. You have probably seen one. Five shiny metal balls hanging in a line from fine wires. If you lift and swing a ball at one end it clacks into the others and stops. Instantaneously one shoots off at the other end and swings up and returns, repeating the process. The momentum of the first ball is passed to the last and back again. The same thing happens if you swing two together and, even more weirdly, if you swing three. Babies get a mixture of frustration and joy from this toy. At first they find it mesmerising and delightful. This quickly turns to resentment when they learn we will not let them grab it.

I am not aware of scientific studies that show this toy to babies. But scientists have looked at babies' reactions to these types of collisions. The original baby billiards study was done by William A. Ball in 1973. I don't know if he got called Billy A. Ball but, perhaps mindful of the teasing he might have received, he did not run his study with billiard balls. He presented babies with a red block and a white block. The red block would move from one side of a platform to another. Behind a screen it would silently collide with a white block, which continued onwards. After they had got used to the situation, Bill removed the screen and showed two events. In one the red block hit the white block, causing it to move. In the other the red block stopped short of the white block with a clear gap between them, but the white block moved off anyway. Babies found this more surprising. They seemed to be born understanding how collisions work.

Later experiments confirmed this and many other aspects of baby physics using a refinement of this method called violation of expectation. The method was developed by American psychologist Elizabeth Spelke and her Canadian Ph.D. student Renée Baillargeon. Essentially, it involves showing babies magic tricks. Babies get to see two or more events, one of which is impossible. If they are surprised by this impossible event this is evidence they understand, at some level, why it was impossible. We say the event has violated the babies' expectations. Their drawbridge task from 1985 is a classic example (Baillargeon, Spelke & Wasserman, 1985), demonstrating that very young babies have knowledge of object solidity.

A flat panel is hinged to horizontal platform and can move like the screen of a laptop or a (tiny) drawbridge, facing the baby. At first the baby gets used to seeing the panel fold all the way forwards and all the way backwards. Then a block is placed behind the panel. Babies see two different events. In the 'possible' scenario the panel folds forward and then back, but the block prevents it folding flat. In the 'impossible' scenario the panel keeps folding all the way backwards as if squashing the solid block completely flat. Babies as young as three and half months consider this 'magic'. They look longer at this impossible event.

Using this violation of expectation method, researchers have found that very young babies know some key principles about the material world. These include object cohesion, solidity, continuity and how collisions work, and are equally applied to blocks, balls and rubber ducks. The experiments are famous amongst baby scientists. Not only did they show that babies are cleverer than we thought, but the experimental method is very clever too. It opened up new ways to ask babies questions. It has rightly made Baillargeon and Spelke very famous in our field, although their conclusions are not universally accepted.

Spelke believes we are born with a built-in set of 'core knowledge' that helps us get started in the world (Spelke & Kinzler, 2007). Her experiments with babies of three months certainly prove they understand a surprising amount. But they have also had a lot of experience by that age. Is it possible they could have learned these things? Everyone agrees babies learn so much, but could they learn everything they appear to understand? Is it nature or nurture? Spelke and colleagues are nativist, believing babies are born knowing these things. The contrasting empiricist view thinks they learn it all. That is the starting point for my own research, and my old lab, Birkbeck Babylab, is famously empiricist. My boss, Denis, would jokingly describe Spelke as the 'enemy'.

I remember meeting Spelke at my very first international conference, in Boston in 2007. The meeting of the Society for Research in Child Development (SRCD) is the largest child-development conference in the world. Even with several thousand scientists in attendance, Spelke was easily one of the most famous people there. Many big names in science have big egos to match. I had seen a few of these 'superstars' across the halls, rushing importantly about, trailing a large entourage. I was presenting a poster summarising my first ever experiments, and to my surprise Spelke turned up with one of her Ph.D. students in tow. They had explicitly come to talk to us because my poster related to her students' work. I was only halfway through my Ph.D., so it was intimidating, but she was charm personified and clearly very supportive of her own student. We had a very constructive discussion and it did not feel like I had just met the enemy.

What is more, on this issue she seems to be right: object knowledge does seem to be built in. Giorgio Vallortigara proved this with the assistance of some cute baby chickens. Whereas Mark Johnson had moved from imprinting in chicks to face recognition in babies, Vallortigara's research went the other way. Inspired by babies, he tried to find the same core knowledge in chicks. Amazingly, he succeeded (Vallortigara, 2012).

Vallortigara managed to run a version of the drawbridge task for the chicks by getting them to play hide and seek. A group of chicks were imprinted on tall red cylinders straight out of the egg. Just like the geese following Konrad Lorenz's wellies, these chicks would run towards tall red cylinders in preference to anything else. To test them, Vallortigara set up an arena with two grey, drawbridge-like panels at the far end. One was large enough to hide the cylinder; the other was sloping away and so was too low to be concealing a cylinder. When he released the chicks at the other end, they ran towards the larger one, the only place that could hide the cylinder.

This gives a nice proof that evolution can build in object knowledge if it wants to. But nature only takes you so far, and human babies have a lot more to learn about objects. Lots more of the actual physics seems to be acquired during nurture. Babies' core knowledge of gravity is limited at best. When you present young babies with an impossibly precarious tower of blocks or a plate dangling way too far off a table, it does not violate their expectations. Only with experience do they learn what works.

Gravity and associated mechanics seem to be among the things babies learn by experience. Waving or bashing an object is great fun if you have never done it before and it tells you about moments of acceleration and centres of gravity. There are so many ways to stack a pile of blocks and so many objects you could pile up that it would be difficult to specify an understanding in advance. It emerges very nicely from play. Recently Misha Denil and fellow scientists at Google DeepMind built a neural network that learned intuitive physics by knocking over randomly stacked piles of blocks (Denil et al., 2016). Knowing DeepMind, that computer is probably world jenga champion by now, but it learned just like a baby.

Babies do not stop there – they actively experiment. A nice study by Aimee Stahl and Lisa Feigenson of Johns Hopkins University demonstrated this with the aid of more magic. Eleven-month-old babies would watch two impossible events, one where a ball passed through a solid barrier and another where a toy car rolled off a table but stayed suspended in the air. When given the toys to play with, babies bashed the ball, testing its solidity and threw the car on the floor to test if it could really fly. A second group of babies saw the same tricks but with the object swapped – the car went through the wall and the ball floated. They bashed the cars and dropped the balls, testing the appropriate hypotheses (Stahl & Feigenson, 2015).

In 1996 I had an encounter with perhaps the most famous scientist in the world. I was finishing my mathematics degree at Cambridge and had a job interview with Stephen Hawking. It is not as impressive as it sounds. I was a very ordinary maths student, especially by Cambridge's or Stephen Hawking's standards. The job was not to assist him with his theories, but with his academic administration. I was worried I wouldn't keep up. I asked him how much maths I would need to know. I watched over his shoulder as he typed the answer, a twinkle in his eye.

THE...

GREEK...

ALPHABET

I didn't get the job but it was a good joke. Understanding the physical universe is less about numbers and more about formulas: generalisations that apply to the world you can see and to all the things you encounter afterwards. This could be learned by experience or you might save time by building them into genes. There is a more elegant solution: design genes to build a very basic set of core principles to help you learn the rest – a mixture of nature and nurture.

It was rather tricky getting this across to the audience of *The Joys of Toys*. The babies were given blocks and, sure enough, they knocked them down, but we did not have time to get across to parents just how much they were learning in the process. We did try a floating-ball magic trick. Using a fan a bit like a hairdryer, you can make a very light ball float in the air stream. We did this with a blue ball while a purple ball sat boringly on the floor. Turning the machine off, we triumphantly presented the two balls to the babies to see which one they would grab. The theory being they would prefer the gravity-defying blue one. Once again, the toddlers were having none of it. They ignored both balls and rushed straight for the machine to press the button for themselves, eager to experiment directly with the device that broke Newton's laws.

Baby Einstein

Play is the highest form of research.

— N. V. Scarfe, education specialist, 1962 (widely misattributed to Albert Einstein)

A few years ago Philip Shemella put his science career on hold to be a stay-at-home dad for his baby daughter. He wrote about his experiences and 'Life in the Baby Universe' for *Physics World* (Shemella, 2013). He learned very quickly that his daughter's knowledge of the gravity of falling objects did not extend to understanding her own gravity, so he kept her away from stairs. Shemella decided the four dimensions of the baby universe are eating, playing, crying and sleeping. He marvelled at her ability to scatter her food in random dispersion to the radius of one arm's length.

A lot of babies' play involves discovering Newton's laws of falling bodies, objects in motion, elastic and inelastic collisions. Meanwhile, new parents are learning first-hand the unforgiving second law of thermodynamics: left to themselves, everything gets messier and messier, always. Plonk any baby who can move around in an empty room with a box of toys and before you can say 'Nicolas Léonard Sadi Carnot', the box is empty and the room is strewn with ducks, trucks and plastic blocks.

At Birkbeck Babylab we would a run a version of this experiment several times a day. When a parent and baby arrived at the lab they would come into our brightly coloured reception area. We gave the parents a cup of tea and sat the babies on the floor next to our boxes of toys. We needed to tell the parents what we would like their babies to do, and we had to explain the science and obtain their informed consent. It takes about five to 10 minutes. In that time, a typical baby will have scattered most of our toys across the room. We also have a big orange bucket of toys to disinfect because many of those discarded items will have been in the baby's mouth.

Shemella decided that the 'eating dimension of the baby universe is closely coupled with the playing dimension' and, watching his daughter play with her food, he thought she had 'a primal urge to make chaos'. Inescapable, increasing chaos is part of our universe, and children as young as four understand that things move from order to disorder. It helps babies learn about time, the fourth dimension, and how fast it flies.

Psychologist William Friedman has investigated the former. In experiments with three- and four-year-olds he showed that they had an intuitive sense of entropy, a measure of how messy or jumbled up things are. To test the arrow of time in babies, he simply played them videos running forwards and backwards. Babies were surprised by water flowing back up into a jug and fallen objects rising up off the floor. But they were equally content when a cookie was broken into pieces as when it was magically reassembled. It could be the babies believed adults could mend broken cookies, just as the four-year-olds understood that adults tidy up after them. Or it could be they are having to learn about the arrow of time (Friedman, 2001, 2002).

My own research has looked at what babies know about how time passes. Working with Denis Mareschal at Birkbeck and Bob French and Elizabeth Thomas from the University of Burgundy in Dijon, our research identified three big problems with existing models of time perception. The first problem is that existing models say there is a clock in the brain. The trouble is, if there were any kind of clock in the brain, we would be better at judging long intervals than short ones, but we are not. Over longer intervals any variation in the ticking of our clock would tend to average out and so, relatively speaking, we would be more accurate. But researchers find, time and again, that errors grow faster than any theory should allow. We are equally bad at judging long and short intervals, suggesting there is no clock in your head. This would also explain why, in 40 years of looking, no one has ever found a clock circuit in the brain.

Secondly, time does not pass uniformly. Our perception of time changes depending on circumstances. As Einstein jokingly observed, 'Put your hand on a hot stove for a minute, and it seems like an hour. Sit with a pretty girl for an hour, and it seems like a minute. That's relativity.'

In fact it is even more complex than that. Imagine you are about to do something nerve-racking, like give a five-minute interview on live television. Five minutes before going on air you are off-camera waiting your turn and there is nothing for you to do but focus on the passing time. Those five minutes feel like for ever. Then you are live and suddenly everything is happening at once. You get to the end in no time and are surprised it is over so soon. Once it is over and you think back on it, the pattern is reversed. You remember little about the waiting, but the interview is full of event. If you did not know otherwise you would swear the interview was longer than the wait. Now that's relativity. Psychologists call this the differential effect of cognitive load on retrospective and prospective time judgements (Block, Hancock & Zakay, 2010). The problem was that no existing model explained both these phenomena simultaneously.

The third problem was that existing models could not explain where timing comes from or what a baby's sense of time would be like. They required a fully assembled clock-like mechanism somewhere in the brain. These clocks had varying degrees of biological plausibility, but in all cases researchers needed it. This was a problem and an opportunity. We were perhaps the first researchers to ask if time perception could be learned. As infancy researchers and empiricists, we wanted to build a computer model that learned like a baby.

We needed to see if babies understood time. Together with Sinead Rocha, our research assistant, Denis and I designed a simple experiment where a teddy bear would pop up on a screen every five seconds. This happened seven times in a row and on the eighth time the teddy stayed hidden; we measured when the babies looked for him. We then tested them again with a faster version, where a purple dinosaur popped up every three seconds. We tested babies from four to 14 months and found that they all looked at the right place at the right time. Their errors were similar to adults' (Addyman, Rocha & Mareschal, 2014).

This was surprising, so to double-check we ran a second experiment to turn the task into a more active game. This time Sinead sat opposite the baby and raised their arms up in the air. She did it seven times, each time saying, 'Ready? … Go!' and leaving a fixed gap each time. As before, on the eighth time we waited to see how the babies responded. Again we saw babies anticipating what would come next and when (Addyman et al., 2016). Mind you, a couple of other experiments were less successful. We tried one task where babies reached for toy ducks and another where they grabbed at a ball on a stick. The trouble was, the toys were too exciting and the babies would not easily let go.

By combining experiments with babies with a computational model that learns like a baby, we came up with a new theory of time perception. In a nutshell, it says that we guesstimate the passage of time based on how our memories fade (French, Addyman, Mareschal & Thomas, 2014). It is a bit beyond the scope of this book to go into the mechanics, but the concept is very simple. Rather than using a special clock circuit in the brain, we suggest our sense of time uses what is already there – our memory of what just happened. The longer ago an event was, the fuzzier your memory.

Our timing accuracy is poor because memories are inherently uncertain. The 'relativity of time' is the result of a combination of two things: how much is happening and how much attention we are paying to the passage of time. Our model quantifies how these two factors interact to create distortions of time. The more that happens, the faster your memories fade, making recent events feel further in the past. Yet with more happening, the less attention you give to the passing of time and it feels like things are happening faster. Relatively speaking!

When writing about our model, I was rather proud when I managed to cite Albert Einstein's famous breakthrough paper on Brownian motion in justification for our fuzziness factor (Einstein, 1905). Brownian motion has nothing to do with Einstein's own theories of time dilation, but it is quite closely related to the concept of entropy. It is the jiggly, random path a big particle takes when it is buffeted by smaller objects, not unlike a little baby crawling around a room scattered with toys. In our model, each of those interactions is an event adding to our experience, and it is the accumulation of fading events that lets us measure the passage of time. When you say it like that, it is obvious this is what time is. Yet, strangely, no other theory worked like that. Other theories clung to a clock. Only by seeing the problem through the eyes of a baby were we able to realise that was not necessary. Babies discover the dimension of time through play.

Categories and Doggeries

One of these things is not like the others,
One of these things doesn't belong.
Can you tell which is not like the others
By the time I finish this song?
— 'One of These Things' from *Sesame Street*, 1969

Where does the idea of a cat come from? We see lots of cats, but how and when do we first start to see that Fluffy, Lucky and Tigger are all individuals from the same family? When do babies know their toy giraffe is the same kind of thing as the giants they see in the zoo? How do they work out their toy cars, trains and diggers are little cousins of the exciting vehicles they see on their travels? When do they acquire abstract concepts like animal, vehicle or food? All the evidence shows that most of this happens sooner than you think. It is one of the great intellectual achievements of young babies and we do not give them enough credit.

How do babies do it? To answer this question, psychologists often reach for the toys. Toys represent a microcosm of the world.

A plastic giraffe or a rubber duck does not share much with a real giraffe or duck. They are made from different materials and have different textures. The physical resemblance is only superficial – not much more than the idea of 'giraffeness' or 'duckness'. This is exactly what categories are: the essence of things. Working in the 1970s, Eleanor Rosch suggested categorisation serves to simplify the world. She thought categories 'carve nature at its joints'. This phrase originates in Plato's *Phaedrus* and expresses the idea that categories are 'real' in a Platonic sense, reflecting true features of the world (Rosch, 1975).

Scientists often give babies toys to see what they understand about categories. For example, you could give babies a mixture of toy animals and toy vehicles and see what happens. American psychologist Jean Mandler did this, and watched very carefully to notice that babies did not play randomly. Some played first with one set then the other, while other babies alternated between the two. Both patterns are non-random, showing babies are treating the animals and vehicles as different kinds of things.

It is worth stopping to consider how this experiment is done. Each baby must be filmed playing with the toys and a researcher must go through the video frame by frame, counting and classifying every touch of every object. They must check these judgements with a second coder and then they must run lots of statistical simulations to see if these patterns of touch are random or not. In some studies there are over 100 babies. Baby research is often labour-intensive and reliant on complex methods to ask simple questions.

Experiments with toys are especially tricky, as babies love toys too much. It is difficult to get them to let go of the cow so you can show them the car.

For this reason, most baby experiments stick to showing things on a screen. I ran a couple of categorisation experiments like this during my Ph.D. In one experiment I Photoshopped leopard-print fabric or swimming-pool blue over the windows of cars and the roofs of houses. We thought babies might use this single highly conspicuous feature to group the objects, but the babies sometimes did one thing, sometimes another. The experiment was inconclusive but did add to evidence that babies' categorisation is flexible and responsive to the world.

My collaborators on the time project, Denis and Bob, have a fantastic set of experiments that prove this. First, they demonstrated that three- to four-month-old babies think cats are dogs but dogs are not cats. Then they showed the opposite. In experiment one, a group of babies saw photos of 10 highly varied dogs followed by a single cat. They decided it could easily fit into the group that had gone before. Another group of babies saw 10 similar-looking cats followed by a dog, and they noticed that this final furry creature was not like the others. The really clever bit came in Denis and Bob's second experiment, where they reversed this strange asymmetry. This time one group of babies saw 10 highly varied cats and decided the dog that followed could be part of that diverse family, while another group saw 10 very similar dogs in a row followed by a cat, and decided this cat didn't belong in the group (French, Mareschal, Mermillod & Quinn, 2004). This shows that for babies, 'dog' and 'cat' are flexible categories that get built by experience and depend upon the similarities that they can see.

You can do a version of this experiment if you take a toddler to the zoo. Depending on the age of your toddler, you may find the bears, llamas and rhinos get triumphantly labelled 'Sheep!' or 'Doggy!' but all lions, tigers, leopards and cheetahs get correctly labelled 'cat'. This shows us two clever things about babies and their categories. First, they are building their world from the ground up in a highly dynamic and flexible way. From three months babies can spot the similarities and differences between sets of objects. Second, this fuzzy matching helps you get along in a complex world.

You do not need many categories before you can put them to some use. Being approximately right is better than being frozen in uncertainty. My friend Megan took her two-year-old daughter to the London Aquarium and everything in every tank, however weird and wonderful, was gleefully labelled 'Fish!'

Imagine you had got through your life without ever encountering a banana. This could equally be a dragon fruit, a starfruit or a persimmon, but let's go with banana. Bananas are the funniest fruit. Encountering a banana for the very first time, you would know at a glance that it was a fruit. It looks organic; it is brightly coloured; it is larger than a pea and smaller than a car. The evidence matches up with your previous experiences of fruit. Maybe it is in the fruit bowl or the fruit aisle – context matters too. You do not yet know what a banana tastes like or if you like it, but all your other fruit knowledge would be a useful guide. Categories do this for us and it is their value. Adults, with our extensive experience, might not encounter new animals, minerals or vegetables very often. Our world is already built. Babies are building theirs and their model needs to be flexible and accommodating.

The Best Toy Ever?

Be humble, be simple, bring joy to others.

— Saint Madeleine Sophie Barat, Founder of the Society of the Sacred Heart (1779–1865)

If you wanted to pick the absolute best toy to give a baby, Sophie the Giraffe is a very strong contender. In her home country of France, Sophie is a national icon, launched in 1961 on the feast day of Saint Madeleine Sophie Barat, founder of the Society of the Sacred Heart, a religious order dedicated to providing educational opportunities for girls. Sophie the Giraffe is a teething toy. She is 18 centimetres tall and made from natural rubber. In 2010 816,000 Sophies were sold in France. In the same year only 796,000 babies were born in France. For many years she was also the bestselling baby toy on Amazon, although she has since been usurped by a purple octopus.

Sophie has a lot of the qualities that make a great baby toy. She is chewable and has all kinds of interesting lumps and bumps that make her interesting to mouth. Tall and elegant, Sophie is also eminently graspable. She is an intriguing three-dimensional object that affords a lot of manual and visual activity. With her long legs and neck, her striking spots and horn-like ossicones,

Sophie is unmistakably a member of the category of giraffes, but she is also unmistakably an individual. Her big round eyes and smiling expression give her character and personality. In my years working in baby research, I have met many infants who were inseparable from their Sophie. I expect one reason the sales figures are so good is from all the parents buying a second, stand-in Sophie, in case she ever gets lost.

Sophie makes a strong case, but I think there is a newer toy that all babies want to get their hands on. Launched on 9 January 2007 and 11.5 centimetres tall, it has gone on to be a far bigger global phenomenon than Sophie. It is more expensive and more magical, although as a physical object it is not much to look at, but if you put them side by side, I can safely hypothesise that any baby born this decade would grab an iPhone over a giraffe. In 2016, 20.2 million smartphones were sold in France. Not many babies have their own smartphones, but almost every baby born that year will have had their hands on one.

Our smartphones are the most the most interesting, compelling and curious things in our own lives. Even a young baby can recognise our fascination with our devices. They might not understand your addiction to the little glowing rectangle you carry everywhere, but they get enough opportunities to see its power over you. Babies want what you've got, and there is no question that babies like smartphones and tablets. Confronted with a screaming baby, there are few more effective pacifiers than handing over your phone. It usually works instantly. But is this just creating an addiction in your infant to match your own? Is it OK to give them tablets to play with?

Plenty of voices warn that screen time is bad for young children, but often without direct evidence or based only on babies' passive television viewing. For example, in 2011 a report from the influential American Academy of Pediatrics (AAP) recommended zero screen time for under-twos. This was before touchscreen devices took off. In 2016 they revisited the evidence; their new report discouraged screen media use for children under 18 months, except for video-chatting like Skype and Facetime. Thereafter, they said, high-quality apps and media should be introduced under parental supervision (AAP, 2011 & 2016). During that period, ownership of these devices increased from under 10% to over 90% of families. The revolution has been fast and the interactive nature of tablets changes the equation dramatically, but research has been slow to catch up.

Recently a group of my former colleagues at Birkbeck decided to tackle the issue. Led by Rachael Bedford and Tim Smith, they won funding to launch the Toddler Attentional Behaviours and Learning with Touchscreens (TABLET) project. They are using a mixture of online surveys of parents and in-depth lab assessments of smaller groups of infants. Their research is still running, but their early results have been surprising. An incredible 99.7% of families in their survey had at least one touchscreen and 51% of babies from six to 12 months use a touchscreen daily, rising to over 80% at two years. This is a toy that we do not grow out of.

The TABLET group found no impact, negative or positive, on most milestones like walking, sitting or language. They found fine-motor control was positively correlated with earlier active scrolling of tablets. Babies who scrolled earlier were also better at stacking blocks (Bedford et al., 2016). This result is correlational, suggesting the two skills are linked: it could be that flicking across the screen improves babies' fine motor control, or it could be that naturally nimble-fingered babies master screens faster. The TABLET group's ongoing lab studies are designed to address this.

In a second analysis they found that greater tablet use was related to reduced sleep and delayed sleep onset (Cheung et al., 2017). Again, the result shows the two things could be linked: maybe babies who naturally need less sleep spend more time on tablets. Demonstrating that tablets cause sleep problems for babies is much harder. It would require careful tracking of babies' sleep and tablet use over an extended period, which the TABLET group do not have the resources to undertake.

Despite these mixed results, the TABLET researchers are optimistic about the benefits of touchscreens for babies. This was one of the last projects my influential colleague Annette Karmiloff-Smith worked on before she died in 2017. Always a champion of progress, she was unequivocal in her view that tablets are excellent toys for babies. In an interview about the study she said, 'Tablets should be part of a baby's world from birth.' She thought they were even better than books: 'Books are static. When you observe babies with books, all they are interested in is the sound of the pages turning. Their visual system at that age is attracted by movement. That is why tablets, which have moving pictures and sound, are very good.' (Ali, 2015).

When I asked what he advises parents, Tim Smith from the TABLET group said, 'The scientific jury is still out about the positive and negative impacts of touchscreen devices on young children. But we can learn lessons from issues like diet and exercise, namely that balance is key. A parent wouldn't feed a toddler only chips. Likewise, they should aim for a varied diet of different types of screen time with real-world physical and social activities.'

If toddlers could choose, they might well opt for chips at every meal and will certainly prefer your smartphone to any other toy there is. They are not even wrong to think that. A smartphone is a magical device with endless possibilities. It is one of the few things that matches the infinite curiosity of a baby.

Chapter Eight: Surprise!

The cure for boredom is curiosity. There is no cure for curiosity.
— Ellen Parr

Babies love surprises. Except when they don't.

Novelty delights them except when it is so surprising that it scares them. The boundaries of fear and delight are constantly shifting. On any given day, squeals of excitement and howls of terror are equally likely. Parents are never entirely sure how new experiences will be received. This does not slow babies down – they are little novelty junkies, always drawn towards things they do not understand (or are not allowed). Yet they also get bored very quickly, their attention frequently moving on to the next new thing. This is good for them because it leads them to explore the world. It is also good for baby scientists. Making babies bored then seeing what it takes to surprise them has been the core method of baby research for the last 40 years.

Boredom: The One Weird Trick of Baby Science

If monkeys could become bored, they would become human.
— Johann Wolfgang von Goethe, German polymath (1749–1832)

One reason I started studying baby laughter is that I was bored of making them bored. Most of modern baby science is built on one ingenious invention called the habituation paradigm. It involves making babies bored and then trying to surprise them again. This experimental design has been used in thousands of experiments with babies. It is the first thing we think of when designing any new study. It is incredibly versatile because it exploits the fact that babies get bored with anything and everything. Babies have an attention span measured in seconds. Scientists like to measure things, so everyone is happy.

The idea of boredom, as English speakers understand it, was invented by the Victorians. In her 2015 book *The Book of Human Emotions*, historian Tiffany Watt Smith explains that the word first appears in English in 1853 as a derivative of the French word *bourrer*, to stuff or force-feed. It occurs in Charles Dickens's *Bleak House* when Lady Dedlock is 'bored to death' by her lonely life. Of course, the experience of being bored existed before we had a word for it. For millennia, languages have had words to describe when things are tedious or irksome. I have not been able to find the original German version of the Goethe quote above, so I am not entirely sure what he thought was happening to humans and not monkeys. In the French it translates as *s'ennuyer*, a reflexive verb literally meaning to annoy oneself. Interestingly, *bourrer* is a transitive verb, which means it gets done to something or someone. To be bored is to be fed up. Tiffany argues that the upper- and middle-class Victorians needed a word for boredom when too much leisure time was forced upon them.

In habituation experiments, baby scientists fill babies so full of an idea that they become bored of it. Then we see what it takes to revive them. We already encountered the habituation method in the previous chapter, where Denis and Bob were testing babies' knowledge of cats and dogs. Given how important it is as a method, it is worth going through it in greater detail. The fact that the method is effective reveals a lot about how babies' brains work.

First we must look at a brain 5 million times smaller than ours, because habituation is a universal property of brains. Understanding this fact was worthy of a Nobel Prize, which was won by Eric Kandel in 2000. The brains he looked at belonged to *Aplysia californica*, the California sea hare, a type of slug. Weighing in at several kilograms and made up of around 35 centimetres of mottled reddish-brown sliminess, they are exceptionally ugly creatures. Nonetheless, Kandel considers them beautiful and their beauty is in their brains. Their entire nervous system has only 18,000 neurons, 50 times smaller than a bee brain. *Aplysi*a brains are tiny but their neurons are giant. Each one can be 50 times larger than mammalian neurons and are so massive you can see them with the naked eye. This made them an ideal laboratory animal for Kandel to study how learning happened.

Kandel was interested in learning and memory, which are closely intertwined. When learning to do something new, you encode it in your memory. Eric Kandel was the first person to work out how this happened at a neuronal level (Kandel, 1976). He did this by teaching his slugs to ignore him. If you poke an *Aplysia* with an electrode, it reflexively withdraws the gill and siphon on its back as a defensive measure. Kandel would wait until the slug went back to normal and then he would poke it again… and again… and again. Eventually, the slug would come to ignore the pokes, learning not to withdraw its gill. Kandel looked at the chain of neurons that controlled the initial reflex and how they changed as the slug habituated. The exact details of the cellular process are not important right now, but isn't it good to know you can get a Nobel Prize for annoying slugs?

Habituation experiments with babies are somewhat different. We certainly do not poke babies with electrodes, we cannot peer directly into their brains and babies are way cuter than slugs. But the earliest experiments were conceptually very similar to Kandel's work. The pioneer of infant habituation, Les Cohen, like Kandel, was working in the early 1970s. He would sit babies opposite a screen in a darkened room with few distractions. Then he would show them a picture like a simple chequerboard and measure how long it was until the baby looked away. Then he would show them the same picture again… and again… and again. Babies, like slugs, got bored. They looked longest at the start but less and less over time (Cohen, 1972).

This is exactly as you would expect. The weird trick in the title of this section is what you do once the babies are bored. We normally define boredom (aka habituation) as a 50% decrease in average looking. To determine this, we keep a running average of babies' looking from the first two pictures compared to the most recent two pictures, using an average because babies can be quite unpredictable. They may easily get distracted by a parent, by their socks or by random baby thoughts. Once they are bored, we test them by showing something different. After a dozen dogs we could show them a cat. After a succession of female faces, we could show a man. If the babies perk up and look longer, it indicates they understand there is a difference. If they stay bored, they are probably not noticing the difference.

Using this method, we can ask babies all kinds of questions and they can answer. We can ask about perception of colour or size or orientation, about categories of animals or people, about concepts like number and relations like sameness or 'in front of'. Using sounds instead of pictures you can test what babies understand about speech or music. Babies can tell dogs and cats apart by five months. At around four to six months babies not only learn to tell male from female faces, but they can know the difference between emotional expressions like happiness, sadness, anger and disgust. Habituation shows cases where young babies can discriminate things older babies and adults cannot. For example, six-month-olds can tell one monkey face from another, a task that ten-month-olds and adults fail. Likewise, at six months babies can discriminate the speech sounds of all languages but by a year they hear only those relevant to their native tongue. This is an example of perceptual narrowing and we will revisit it in the chapter on language (Maurer & Werker, 2014).

One important refinement of this method is to include

something super-exciting at the very end. This is to check the babies are still paying attention, as they sometimes zone out. In my Ph.D. I was habituating babies to some rather dull shapes, which looked like outlines of a house with a big white arrow on it. Each one was slightly different. I was interested in whether the babies learned the average. The trouble is, the babies might know the difference but could be so bored they just do not care any more. Therefore, all my habituation experiments ended with a photo of a bunny rabbit. My experimental results were mixed but I could very strongly conclude that babies like bunnies.

Once I had survived my Ph.D., I decided to celebrate by getting my left arm tattooed with various images from my research. Naturally I had to include the rabbit, although with a nod to my time-perception research, I transformed it into the White Rabbit from *Alice's Adventures in Wonderland*, carrying a large pocket watch to measure how quickly I made the babies bored.

The swiftness with which babies get bored is very convenient for baby scientists, as it means we can run an experiment in around 10 minutes. This is helpful because we often do not have long with any given baby. The experiment is not the only thing that makes the baby fed up: the whole experience of visiting the lab and meeting new people can be exhausting. We deliberately try not to get the baby too excited before the study in case it affects their ability to concentrate. If you are cunning and organised, you might run two or three studies in a single visit, but you always put the most important one first.

The speed and universality of infant habituation also gives lots of clues as to how our brains operate. Kandel's slugs were learning by permanently strengthening certain wiring inside their tiny brains. Human brains are more flexible than this. Sylvain Sirois and Denis Mareschal make a good case that infant habituation involves the interaction of two brain areas. It is a combination of short-term inhibition in the hippocampus and long-term potentiation in the cortex (Sirois & Mareschal, 2004). The hippocampus is the gatekeeper to long-term memory. When something new happens to you – or a baby – the hippocampus keeps a short-term note while comparing it to previous experience. If the new thing is like lots of old things, the hippocampus is inhibited, meaning we are not as interested. If it is unfamiliar, then the hippocampus is not inhibited. The more active the hippocampus, the more likely information about the event gets encoded into long-term memory by strengthening connections between neurons by long-term potentiation, just like in slugs.

Habituation is the workhorse of infant research and the engine of infant exploration. It is just one mechanism of learning, but it is an important one for babies, who experience so many new things and have so much to explore. Habituation keeps them learning, but it also keeps them moving on to the next new thing and the next. At the same time, habituation on its own does not seem to capture the full joy of being a baby. They do not just act to avoid boredom – they actively seek out interesting things. They delight in their play and revel in their discoveries. There is clearly more going on.

Goldilocks and the Zone of Optimal Experience

When Silver-hair came into the kitchen, she saw the three bowls of porridge. She tasted the largest bowl, which belonged to the Big Bear, and found it too cold; then she tasted the middle-sized bowl, which belonged to the Middle-sized Bear, and found it too hot; then she tasted the smallest bowl, which belonged to the Little Bear, and it was just right, and she ate it all.

— *The Three Bears*, Robert Southey, English poet, 1837

The first experiment of my Ph.D. was also about baby boredom, but it did not involve habituation. Instead we showed babies long sequences of looming coloured shapes. A yellow square would loom towards them in the middle of a screen, then a blue triangle, then a red circle, then maybe a yellow square again, and so on. There were six shapes in all. In half the cases there was a repeating structure, with the shapes coming in pairs: red always followed blue, green always followed yellow, pink always followed turquoise. In the other half, the sequences were completely random. We found that babies looked longer at randomness (Addyman & Mareschal, 2013).

Before any weary parents scoff that of course babies love to gaze upon chaos, I need to explain there was more to it than that. These types of tasks are often used to study infant language-learning abilities. The structured sequences are called 'artificial grammars'. The individual shapes can be thought of syllables and their pairs as words. The structured sequence was a simple language with just six syllables and three two-syllable words, while the random sequence was a babble of syllables.

Our experiment found babies considered the grammar less interesting than the nonsense. They tuned it out faster because it had more repetitive bits. We concluded that babies' exploration of the world is guided by the complexity they encounter.

This was not a new idea. When he was developing the habituation method, Les Cohen speculated that babies' interest in pictures would show an inverted U-shaped pattern. If they were too simple, babies would get bored quickly; if they were too complex, babies would not comprehend what they were seeing and get bored; but if they were just right, babies would stay engaged the longest.

This is an appealing, intuitive idea, but it was many decades before anyone tried to quantify it. This happened when infant psychologists Celeste Kidd and Dick Aslin teamed up with computer scientist Steve Piantadosi (Kidd, Piantadosi & Aslin, 2012). They used visual sequences and, like my study, they found babies were guided by surprise and 'interestingness'. Their method and equations were more sophisticated than mine and they were able to show the full U-shaped curve, just as Les Cohen had predicted. Babies were engaged most by things with just right level of complexity. They called this the Goldilocks Effect after the choosy little home invader. (In Robert Southey's original story the sleepy porridge thief was a silver-haired old lady; only later was she transformed into a child with golden locks.)

I asked Celeste Kidd where her study had originated from. 'We were trying to understand the link between babies' expectations and where they look. People had been theorising about this for a long time, but all those old theories of curiosity were articulated in human language, which is very ambiguous.' And worse, 'none of them are right'.

For example, in Jean Piaget's early theories of infant development from the 1930s, he talked about babies engaged in an ascending cycle of assimilation and accommodation. Accommodation is when the baby adjusts their behaviour to new things they are encountering in the world. Assimilation happens once the baby has learned a new rule and starts finding things that fit with it. First, I must learn to grasp a spoon in a particular way. Then I discover I can scoop or bash things with it.

Piaget thought these cycles were well structured and proceeded in stages, like a sequence of puzzles a baby must solve to unlock the next level of understanding of the world. Looking backwards from an adult perspective, this is a rational post hoc explanation of how babies learn, but the point of Celeste's research is that it does not seem this way to the baby. The problem was noticed by psychologist William James way back in 1890. He pointed out that experience is an active process and 'only those items which I notice shape my mind; without selective interest, experience is an utter chaos' (James, 1890, p. 402).

The Goldilocks Effect is about what is just right for that baby at that time. You often hear it said that babies are little sponges, but it is the wrong metaphor. They do soak up information, but not in a passive way like a sponge. They are more like magpies or collector crabs actively seeking out shiny things. The things that capture a particular baby's attention on a particular day depend on how surprising they are for them. For one it might be the swish of curtains, for another the crinkle of a crisp packet. A morning's activities might explore putting things on other things, while the afternoon includes babbling and pulling off socks.

In one delightfully weird study from 1970 Tom Shultz tried to gauge babies' understanding of new experiences by measuring their smiles (Shultz & Zigler, 1970). He dangled a toy clown in front of three-month-old babies and waited until they smiled. For some babies, he held the clown still; for others, the clown would be swinging gently backwards and forwards. Babies smiled much faster with the stationary clown. Shultz thought the swinging made it more complex for the babies and so their smile spread more slowly.

If you type 'surprised baby' into YouTube, you will find many variations of Tom Shultz's experiment. In a typical example of the genre a baby (anywhere between two and 12 months) is filmed sitting in chubby-cheeked contemplation of the world when a well-meaning parent spins a swirly toy or bops a bouncy puppet. Almost without exception the babies jerk backward in shock at the unexpected movement. Lips wobble. There may be laughter or there may be tears. The stronger the reaction, the more times the videos are likely to get shared, but with a hefty advantage for tragedy over comedy.

One lesson is that adults are terrible. The other is that babies sail a tempestuous sea. Surprises can delight or enchant, frustrate or frighten. They live in a cluttered, chaotic world that does not make sense. To make matter worse, the world is stochastic. Stochastic is from the ancient Greek for 'guess' and is just a scientist's fancy word for 'unpredictable'. The world is random but not totally so. Roll a dice and you cannot predict whether you get one or six, but you will never get seven or water buffalo.

Our experiments show that babies are sensitive to likelihoods in their world and use them to inform their explorations. They actively select the things they can learn best from. In this sense I would claim, like Goldilocks in that moment, that they are happy. I would go further and say they are living meaningful lives. I cannot easily prove it, but I strongly believe babies are experiencing a deep existential satisfaction that comes from time spent in the zone of optimal experience. Often just known as 'the zone'.

Being 'in the zone' is a phrase associated with sporting excellence, but it comes from the field of positive psychology. It was coined by Hungarian psychologist Mihaly Csikszentmihalyi. Starting his investigations in the 1970s, he wondered what made people happy. He was inspired by Abraham Maslow's famous work on the hierarchy of needs. Maslow, an American psychologist, said that after basic needs like food, warmth and shelter are met, we still crave companionship, recognition and meaning. Maslow imagined these as a pyramid with physiological needs like food, oxygen and water at the base, building up through security, love and confidence to a peak of 'self-actualisation', reached in rare occasions where someone achieves their full potential.

Csikszentmihalyi thought this put too much emphasis on elusive peak experiences and undervalued everyday success. Initially he studied the absorption and satisfaction experienced by artists as they create new work. He quickly realised this same state was shared by remarkably happy people from all walks of life. As he outlines in his book, *Flow: The Psychology of Optimal Experience* (1990), he studied everyone from musicians, athletes and chefs to prisoners, farmers and production-line workers. They all entered a 'flow state' where they became absorbed in doing something well. The happiest people were the ones who reached that state most often. It happened because they were constantly challenging themselves, refining their skills. This confirmed a two-millennia-old prediction of Aristotle, who speculated that pleasure consists of achieving mastery of the world.

Following the publication of Csikszentmihalyi's book, many Montessori teachers pointed out that their schools cultivate this same mindset in their pupils. Csikszentmihalyi studied Montessori primary-school children and found that this was the case. It inspired him to speculate that the same holds true all the way down into infancy. He never found a way to test his theory with babies. His research method, 'experience sampling', involves interrupting people at random points in their day to ask them what they are doing and how focused they are. Obviously, this will not work with babies, although they undoubtedly spend a lot of time in 'the zone'. Flow is found when you get the balance between boredom and anxiety just right. It plays with our natural tendencies 'to seek continuity (comfort) in the face of overwhelming change, and change (stimulation) in the face of numbing continuity' (p.500, Rathunde & Csikszentmihalyi, 2007).

Curiosity: Why Babies Get out of Bed in the Morning

We are driven by the usual insatiable curiosity of the scientist, and our work is a delightful game.

— Murray Gell-Mann, winner of the 1969 Nobel Prize for Physics

Scientists love their own curiosity. Murray Gell-Mann, quoted above, had eminent company with Einstein, who described himself as 'passionately curious', and palaeontologist Mary Leakey, who felt she was 'compelled by curiosity'. Embryologist Christiane Nüsslein-Volhard, discussing her Nobel Prize for Physiology and Medicine, saw her scientific career as natural continuation of the 'big curiosity' she had possessed as a child. This is perhaps no surprise. It is part of the job description of a scientist to poke around at the edges of their own understanding.

In baby science we go one step further. We are curious about curiosity itself. We are enthralled by babies' own sense of wonder, and we delight in their delight. We ponder deeply the thoughts of philosophical preschoolers with their constant refrain of 'Why?' and we commonly repeat the line that 'babies are little scientists'. In fact, Alison Gopnik from the University of California, Berkeley, takes it further still. In a paper entitled 'The Scientist as Child', she argues there are deep and important similarities between the ways children and scientists learn about the world. Moreover, since childhood comes before science both individually and collectively, she says, 'The moral of my story is not that children are little scientists but that scientists are big children' (p.485, Gopnik, 1997).

Gopnik was not the first to make this link. The American philosopher John Dewey came to a similar conclusion 100 years earlier. Today, Dewey is best known as a philosopher, but he was also a psychologist and an educational reformer. When he moved to the University of Chicago in 1894, he did so on condition he could set up the Laboratory School, a working school with nursery and primary teaching where progressive educational ideas could be trialled. By 1901 it had 140 children and 33 teaching staff. It still exists today as a private school, with more than 2,000 students with fees of over $30,000 a year.

Based on his observations of children at the Lab School, Dewey wrote a book called *How We Think* (1910). It was a short book but one that changed the world. In one section, discussing how children learn, he analysed the steps involved in 'a complete act of thought'. He wrote:

> Upon examination, each instance reveals, more or less clearly, five logically distinct steps: (i) a felt difficulty; (ii) its location and definition; (iii) suggestion of possible solution; (iv) development by reasoning of the bearings of the suggestion; (v) further observation and experiment leading to its acceptance or rejection; that is, the conclusion of belief or disbelief. (p.72, Dewey, 1910)

As historian of science Henry Cowles recounts, this single paragraph changed how scientific thinking was understood. It became the textbook description of the scientific method and is one of the most widely quoted passages in the philosophy of science. Apparently this annoyed Dewey, who was trying to explain how we all think, not just children or scientists (Cowles, 2017).

Dewey's paragraph is a precise, if somewhat dry, description of problem-solving, scientific or otherwise. It works well as a model of how babies, children and the rest of us progress when confronted with a 'felt difficulty'. It does not explain what gets us into those difficulties in the first place. Curiosity is the answer. Much earlier in the book Dewey explains that 'wonder is the mother of all science' and 'eagerness for experience, for new and varied contacts, is found where wonder is found'. Curiosity is the engine of our difficulties and of their resolution.

Nowhere is this more apparent than in the daily lives of babies. Most achievements are not goals in themselves – they start out as accidental discoveries made in all babies' delightful games. All day long babies are constantly moving and constantly observing their effect on the world. Many wonderful things happen in the process of trial and error. A baby lying on her back who cannot yet roll over spots a colourful toy off to her left; she reaches for it and accidentally rolls herself over. A baby trying to grab two things accidentally drops a small block into a pot with a satisfying clunk. The rewards of actions are noticed, but the connection between cause and effect is not.

The babies' difficulties come as they try to repeat or extend their achievement.

Babies often surprise themselves with their new tricks. A baby cannot know in advance where a sequence of skills ultimately leads, but each is accompanied by a new set of unexpected goals. Secret doors opening to whole new worlds. For example, sitting unsupported frees up both hands to explore objects more effectively, but this has difficulties of its own. Babies must have dexterity and coordination to pass Sophie the Giraffe from one hand to another or turn her to a preferred angle. Understanding the objects she picks up widens the horizon of the baby's attention. The toy that is out of reach now becomes the most desirable. Crawling happens and then the geography of the world suddenly comes alive to the baby. As Dewey says elsewhere, 'arriving at one goal is the starting point to another'.

Short attention spans are compensated by huge determination. Karen Adolph and colleagues carefully tracked 151 babies as they learned to walk. Babies averaged over 2,000 steps and 17 falls per hour. Learning to walk takes time and large amounts of practice, but the pay-off is huge. Walkers can cover much more distance much more quickly than crawlers (Adolph et al., 2012). At first this might not seem like a cognitive triumph – walking is action, not thought. But the real achievement of walking is to transform the baby's experience of reality, and the motivation to keep getting up after each fall is central to the process. An adult sees that the baby has acquired a new physical ability; the baby sees a whole new world, with more opportunities and new difficulties.

Alison Gopnik does not cite Dewey in her article, but her work takes his ideas forward into the current century. She is a leading advocate for something called 'theory theory'. As a 'theory theory' theorist, Gopnik sees babies as problem-solvers par excellence and believes their success comes because they expect problems to have solutions. She thinks babies are highly successful at learning about cause and effect because they come with an in-built theory that this is the way the world works. As theories go, it is a pretty good one, albeit very 'meta' with brain-twistingly recursive aspects. For example, is the fact I find theory theory appealing attributable to theory theory?

For now all we need to know is that theory theory makes two large advances in our understanding of understanding in babies. Firstly, it takes the nativist versus empiricist debate in an interesting direction. Secondly, it does this by bringing some very heavyweight conceptual machinery down into Babyland. Even if theory theory turns out to be wrong, it has already changed the way we make theories about babies.

Let's take this in reverse order. Theory theory claims even very young brains can solve problems about cause and effect, and they can do this by having things like scientific theories in their heads. In a simple case we can see how this might work. *If* I bash these pots and pans with this wooden spoon *then* it causes a pleasing cacophony. But inferences quickly get a lot more complex. *If* I bash this pot *and* mum is nearby *and* she is in a good mood *and* she is not trying to use the pan *or* talk on the phone *then* she might find it pleasing too… for the first few minutes.

Even the simple cases are not completely straightforward. As every scientist knows, all observations are unreliable. Babies experience this too: maybe an uncoordinated swipe misses the pan entirely, or it does connect but the baby's fingers get in the way? Or the baby gets distracted and does not notice every bang. So how do you draw the right conclusion from your unreliable observations? The solution was discovered in the 1750s by the Reverend Thomas Bayes. Bayes' rule is a simple law of probability that lets you pick the best hypothesis to explain your unreliable data.

The formulas for Bayes' theorem look mysterious, and most explanations given by statisticians only make things worse. But we all do Bayesian inference many thousands of times a day and do not realise. Let me give you a simple example. Ordinary probabilities can give us predictive text, which follows 'Miley' with 'Cyrus' or 'Washington' with 'DC'. Bayes' rule and its conditional probabilities are what allow the modern Google search box to be even cleverer. Because your favourite search engine knows about you personally, it knows to follow 'Miles' with 'Davis' for jazz fans and with 'per gallon' for car enthusiasts. It knows to follow 'New York' with 'weather' for you but with 'Knicks' for your brother, the sports junkie. We do this too. We adjust our expectations according to where we are, what we're doing and who we're with.

Suppose I show you a fish tank filled with 80% white ping-pong balls and 20% red ones. I cover the box with a cloth and, without looking, I draw out five balls. Four are red and one is white. You would be surprised by this, wouldn't you? It seems 'unlikely', given what you know. You would be right to be surprised. Amazingly, when six-month-old babies see this in an experiment they are also surprised. But what if I was looking as I drew out mainly red balls from a container of mainly white ones? Then you would infer that I prefer red ones. Eleven-month-olds can do this too. If they encounter a person who really likes red balls, they are not surprised if she picks out red balls when she can see into the box, but they are surprised if she does this while blindfolded (Xu & Kushnir, 2013). Most of our own inferences are like this; they happen when we judge what we expect other people to do based on what we know about them.

We normally call this intuition because we cannot easily explain how we do it. For a long time, statisticians could not explain it either. Bayes' theorem worked well for picking one hypothesis for one set of data. If everyone coming into the building is wet, it must be raining outside. It could not cope with a complex, messy real world with multiple interacting factors, agents and sources of uncertainty. Why did half the class turn up late today? Then, in 1982, computer scientist Judea Pearl solved causality. In a four-page paper he demonstrated that Bayes' theorem could be extended to more complex cases. He drew graphs of how all the factors interacted and provided an elegant recipe to balance things out (Pearl, 1982). Bayes' theorem was generalised to Bayesian networks, which could be analysed with Pearl's belief propagation algorithm. Not many people understood him, so Pearl had to expand his four-page argument out into three books, and then his beliefs propagated widely. The original paper was cited by 777 other authors. The books have been cited by 40,729.

This is not the final word on causality, and vast armies of statisticians and machine-learning experts are concerned with how to make even more effective causal inferences. But the rest of the story is more technical and philosophical than we need to worry about. Suffice it to say, Judea Pearl's methods were a giant leap forward.

Alison Gopnik and other theory theorists, in collaboration with mathematically inclined cognitive scientists like Josh Tenenbaum, are making baby steps to applying the same ideas to infant learning. Most exciting for developmental scientists like me, this brings something new to the nature–nurture debate. Nativists and empiricists both agree that babies achieve remarkable things in the first few years. The nativists always insist that evolution builds in lots of core knowledge to get babies started, while the empiricists champion all-powerful statistical learning mechanisms. Both are short of good explanations for where abstract knowledge comes from. There appeared 'to be a vast gap between the kinds of knowledge that children learn and the mechanisms that could allow them to learn that knowledge' (p.281, Gopnik & Tenenbaum, 2007). Bayesian methods may provide the tools to build a bridge over that gap.

Neither the nativist nor empiricist accounts would have satisfied John Dewey. They do not explain the great leaps in understanding that babies and children make, nor the very active role they play in their own process of discovery. They can't easily explain the curiosity that drives babies forward, nor the delight they experience in all their little 'Ahas' and 'Eurekas'. The Bayesian approach seems to offer that possibility. It gives hints of how babies can learn from a single example, or solve problems in one area with insights from another. As a baby scientist I totally love the idea that babies are little scientists. I am equally gleeful at the suggestion that I am just a big kid.

Which leads to the final part of the puzzle of curiosity. There is a strong emotional element, which these philosophical accounts often underplay. Rational theories of optimal probability are all very well, but our delight is visceral. Alison Gopnik feels this too. In her book *How Babies Think* (1999), written with Andrew Meltzoff and Patricia Kuhl, she writes of 'the agony of confusion and the ecstasy of explanation' (p.162, Gopnik, Meltzoff & Kuhl, 1999). What drives us to feel our ignorance and our enlightenment so strongly?

Gopnik sketches an explanation in terms of evolution. Undoubtedly we are a problem-solving species. We live by our wits and make our brains our biggest investment. They are bought at the risk of death in childbirth and paid for daily with a huge number of calories to keep them running. The reason our brains are so large is the same reason we are born so helpless. Our brains cannot be prewired with too much information. We have too much to know and hardwiring is too hard to undo. A more elegant solution is to build a general-purpose problem-solver and let it solve whatever problems it encounters. That's a baby.

Babies resemble little scientists, armed with brains that work on a principle of inference and conjecture, Bayesian brains that can build complex, hierarchical networks of cause and effect. Remember, all our science and cleverness might be a side effect of our skill as babies. As Gopnik puts it in *How Babies Think*, 'Five hundred years ago a natural activity of children was transformed into an institutionally organised activity of adults.' It was the babies who came first, and their drive for explanation is integral to our survival and success as a species. Curiosity may kill cats, but it is what keeps us alive.

Security Blankets

Life is an inevitable & emergent property of any (ergodic) random dynamical system that possesses a Markov blanket. Don't leave without it!

— @FarlKriston, 12 Jan 2015, anonymous Twitter parody of Professor Karl Friston

Professor Karl Friston is probably the most influential scientist you've never heard of. He works at the world-famous Wellcome Trust Centre for Neuroimaging at University College London. He has been there most of his career. Back in 1991 he invented statistical parametric mapping. SPM is a statistical technique for analysing the data from brain-imaging experiments. SPM is also a set of software that does the analysis for you. The elegance of the method and the fact Friston gave away his software for free has led to SPM being referenced in about 90% of all brain-imaging studies. As a result, Karl Friston is the most widely cited neuroscientist alive.

Most of us would have been very happy with that, but Friston's contributions did not stop there. He worked with Chris Frith to develop a highly influential account of schizophrenia and invented something called dynamic causal modelling. He is author or co-author of over 1,000 scientific papers. This is a mind-boggling number. For comparison I have written fewer than 20. This is a consequence of his eminence but also evidence he is a very practical researcher who stays involved in the nitty-gritty. Friends who work with him tell me he is an affable and generous colleague. Friston's many, many awards include Fellowship of the Royal Society and something called the Golden Brain Award. He is undoubtedly a worthy recipient. He is famous among brain scientists as perhaps the brainiest of them all.

Karl Friston's most recent idea is his biggest yet. The free-energy principle (FEP) tries to explain not only what brains do, but possibly even life itself. But it is also making Friston infamous, as the nerdy but well-meaning mockery of the @FarlKriston account shows. The free-energy principle is very hard to comprehend and Friston's explanations and equations usually only make matters worse. I will do my best to translate. But if you found the last section bamboozling, now might be a good time to reach for your security blanket. Here's a relatively tame example of Karl explaining it in his own words:

> The free-energy principle says that any self-organising system that is at equilibrium with its environment must minimise its free energy. The principle is essentially a mathematical

> formulation of how adaptive systems (that is, biological agents, like animals or brains) resist a natural tendency to disorder. (p.127, Friston, 2010)

That makes it sound important, doesn't it? Apparently it can explain everything from the existence of 'life as we know it' (Friston, 2013) right up to Freudian theory and psychedelic drug experiences (Carhart-Harris & Friston, 2010).

The secret is nestled in our Markov blankets, which are a supercharged version of Judea Pearl's Bayesian networks. They provide a statistical way to represent the boundary between an organism and the world. The mathematics gets very complicated, combining Bayesian statistics, information theory and entropy to explain how life can survive in the face of the chaos of the universe. But in some sense the free-energy principle states that life is about trying to avoid being too surprised by the future.

Knowing what might happen next sounds like a good survival strategy. For Karl Friston, life is anything that can predict its own future. From single cells to Sigmund Freud, he wraps us each in a Markov blanket and sends us out to do battle with the unknown. Describing organisms in this way has some useful features. Action, perception and learning all become mathematically well-defined properties of the system. Perception provides information to optimise future predictions, actions move us out of uncertain (dangerous) situations, and learning is about updating internal states and beliefs about the external world. This might seem a very abstract way of looking at things, but its supporters see it as a general framework that can be applied as easily to bees as to babies.

Critics of Friston's theory say there is nothing easy about it. They view it as an interesting intellectual exercise but say the free-energy principle and the closely related Bayesian brain hypothesis are too general to be useful in the real world. FEP is a lot more abstract than SPM. It is not easy to see how it can be used to predict how adult or baby brains will react to the world. But this style of reasoning is already being used to understand what happens in real brains.

My favourite experiment of this kind involved a group of ferrets that went to the cinema. In what was clearly a naked attempt to win an Ig Nobel Prize (a jokey award given out for research 'that first makes people laugh, and then makes them think'), József Fiser, Chiayu Chiu and Michael Weliky at the University of Rochester got ferrets to watch *The Matrix* on DVD. The choice was deliberate because, like Neo and friends, the ferrets had wires coming out of the backs of their heads. This allowed the scientists to watch what they were thinking. The ferrets would watch the film all day and then dream about it at night. In doing so they helped Fiser and colleagues work out a lot more about how brains are Bayesian predictors (Fiser, Chiu & Weliky, 2004).

József Fiser is the sort of scientist Hollywood might dream up. He is tall, charming, handsome and impeccably dressed, a Hungarian who speaks English with an American accent. His work is in psychology and neuroscience but with a strong mathematical element. If they made a film about him, there would be a whiteboard of equations in the background. Using *The Matrix* for this research seems like a doubly prophetic choice. In adult ferrets, the scientists discovered patterns of neural activity that correlated significantly with the images on the screen, while baby ferrets were more confused. Moreover, the adults kept on thinking about the movie after it had finished. This was pretty cool, but the most surprising thing was that the ferrets' brains were not just passively reproducing what they saw. They could dream about it and their dreams appeared to actively improve their models of the world. Like Neo in the film, they were bending their existing expectations to fit their new reality. Or in the language of Karl Friston, they were minimising their prediction errors via a Gibbs sampler over the probability space.

Still with me? Perhaps now might be a good time to mention Douglas Adams. In that wholly remarkable book the *Hitchhikers Guide to the Galaxy*, he relates that one of the highest compliments intergalactic hitchhikers can pay to one another is to say they are 'someone who knows where their towel is'. There are, of course, many practical uses for a towel when travelling the universe, but a towel's greatest value is psychological. If you have hitched across the galaxy without losing your towel, you are probably doing OK.

Babies and young children are more likely to carry a security blanket or soft toy than a towel on their adventures. Some estimates suggest that up to 70% of children have a strong attachment to a particular object. This seems to be largely a Western phenomenon, possibly a result of many more children sleeping separately from their parents than in Eastern cultures. The standard explanation was that these 'attachment objects' are a substitute for the original 'object', the mother and her breast. Research does not support this. The object can provide security in novel situations, but it seems to be independent of a child's attachment to their mother (Donate-Bartfield & Passman, 2004).

Donald Winnicott thought attachment objects were a reminder of security and love. I think this is correct. However, Karl Friston and the ferrets let us see security blankets and velveteen rabbits in a wider context. Babies and children use these objects because humans need security as we build our worlds. The ultimate aim of life is to explore enough of the world that you can survive surprises. We will never be able to expect the unexpected, but we can and must reduce its scope and impact. To survive we must change our minds many times. Like the ferrets, we do this by improving in a Bayesian way, updating our beliefs to better fit our experience.

Babies are surprised every day and must continually confront uncertainty and explore the unknown. This is exhilarating and exhausting. It is not enough to add knowledge about the world; they must change their expectations and experience a new existential crisis every day. A parent, a teddy or a security blanket is a reassuring element of continuity and predictability. If babies know where that is, they know where they are. Perhaps this prevents the Markov blanket from unravelling?

It is hard to appreciate what a wild ride daily life must be for babies. Adults do not change their beliefs very often: we have worked our whole lives to feel that we are right about most things. After all, in Friston's theory that is the whole point of life: being less surprised over time. The best analogy I can suggest is to imagine your home planet gets destroyed and your best friend turns out be an alien who takes you hitchhiking across the remainder of the galaxy.

I might be biased here. Not only am I keen to meet aliens, I also still have a security blanket. I had one when I was little. I was so attached to it that my mother knitted a large elephant and sewed the tatty cotton rag onto his back. This was meant to deter me, but inevitably I ended up dragging the elephant around everywhere. The original blanket disintegrated decades ago. It was replaced in my affections by a cellular blanket my mother brought home one day from hospital. The blanket wrapped a parcel containing my baby sister. No doubt I seemed alien and friendly to her. I still find cotton cellular blankets very soothing. Maybe you do too. Around 30% of adults keep an old teddy or similar childhood memento. By my estimates, Charlie Brown's friend Linus van Pelt must be into his seventies by now. I imagine he still carries his blanket some of the time.

As luck would have it, just as I was finishing writing this section, Karl Friston came to my university to give a lecture. This was my chance to hear him in his own words. Would I be bamboozled? His opening was not promising: 'I can give very good lectures. This is not one of them.' But he was wrong. He had us imagining ourselves as hungry owls and playing logical guessing games. There were some of his infamous equations, but he guided us through them gently. His reassuring, unhurried delivery was no doubt acquired during his early training as a psychiatrist.

His summary of the purpose of life fits very well with the ambitions of our babies. When confronted with the big mysteries of the universe, we are compelled to explain them (even if only to explain them away). 'The brain is in the game of explaining the sensory impression at hand,' he said. This is a game of chance and we are all born with an intrinsic motivation to play it. We all keep score, with the information gains measured in 'Bayesian surprise' (or minimised free energy).

Afterwards I told him about this book and asked if he had any insights into how this must feel for babies, who play the game so much more intensely than adults. He could not much improve upon the hitchhiking analogy. And, wise man that he is, he also turned the question around: 'This is why we are scientists, isn't it? To keep exploring and to try and recapture that feeling of joy.'

At the end of his famous four-page paper, Judea Pearl stated his hope that his Bayesian networks would become 'a standard point of departure for more sophisticated models of belief maintenance and inexact reasoning'. Be careful what you wish for. I do not think he could have predicted ferrets watching *The Matrix* or Karl Friston draping Markov blankets over all life on earth. 'In truth it's blankets all the way down. So cuddle close and keep that free energy minimal.' (@FarlKriston, 8 Dec 2017)

Peekaboo

Peeeek-aaa	*Boo!*	*(English)*
Kuu kuck	*Daa!*	*(German)*
Inai inai	*Ba!*	*(Japanese)*
Naaaaan	*Ku!*	*(Xhosa)*

Now that we understand boredom, surprise, curiosity and Markov blankets, we might appreciate the magic of peekaboo. Peekaboo is the ultimate in infant comedy. When I ran my baby laughter survey in 2012 I asked the question: 'What is the funniest game to play with your baby?' I had responses from parents in over 20 countries. In every one the most common answer was peekaboo. What is so funny? There is nothing adults would recognise as humorous about it and children do seem to grow out of it by two years old. Fortunately, the research covered in this chapter lets us get half the answer. The other half comes in Chapter Nine.

This also lets us explain the universal appeal of the game. We do not know if every culture has a version of the game, or when our species first started playing it, but I can guarantee that every baby in the world would like to play it. In 1993, Anne Fernald and Daniela O'Neill conducted a very thorough survey of all that we know about peekaboo from psychological and anthropological research. They concluded that it spread far across the globe and always shared many similarities. They recorded mothers playing the game in at least 17 different native languages. The words changed but the acoustic properties were remarkably constant. Even if you did not know the language you would recognise the game. So would a baby. The biggest fans of peekaboo are babies under a year. They do not have a language of their own yet as they do not need one. That is part of the appeal.

In the earliest forms of the game, with babies under three or four months old, hiding is not too important either. New parents will spend lots of time just staring and cooing at their little miracles. Together they discover a mutually rewarding game: when mummy or daddy looms a little closer to the baby, getting clearer in the baby's short-range vision, it provokes a little smile or squeak. Peekaboo has begun. It does not yet need all the theatrics, there is no script and very few stage directions. But like all good comedy, the secret is in the timing. Parents will instinctively adapt their rhythm to keep their baby entertained.

As they play peekaboo with these young babies, parents are learning all about habituation. To keep getting the squeaks and the smiles, a parent must carefully attend to the excitement and boredom of the child. They play with the baby's interest and expectations to get the biggest smiles and coos in return. Californian infancy researcher John Watson called this 'the game'. He found that by three months old babies respond better when the timing is slightly unpredictable (Watson, 1972). Watson was radical in his claims about the importance of peekaboo-type games:

> 'The Game' is NOT important to the infant because people play it, but rather people become important to the infant because they play 'The Game'. (p.338, Watson, 1972)

Perhaps he had seen the multimillion-dollar success of psychiatrist Eric Berne's 1964 pop-psychology bestseller *Games People Play* and wanted in on the action. Although curiously, Watson does not cite Berne in his work.

Personally, I think Watson was exaggerating. Peekaboo is important and enthralling to babies not for itself but because it inhabits a Goldilocks zone of its own. Peekaboo is statistical, it is rule-based, it is surprising, and it adapts. It appeals to babies on all these levels and the game grows with them. From five or six months, babies begin to enjoy the game proper. You hide and they can anticipate your return. They are surprised and highly delighted when you do. It is not true they think you stop existing. Psychologists used to think so. In Jean Piaget's theories, babies under one year lacked 'object permanence'. He thought their tiny minds lacked the conceptual machinery to track things that were not there. Out of sight was out of mind.

Thanks to Renée Baillargeon and Elizabeth Spelke's magic tricks mentioned in the last chapter, we know babies are better at this they get credit for. You hide and they seem to forget because of their very short attention span. If you are out of sight their mind might fill with something else. But you come back and they remember what game was being played. They even knew you would return.

At first this is something purely statistical, just the vaguest sense of the structure of the game, but keep playing peekaboo and the consistent pairing of expectation and reward means it evolves into something more. It may even be a baby's first explicit theory about the world, her first scientific hypothesis, shaped by the eager complicity of adults who already know the rules. Each squeak of pleasure at the return of the adult marks another prediction confirmed. As American psychologist Jerome Bruner wrote about peekaboo and the learning of rules: 'It is hard to imagine any function for peekaboo aside from practice in the learning of rules in converting "gut play" into play with conventions' (p.184, Bruner & Sherwood, 1976).

Playing peekaboo, babies are learning a lot more than just that you will return. The conventions Bruner was referring to are all within the realm of conversation and social connection. They are learning not just from you, but from themselves. Karl Friston's equations help us here, although we can't apply them directly. At least, I can't. But they remind us that perception and action are two sides of the same coin. Babies learn as much from their own actions as from yours. Your laughs and smiles are valuable data about their behaviour. It is their first taste of a sense of agency and it tastes good.

Peekaboo starts with a familiar face resolving out of the fuzzy middle distance. It builds statistically as parents tweak their timing to keep their baby 'in the zone'. As the baby grows, that zone expands and the baby learns to anticipate the surprise. What matters is not to predict exactly when you return but to realise that you always do. There is delight in being right, which grows greater when they realise they are an active participant. 'The game' now has two players and the realms it explores are greatly increased, but babies' curiosity still compels them to face mysteries head on.

John Watson is wrong when he says that playing this game

makes people important to babies. Babies are born social; there is nothing more fascinating to them than other people. There is nothing more enigmatic either. The real magic of laughter and peekaboo is how they connect babies to other people.

Chapter Nine: Laugh and the World Laughs with You

Laughter is the shortest distance between two people.
— Victor Borge, Danish comedian and musician (1909–2000)

Victor Borge's quote is easily my favourite summary of the essence of laughter, and if laughter is the shortest distance between two people then peekaboo proves it. This surprised me when I first started studying baby laughter, but the further I went the clearer it became. Connection is the core of laughter and is the reason babies laugh so much and inspire laughter in everyone else. Laughter exists to connect us and peekaboo is pure connection.

Peekaboo Reloaded

Oculus animi index. — *Latin proverb*
Les yeux sont le miroir de l'âme. — *French proverb*
The eyes are the window to your soul. — *English proverb*

Surprise only takes you so far when trying to understand the global appeal of peekaboo. Eye gaze takes us the rest of the way.

The best thing about the game of peekaboo for babies is that you are playing with them. You are playing it as equals, and to play it effectively you must give them your full attention. This is what provokes their delight and where they learn.

Once babies are familiar with the game, and they know enough to realise that you will come back, the real game for them is to learn how to have a conversation. Peekaboo is pure social interaction stripped of all the confusing words, content and external references. It is the simplest conversation you could have with someone. It needs to be simple for babies, but it is still rewarding and packed with meaning.

Any adult should recognise this. Just think about a time you swapped glances with a potential romantic partner and the rush of reward if the glance was reciprocated and became a mutual gaze. One disarming thing about small babies is how they can hold your gaze for such a long time. Enter a staring contest with a small baby and you will lose.

Eye contact has a powerful effect on us. We saw in Chapter Two how Mark Johnson showed that newborns will turn towards faces. In a later study with Teresa Farroni, they found that newborns preferred it when we are looking directly at them (Farroni et al., 2002). It is likely that the whites of our eyes have been optimised by evolution for communication. The shape and colouration of our eyes let us signal to each other who and what we are looking at. Out of 88 primate species humans are the only one with exposed, white sclera (Kobayashi & Kohshima, 2008). Other primates disguise their gaze; we advertise it.

Mutual gaze even appears to synchronise our brainwaves. Research on adult communication has found that during conversations our brains fall into step with each other. This has been shown by getting two people to wear electroencephalogram (EEG) hairnets and simultaneously recording their brain activity while they interact. Amazingly, this even seems to happen with babies. Researchers from Cambridge recorded infant brainwaves as they listened to an adult reciting nursery rhymes. In some conditions the adult would be looking at the baby; in others the adult looked off to one side. The babies always found the adult interesting, but the brainwaves of the two synchronised the most when there was mutual eye contact (Leong et al., 2017).

The senior author on that paper was my friend Sam Wass. We did our Ph.D.s at the same time. When Sam talks about this research he is keen to emphasise that 'this is not telepathy' precisely because that is what it looks like. It can be literally true to say that you are on the same wavelength as someone else, but it is a skill you must master. To adults this becomes invisible, but babies are just joining the conversation. Peekaboo and other 'conversations' with adults are where they learn how to do so. From the first few months many parents are convinced a baby's little coos and squawks are answering them, but it is through eye contact that we construct this understanding of others. As the main researchers into adult brain-to-brain synchrony say, 'Cognition materialises in an interpersonal space' (p.114, Hasson et al., 2012).

The mysteries of peekaboo have even caught the attention of Kool A. D., the 'baby correspondent' for ultra-cool website

Vice.com (yes, that is his name and yes, Vice has a baby correspondent). As you might expect, he plays parenting for shocks and laughs. But that is exactly what a lot of parenting is and he can be very perceptive:

> Another aspect of 'Where's the baby?' is peekaboo, a game where you're literally asking the baby itself, in the third person, where it is. So you ask the baby: 'Where's the baby?' and the baby, who is having a hard enough time learning how to say basic one-syllable words, now has to imagine itself as some sort of objective third party? An avatar of itself? And then locate that avatar in a space whose parameters are completely unspecified? That's a lot to ask of the baby. Pretty trippy little game if you ask me. (Kool A.D., Vice.com, September 2015)

Kool A.D. is completely correct that peekaboo must be trippy for a baby. This ought to make us wonder why they respond so positively. Babies learn from every interaction and laugh at the strangest things. But strangeness often = fearful = tearful. Peekaboo provokes strong emotions that are almost always positive. It spills over into laughter and that laughter is not simply contagious; it exists to be shared. This sharing is the beginning of mind-reading.

A Laughing Party

We do not inherit the land from our ancestors; we borrow it from our children.

— Navajo proverb

In Navajo culture a baby's first laugh is a very important landmark. It marks the baby's passing from the spirit world fully into the human realm. From when the new baby is a couple of months old, friends and relatives will ask, 'Has your baby laughed?' It is an honour to be the person who first makes the baby laugh. It also involves an obligation, as you then have to organise and pay for a laughing party for the baby. I learned about this from Pastor Mark Charles, a Christian preacher and social activist from the Navajo nation. He had described it briefly online (Charles, 2012) and I called him up to find out more.

The first thing I learned was that the baby's first laugh is important because it is as an intentional and social act. Navajo people believe babies are of born of 'two worlds', the Earth People and the Holy People. The first laugh is an early sign of autonomy that signals the baby's choice to become fully part of the Earth People. Thus it is celebrated and the baby is welcomed to the community. The laugh is expected at around three to four months, the same age range I found in my survey of baby laughter. It was Mark's teenage niece who made his baby daughter laugh. She was very pleased, but horrified that she would have to foot the bill for the laughing party. (She didn't.)

At the party the hosts help the baby give out small gifts to attendees, including rock salt, sweets and even money. Symbolically, this trains the baby in generosity and introduces them to members of their community. For Mark's daughter the ceremony combined traditional Navajo worship with Christian prayers and hymns. Mark worried that the mixed theology could offend traditionalists on all sides of his American, Navajo and Dutch extended family, but he underestimated the magic power of a small, smiling baby. The party was a great success.

As someone who studies infant laughter scientifically, I am a huge fan of this tradition. The Navajo know that laughter is social glue. They clearly understand that laughing is about connection and communication that can cross generational divides. The Navajo culture assumes that the baby's laughter will be caused by someone, not by something. They know laughter is social first and humorous second. Their ceremony celebrates the first laugh in a symbolic way that connects deeply with the reason why laughter evolved and why it exists at all.

It is not impossible to imagine an entirely serious world where no one laughs or has a sense of humour. Maybe there are a few people among your friends who are like this and, certainly, among your acquaintances. On an individual level laughter does not seem essential to our existence, but across all cultures and communities it is universal. You never find a community without laughter. When something is universal that's a big clue it is important to our species. The other big clue is that laughter is so enjoyable. Things that are fun usually have some evolutionary benefit behind them, sex being the most obvious example. Therefore it seems that laughter has been favoured by evolution but if so, what is laughter's purpose and how did it evolve?

For traits less obvious than sex, evolutionary explanations must balance telling fun origin stories with the need for concrete evidence. For many physical characteristics this is possible. For example, you might find evidence of 'how the elephant got its trunk' in the fossil record, and a computer simulation of the physical effectiveness of camouflage might explain how the zebra got its stripes and the leopard got its spots. It is much more challenging when trying to account for behaviour, especially human behaviour.

The best story about the origin of laughter is told by Robin Dunbar, emeritus professor of evolutionary psychology at the University of Oxford. He is most famous for Dunbar's number, which is an estimate of the typical size of our social groups – 150 members. It crops up in many contexts, from the size of Roman legions to that of corporate divisions. Even in modern, dense urban environments, it is the approximate number of our active social contacts. It is an average; some people will have many more, others less. Crucially, 150 was also the estimated size of our villages and tribes across many hunter-gather societies and is thought to be the group size of our hominin ancestors. This contrasts with a maximum group size of around 50 found in other primates.

Robin Dunbar originally settled on a human social-group size of 150 by predicting group size from brain size. He compared our giant brains to those of gibbons, chimps, macaques and our other monkey cousins, and concluded that our group size ought to be around 150. Dunbar's social brain hypothesis suggests that the complexities of living in bigger social groups requires bigger brains. The more individuals there are, the more relationships there are to maintain and keep track of. But primate social groups are held together by mutual grooming and this creates a problem because the time and effort required for mutual grooming puts an upper limit on group size of 50.

In just 2 million years our branch of the primate family tree, the hominins, has seen our group size and our brain size triple. Dunbar believes that laughter made this possible. It helped replace the need for intensive one-on-one grooming with a form of collective social bonding that could take place in larger groups. Laughter, singing and conversation can all be simultaneously shared by groups of more than two people. Dunbar argues that laughter came first, supplementing grooming to help keep those ancient clans together as they grew in number.

He offers four reasons for this. First, we were already laughing. Our cousins the chimpanzees and other great apes laugh, and it is safe to assume our common ancestors all had this ability. Laughter existed and was a behaviour that could become more important. Second, laughter also comes before language. You do not need language to laugh or make someone laugh. (Any preverbal baby would tell you this, if only they could talk). Third, communal laughter is both a highly contagious and a highly social activity. Fourth, just like grooming, laughter triggers the release of endorphins, the brain's pleasure chemical. It is, in effect, 'grooming at a distance' (Dunbar, 2012, 2017).

We will never know for sure if laughter was the touch of magic that made us more than monkeys, but the story is very compelling, and the evidence does add up. Laughter is a positive social signal that is hard to fake. Just try laughing genuinely in the company of your worst enemy or while angry with someone. You cannot do it – at least not convincingly. Laughter is energetically costly and it empties our lungs, making us vulnerable. It is what biologists call an honest signal (Bryant & Aktipis, 2014). As a result, laughter improves the quality of social interactions and helps social cohesion.

Dunbar even tried to measure the multiplying effect of laughter. He and his French collaborator, Guillaume Dezecache, went on pub crawls around Oxford, Calais, Lille, Paris and Berlin eavesdropping on people having a good time. They counted the laughs and the size of the groups that laughed or chatted together. Laughter groups averaged 2.72 people while conversations averaged 2.93 (Dezecache & Dunbar, 2012). This supported Dunbar's idea that laughter is 'social glue' that can supplement grooming.

This also kept up a great tradition of laughter researchers spying on people having fun. Laughter pioneer Robert Provine sat in college canteens observing laughter and also found this social-lubricant role for laughter (Provine, 2001). My favourite example was Lawrence Sherman who in 1975 videotaped nearly 600 hours of three- to five-year-olds in preschool class and carefully measured how giggles, glee and hysteria spread through the group (Sherman, 1975). This delightful study won an Ig Nobel Prize in 2001.

You will notice one thing missing from Dunbar's account: there are no babies. This is sad. Evolutionary psychologists should know better than most that 'the children are our future'. The way that species care for their young is very strongly determined by evolution, and humans are no exception. Babies laugh and make us laugh more far more than adults do. Dunbar does talk about laughter evolving for bonding but, curiously, he does not talk about the bond between parent and infant, perhaps because it does not fit his group-size model. Although our ancestors increased the size of their social groups by a factor of three, parents did not start having three times as many babies. Parents must bond with their children but baby laughter does not fit into his evolutionary story. This overlooks that our babies are harder to raise. They are more helpless and more demanding than baby apes and primates, and have far more to learn. There is a huge pressure for us to connect with and bond with and cope with our babies. A friend of mine puts it very succinctly: 'If my baby had not made me laugh I might have thrown him out of the window by now.'

The Navajo laughter party is not a great guide to the distant past. For all we know, the tradition may only be a few hundred or thousand years old. It does not help us understand what life was like for our ancestors on the African savannah 2 million years ago. But it does highlight the way a baby's laughter is something valuable that can be shared among the whole community. Early hominins lived in large social groups that persisted over time and generations. Laughter was one of the first mechanisms for binding that group together to the benefit of all. Grooming may be the shortest distance between two primates, but laughter is the shortest distance between two hominins. Better than language or grooming, laughter has the advantage that it can be shared as equal partners by any two people, however big or small, young or old.

What Are Emotions?

Emotions do not exist to be locked away inside individuals.

— Vasudevi Reddy and Colwyn Trevarthen,
developmental psychologists, 2004

If laughter evolved as a social glue, central to this role is that it expresses emotion. The most infectious thing about a laughing baby is their absolute delight. It may seem a truism to say that 'babies laugh because they are happy', but this challenges us to answer the question: what is happiness? While we are about it, we might as well try to explain anger, sadness, worry and the rest. It should not surprise anyone that emotions are still mysterious to science. Many theories have been proposed and few have been discarded.

The race for a comprehensive theory of emotion is still wide open. Perhaps it will always remain so; no scientific theory could catalogue all the nuances of our adult experience. In *The Book of Human Emotions*, Tiffany Watt Smith describes 156 different emotions. She readily admits this list is not comprehensive and that the categories overlap and blur at their edges, changing over time and by culture. Tiffany's goal as a historian of emotion is to offer an argument against the tendency to reduce 'the beautiful complexity of our inner lives into just a handful of cardinal emotions' (Watt Smith, 2015).

It is a tendency that has always been there. Tiffany describes the *Li Chi*, a book from the Confucian era, around 500 years BC, that lists seven essential feelings: joy, anger, sadness, fear, love, dislike and fondness. Two-and-a-half millennia later and little has changed. In the 2015 Pixar film *Inside Out*, the main character, a young girl called Riley, is shown with five emotions: joy, anger, sadness, fear and disgust. Modern science usually settles on a list of about nine 'basic emotions'; happiness, sadness, anger, fear, parental love, child attachment, sexual love, hatred and disgust (Oatley & Johnson-Laird, 2014). These lists seem reasonable in as far as they go, but the best theories are not about listing emotions; rather, they explain why we have emotions at all.

One of the first people to realise this was Charles Darwin. In a work of visionary genius, Darwin advanced one the first ever scientific theories of emotions. His book, *The Expression of the Emotions in Man and Animals* (Darwin, 1872), proposed that our emotions evolved for our survival. Of course, he would say that, wouldn't he? But like all of Darwin's work it was supported by decades of patient accumulation of evidence. He compared the anger displays of many species and included many observations of babies. Darwin kept detailed biographical diaries of several of his children, wondering at their frowns, blushes, and laughs. On a theoretical level Darwin's account was a bit thin: all it really says is that emotions are universal, valuable and shared with animals. But it was a very radical proposal for its time.

About a decade later, William James and Carl Lange independently decided that emotions were reactions to bodily states. For example, fear might be how we interpreted our racing hearts. For James, emotions are literally feelings, 'We feel sorry because we cry… not… we cry… because we are sorry' (James, 1884). In this view emotions happen after the fact and are what philosophers call 'epiphenomena'. The theory suggests that if you carefully measure how a person is reacting physiologically, you can tell what emotion they are experiencing. The James-Lange theory feels unsatisfying to me because it relegates emotion to a passive role. But it does have two important strengths. It points out that our physiology strongly influences our mental state and that emotions depend upon interpretation of experience. Contrary to early views of the theory (popularised by John Dewey), neither James nor Lange ever insisted on a single emotion for each physiological reaction. They would accept that a racing heart and sweaty palms could be interpreted as fear in some situations and as love in others (L. B. Feldman, 2018).

Jaak Panksepp, who we met tickling rats in Chapter Seven, believed our emotions exist to tell us what supports or detracts from our survival. He thought we have seven emotional systems: ancient systems of FEAR, RAGE, LUST and SEEKING, and more modern mechanisms for CARE, PANIC and PLAY that are unique to social mammals. He capitalised the words to emphasise that they have very specific scientific meanings (Panksepp, 2005). Each system serves a specific goal and can be mapped to equivalent brain areas in many species. Take the PANIC system, which rules babies' separation anxiety. Panksepp believed it operates in the brain with the same neurochemistry as physical pain. The pain of separation is real pain and prompts the infant to act, usually calling out to the mother in distress. The return of the mother releases opioids and oxytocin, which relieve the pain. The brain circuitry goes back to the imprinting in chicks and the survival value is clear in both cases (Herman & Panksepp, 1981).

As well as his laughing rats, Panksepp looked at sadness in chickens, what makes guinea pigs cry and mother-infant bonding in sheep. He spent decades researching emotion in animals and insisted that they feel things in the same way we do. He believed there is an emotional consciousness common to humans and animals, and a cognitive consciousness that comes later with the use of language. Emotions colour our world, and the conscious experience of joy or rage is essential to humans and animals alike.

This is an unpopular viewpoint. Plenty of scientists are dismissive of the experience of animals. They cite Morgan's canon and say science can only ever study animal behaviour. They criticise Panksepp because they do not believe animals have the consciousness necessary to experience or interpret emotions. In Panksepp's view, these scientists are looking down the wrong end of the telescope. It is the experience that makes the emotion, and experiencing emotions was how and why consciousness evolved. We may have to describe animal emotions with human labels, but FEAR came before 'fear' and SEEKING before 'pleasure'.

In my view, the most compelling case against Panksepp's critics is that anyone who is dismissive of animal emotions also has to dismiss all the emotions of preverbal babies. Some researchers do argue precisely this. Lisa Barrett Feldman, a professor of psychology at Northeastern University in Boston, argues that emotions are entirely conceptual, and so animals and newborn babies cannot have them. Here is what she says about babies:

> Babies don't know what telescopes are, or sea cucumbers or picnics, let alone purely mental concepts like 'whimsy' or 'schadenfreude'. A newborn is experientially blind to a great extent. (p.113, L. B. Feldman, 2018)

The quote comes from her 2017 book *How Emotions Are Made*, in which she describes her own theory of constructed emotion. She contrasts this with what she calls the 'classical' view of emotions shared by Darwin, Panksepp and others. As I said at the outset of this section, no one theory of emotions covers all the ground yet, so it's worth looking at this opposite perspective. To do this, let us go back to *Inside Out*.

In that film, each of the basic emotions is personified as a character inside Riley's mind. Joy appears when Riley is a newborn baby seeing her blurry parents for the first time. Her job, it seems, is to press buttons that cause Riley to respond and then collect the memories associated with her actions. She is shortly joined by Sadness and the others, and each interprets situations and responds according to their nature.

Joy delights, Anger gets cross, Fear worries, Disgust dislikes things and Sadness is sad. If we forgive the artistic licence of little people inside your head pressing buttons, it is a wonderful depiction of the classical view of emotions. Indeed, the chief scientific advisor to the film was Paul Ekman, a champion of the idea that emotions are universal biological drives (Keltner & Ekman, 2015).

The outer plot revolves around the 11-year-old Riley having to adapt as her family move from Minnesota to a new home and new school in San Francisco. The inner plot revolves around Joy trying to understand the purpose of Sadness. It is a good film, so I won't spoil it for you. But it is not giving too much away to say that the emotions learn to work as a team and Riley learns that other people struggle with their emotions too. At various points we see into her parents' heads, with their own teams of five emotional essences at their controls. It is a story, Barrett claims, that would be recognisable to Aristotle, Plato and even the Buddha, but she argues that it is built on a myth. Barrett does not believe there are universal emotions. Your emotions are not fixed by evolution but are constructed as part of your culture.

Barrett's theory has no problem with there being hundreds of subtle emotions like those listed in Tiffany Watt Smith's *Handbook*. In fact, Barrett is the editor of her own *Handbook of Emotions*, an academic volume running to over 900 pages. We can have countless complex emotions because our highly social lives and big brains create that complexity. But then Ekman and Panksepp do not have any problem with the existence of complex emotions like embarrassment, ennui or exasperation. Where Barrett's theory differs is that she does not think happiness, anger or sadness are any more natural or biological than 'technostress' (caused by new technology) or *Torschlusspanik* (the fear that time is running out, often specifically applied to women who haven't had children and want to conceive before it's too late).

That does not mean that in Barrett's version of the film there would be 156-plus characters all clamouring for attention in Riley's head. That would be a terrible movie and it would be committing the error of essentialism. Just because we can classify a set of behaviours as 'anger' does not make anger a real thing. According to Barrett, Plato, Darwin and Panksepp all commit this error. Plato we can forgive – essences and Platonic ideals were kind of his 'thing'. Barrett gives Darwin a particularly hard time, and she has a point. His theory of evolution removed the need for essentialism from biological classification, but his book on emotions went the other way. Barrett notes that Darwin says, 'Even insects express anger, jealously and love' (p.350, Darwin, 1872).

Why is this an error? Let's look at anger. In several chapters of *How Emotions Are Made*, Barrett deconstructs anger to show it is not a single, simple thing. First, she takes aim at Ekman's famous work, supposedly showing that expressions of emotion are universal. Her research shows that facial expressions or physiological signals are highly ambiguous. You can be angry without giving any outward sign of it. Second, there is ambiguity in language. 'Anger' might mean annoyance, irritation, rage or fury. Some languages, such as that of Utku Eskimos, have no concept of 'anger', while Mandarin has five or more different 'angers'. Some languages cannot even translate our Western notion of emotion. Finally, Barrett asks, 'Is a growling dog angry?' As you might guess, her answer is that 'there is no clear evidence that any non-human animals have the sort of emotion concepts that humans do', even dogs, which we have been breeding for their loyalty and understanding of us for millennia. The best we can say is that dogs have raw feelings, but this is a long way from emotion. With insects, we can't even identify raw feelings.

It is in the way they approach the emotions of babies where the gulf between these theories comes into focus. Barrett, for whom emotions are conceptual, spends a lot of time discussing infant pattern-recognition abilities and how they learn words and concepts, the mental prerequisites for her cognitive concept of emotions. Panksepp, for whom emotions are feelings, does more to evoke our empathy but usually cannot help reducing things down to biology and brain areas (Panksepp, 2001). It is notable that neither camp engages directly with the experience of the babies themselves. Yet I think this is precisely where we will find a better sense of what human emotions are and how they build on the basic feelings we share with other animals.

Emotion is about more than just classifying feelings; it is about experiencing them. A baby may not know that their sadness is 'sadness' or their happiness is 'joy', but there is something real in their experience. I am sure that Barrett and Panksepp would both acknowledge this, but there is not much space in their theories for the subjective sense of emotion, its 'phenomenology', if you wanted to be fancy. I do not believe a comprehensive theory of emotions exists yet, but such a theory would not be complete if it did not encompass the primal emotional experience of infants.

Of course, this is what psychoanalysts have been saying all along. For the past 70 years infant observation has formed a key component of training for many psychoanalytic psychotherapists. Introduced as a method by Esther Bick and John Bowlby at the Tavistock Clinic in 1948, infant observation involves the trainee therapist visiting a mother and baby for one hour every week from birth to two years. The trainee's job is just to observe, something that is harder than it first appears. The observer tries to remain neutral, but alert to the stresses of the parents, the jealousies of older siblings, the anxieties and anger of the baby. They must also be aware of their own reactions to this emotionally intense environment. This makes it good training for becoming a therapist. Additionally, observers meet every week in small group seminars to discuss and interpret their experiences.

Psychoanalysts use infant observation to support their beliefs that our main emotional responses are learned in infancy, but they are often adamant that their observations only be interpreted in context of their own theory (Rustin, 2009). This leads to accusations of circular reasoning and makes scientists dismissive of psychoanalysts' claims. There are undoubtedly many valuable insights to be gained from these *Closely Observed Infants* (Miller, 1989). The trick will be to put the emotions of infancy into a scientific framework.

But scientists should heed therapists' warnings that this won't be straightforward.

There have been some attempts to build bridges. Sue Gerhardt is a psychotherapist and founder of the Oxford Parent Infant Project, which provides psychotherapeutic help to new parents. In her excellent book *Why Love Matters*, she tries to integrate the scientific findings of Panksepp and others with her own psychoanalytic insights. The book was written before the breakthrough work of Michael Meaney on cortisol and stress described in Chapter Six. Nonetheless, it recognises that 'our physiological systems and our mental systems are developed in relationship with other people – and this happens most intensely and leaves its biggest mark in infancy' (p.10, Gerhardt, 2004).

Travelling in the other direction, child psychologists Vasi Reddy and Colwyn Trevarthen have been trying to bring the subjective into the objective world of science. Trevarthen is an 87-year-old New Zealander based in Edinburgh who has been studying infants for over 50 years and is still working to understand the minds of babies. Reddy is originally from India but is based at the University of Portsmouth. She's been working on the question a mere 30 years, having done her Ph.D. at Edinburgh with Trevarthen. As they explain their aims better than I can, I will let them speak for themselves:

> Anyone, including a researcher, has to be emotionally involved in sympathy with the infant in order to fully understand why that emotion has come about, and what purpose or effect it may have in the child's experience of life. A lot can be learned

> from intimate and 'respectful' engagement with babies' actions and feelings, and we suggest that this way of observing alters not only the empirical picture of what a particular infant at a particular time is capable of doing and feeling, but also the whole theoretical story about how infants develop, what they are motivated to experience and to be changed by. (p.10, Reddy & Trevarthen, 2004)

In practice this means trying to imagine what consciousness must be like for a baby and paying attention to the importance of intersubjectivity in the creation of emotions. Consciousness is a huge and mysterious topic. The consciousness of babies is a mystery times a mystery, wrapped in a diaper. A deep dive into this fascinating topic is sadly beyond the scope of these two short paragraphs, but the interested reader will find plenty to twist their minds around in Reddy's book *How Infants Know Minds* (Reddy, 2008) and Trevarthen and Reddy's joint contribution to the *Blackwell Companion to Consciousness* (2017). It's sufficient to say that they believe that 'infant consciousness is active, emotional and communicative' and that infant emotions are more than just interpersonal: they are intersubjective. Intersubjectivity is not a familiar concept in the West but compared to consciousness it is a simple idea. It says that emotions do not merely communicate an internal feeling or send signals from one person to another; they are often constructed in the space between individuals.

There is not much research on this yet, so let me end this section with an anecdote about my work, and an observation about a procedure invented in 1978, both of which show how emotions exist in the space between us. When Sam Wass and I worked in the same office, I could always tell when he was trying to write computer code by the amount of frustrated swearing coming across the desk partition. I could completely sympathise: I gave up my previous career in finance because I hated trying to get computers to obey me. Having the benefit of the same experience, the problem was that I sympathised too much; the only cure was to try and help him out. Usually I could not, and we would both be in a state of deep vexation at his impassive silicon nemesis. From Watt Smith's book I have since learned that this is 'technostress'.

The 'still-face' procedure was invented by Edward Tronick and colleagues at Boston Children's Hospital in 1978. Just down the hall from where Richard Ferber was teaching parents to ignore babies to promote self-soothing, Tronick would tell parents to sit opposite a young baby and simply do nothing. They were to sit motionless and impassive with a 'neutral face', not reacting to the baby. The response from the babies is very well summarised by the abstract of the original paper: 'The infants studied reacted with intense wariness and eventual withdrawal, demonstrating the importance of interactional reciprocity and the ability of infants to regulate their emotional displays' (p.1, Tronick, Als, Adamson, Wise, & Brazelton 1978).

The response is highly predictable and has been replicated many times. As a result, the procedure has been used in thousands of studies. Sometimes the researchers are investigating emotional reciprocity between mothers and infants. At other times they require an ethical and harmless way to make babies a bit angry. In this respect, the still-face procedure is outwardly almost identical to peekaboo, but emotionally it could not be more different.

Why Are Babies So Funny?

When I was a kid, I told my mother I wanted to grow and be a comedian. She said, 'You can't do both.'

— Jimmy Carr, comedian, aged 45

William Nilsson was born in Sweden in 2006. He is currently a teenager but might forever be known as the Laughing Baby. One day when he was around seven months old, William was sitting in his high chair when the microwave binged. For some reason he found this very amusing and started laughing. His father quickly grabbed a camera to make a short video to send to William's grandma. Dad did his best microwave impressions and his cute little blond, blue-eyed baby cackled like a witch with every 'bing' and 'dong'. As well as sending it to grandma, William's father uploaded it to YouTube. Within a very short time it had tens of millions of views. When the Queen visited Google's newly opened headquarters in London in 2008, the staff played her William's giggles. Also in 2008, *South Park* included him in an episode about viral internet stars, along with the Sneezing Panda and the Star Wars Kid.

William Nilsson is far from the only laughing baby on the internet. Back in the distant past, before 'Gangnam Style' and

'Despacito', when Justin Bieber was still a teenager singing his bedroom, funny baby videos were one of the few things giving cat videos a run for their money. While William accumulated 80 million views, 'Charlie Bit My Finger – Again!' has nearer half a billion. It is a tragical comedy or comical tragedy of a young boy who cannot believe his grinning baby brother just bit him – again. For a while it was the most viewed video ever. It is one of thousands posted by proud and enchanted parents showing their their adorable offspring, although there is nothing remarkable about any of the babies in these videos. The laughing baby is just a baby laughing. Charlie is just being Charlie. Like him or not, Justin Bieber has talent, but these babies are just regular babies. Yet unlike Bieber, they have universal appeal. Why is that?

Cuteness seems easy to account for. Evolutionary psychologists argue that babies' cuteness and our appreciation of it are built in to serve a biological purpose. Given the huge investment we make in pregnancy and childrearing, this makes sense. One could imagine genes that made us cherish babies would be selected for. Undoubtedly, we are beguiled by their button noses, chubby cheeks and soft skin. We adore their small faces with high foreheads. Konrad Lorenz called this *Kindchenschema* – 'baby schema' in English. We can think of it as a counterpoint to imprinting, whereby adult organisms are irresistibly drawn to infantile features and treat babies favourably. This works with kittens, puppies and other baby animals. The effect seems to get stronger the more you exaggerate it, as Walt Disney discovered to his profit. The big-eyed baby-faced characters of animated films seem to become ever more extreme, and I am curious where they have left to go after the Minions. In a similar vein, Vasi Reddy believes a form of artificial evolution has made teddy bears progressively cuter, as young children select the most baby-faced versions (Morris, Reddy, & Bunting, 1995).

Kindchenschema is a cute theory but, like everything else in evolutionary psychology, how do we prove it? Behaviour does not fossilise, so there is no direct evidence of doting parents in the fossil record. Nor can cuteness be taken for granted. Anthropologists are quick to point out that our Western adoration of bonny babies might be a local cultural invention. American anthropologist David Lancy argues that 'if one is not inclined to view the baby as an adorable cherub, then many infant characteristics, such as the lack of speech, its softness, lack of motor control, crying and screaming, constant runny nose, diarrhoea, lack of teeth/hair and mobility might be seen as anomalous, bestial or frightening' (p.77, Lancy, 2014). Worse still, infanticide is equally 'natural'. In mountain gorillas, infanticide is a notorious 'rational' strategy used by dominant males when they usurp a rival (Robbins et al., 2013). In humans too, research by anthropologist Laila Williamson shows that 'infanticide has been practiced on every continent and by people on every level of cultural complexity, from hunter gatherers to high civilizations … Rather than being an exception, then, it has been the rule.' (p.61, Williamson, 1978).

Besides, cuteness is not funniness. Mickey Mouse and Hello Kitty are endearing, but they are not very amusing. I think it is funniness that will save the day. Laughter shortens the distance between us and our babies. It connects us with these endearing but anomalous invaders. What makes babies so funny? Traditional scholars of laughter and humour do not have many answers. Mostly, they do not consider laughing babies to be interesting or relevant. Babies are beneath them. Theories of humour fall into three broad categories focusing on incongruity, superiority and emotional release respectively. Funny babies do not fit any of these. To be fair, babies do not tell many jokes, but this is a massive blind spot in theories of humour, as babies are undoubtedly natural comedians.

The incongruity theory says jokes usually have a punchline that takes you in a clever or unexpected direction. For example, 'Little babies get delivered by a stork. Bigger ones may need a crane.' This theory is an old one and it makes a lot of sense. It is attractive to intellectuals, who usually write unfunny things about it. Philosophers Immanuel Kant and Arthur Schopenhauer both dissected jokes in this way and it is fair to say neither was known for his sense of humour. The most influential version of the idea was put forward by Hungarian writer and polymath Arthur Koestler in his 1964 book *The Act of Creation*. He argued that artistic creativity, scientific discovery and humour all involve unexpected 'bisociation' between two different frames of reference. A recent book *Inside Jokes: Using Humour to Reverse-Engineer the Mind* (Hurley, Dennett & Adams, 2011) follows the same tradition, although it does at least contain some good jokes.

The superiority theory populates jokes with winners and

losers. Normally, the joke teller and the audience are the winners at the expense of the object of ridicule, as in the joke: 'Politicians are like diapers. They should be changed frequently… and for the same reason.' Sigmund Freud was a big fan of this theory; in 1905 he wrote a whole book on *Jokes and Their Relation to the Unconscious.* It contains a lot of jokes, but none of them translate very well from the original German. Contrary to his usual view that everything starts in infancy, he thought it was the intellect rather than the infantile that was the source of most amusement. When it came to humour, he took a very Victorian view that children should be seen and not heard. In Freud's view, 'children do not strike us in any way comic' and 'children are without a feeling for the comic'. He admitted that children's laughter can express playfulness or pure pleasure, but, for Freud, the main explanation for children's laughter is that it shows superiority or schadenfreude. In one typical example he imagines a young child laughing at someone falling over because they are pleased it was not them. Silent-movie star Oliver Hardy agreed this was secret of his success: 'One of the reasons why people like us, I guess, is because they feel so superior to us. Even an eight-year-old kid can feel superior to us and that makes him laugh' (p.46, McCabe, 1966).

As we saw in Chapter Three, the emotional release theory originates with Herbert Spencer and, if we are honest, it is a bit shit. Freud was a fan of this theory. In his mind, jokes – like dreams – are a window into the darkness of our subconscious. If superiority is all about the ego asserting itself, then release involves the wild and unruly id breaking free. A theory based on the emotional impact of jokes seems like it ought to suit babies better. Sadly, this one does not fit either. There is nothing about funny babies that conflicts us or causes the release of anything pent up – except perhaps warmth and fellow feeling. Which is not what had Freud had in mind.

Psychologists dismiss the id, the ego and superego on the pedantic grounds that there is absolutely no evidence for them. However, the release theory does explain the appeal of offensive, sexual or plain gross jokes. It might explain why the only good baby joke is a dead baby joke. There aren't many good jokes featuring babies, but there are a hell of a lot of dead baby jokes. They are all variations on the same joke, drawing their shock and humour from the inappropriateness of joking about dead children. About the only one I felt comfortable including in this book was this one: 'What's the best part about dead baby jokes? They never get old.'

To understand the funniness of babies, we need only think about the most popular comedians of 100 years ago. They were all clowns. Charlie Chaplin, Buster Keaton, and Laurel and Hardy conquered Hollywood; Charles Adrien Wettach, when dressed as Grock the Clown, was the highest-paid entertainer in Europe. Babies are certainly clownish. And it is not just the baggy clothing, clumsiness and pratfalls. They share the foolish innocence and the exaggerated emotional responses. They are alien and unpredictable, although they are much less scary. I do not have exact statistics, but I guarantee brephophobia – the fear of babies – is a lot less common than coulrophobia – the fear of clowns.

Infancy researchers, unlike theorists of humour, have long recognised the comic, clownish qualities of babies. Eminent Victorian psychologist James Sully noted in his 1897 book *Children's Ways* that: 'The sense of the comic in children is a curious subject to which justice has not yet been done.' His next work – a book-length *Essay on Laughter* (Sully, 1902) – attempted to fix this. He criticises philosophers like Henri Bergson for being too high-minded about laughter and often reminds his readers that theories of humour should not overlook the joy we get from simple low humour like clowns. Sully thinks this is a pure and playful type of laughing, as when a baby laughs at 'a dancing sunbeam' on their nursery wall. The same debate reoccurred in the 1970s as researchers argued over when babies could first experience humour. Mary Rothbart saw potential already present in the very first laughs and playful attitude found in four-month-olds. By contrast, Paul McGhee took the intellectual view that humour is impossible before 18 months, when infants can first understand make-believe.

Most parents would wonder what there was to debate. They would agree with Sully and Rothbart that their laughing babies can already share a joke from a very young age. Vasi Reddy found this when she interviewed 32 parents of babies between seven and 12 months (Reddy, 2001). She found that parents always found reasons for their babies' laughter; it was not random or mysterious. Interactions strongly resembled clowning, with parents acting in an exaggerated or 'silly' manner or violating norms to elicit laughter. The parents were acting deliberately and were aware of the emotional response they were evoking. The babies got the joke. More recently, Reddy has been interested in cases where babies turn the tables and start teasing their parents (Reddy & Mireault, 2015). She believes that the laughter shared by a parent and child is not some incidental side effect of their interaction. Rather, this interactive, social element of humour is likely to be a key part of their learning and nurturing relationship. As such, it is also likely to be central to any truly comprehensive theory of why we laugh when we do.

My favourite book about jokes and joking is *The Naked Jape* by comedians Jimmy Carr and Lucy Greeves (2006). Not only is it funny but, drawing on their huge experience of as performers, the authors are dismissive of the academic theories of humour that overlook the live and immediate nature of comedy. Their own advice on how to tell jokes comes down to five rules of thumb: pick your moments, know your punchlines, be relaxed, use few words, and enjoy yourself. To a degree, I would argue that babies do all of these. Good comedy is more than jokes and juxtapositions. It involves charisma and a connection with the audience. Watch any good stand-up comedian and you'll see they do not need many punchlines. They win us over with charm and invite us to share their joke. Even when comedians insult their audiences, they are careful to keep most of the room on side. Babies have built-in charisma. All things being equal, babies are likeable and charming. You want them to be your friend. As with the best comedians, we are laughing with them, not at them.

Babies are more than clowns – they are masters of

observational comedy, and an inability to speak does not hold them back. Good observational comedians do not need many actual jokes. Britain's most successful comedian, Peter Kay, even jokes about his lack of jokes. In 2010 Kay played 15 nights in the huge O2 Arena on the Greenwich Peninsula in London. The show was seen by a world-record 1.2 million people. In the recording, he thanks the audience for coming to see '20 minutes of comedy dragged over a two-hour show'. He starts with a few terrible one-liners before getting all the real humour from observations of everyday life. When American stand-up Jerry Seinfeld riffs about airline safety announcements or chopsticks, he rarely says anything you did not already know. Observational comedians point out things we all recognise but from a different angle. They invite us to share in their carefully crafted delight and wonder at the world. Comedians like this make us feel good about life and its absurdity.

Babies do this too, without even trying. A baby laughing at popping soap bubbles or an excitable dog calls our own attention to a delight we had forgotten but can still appreciate once it is pointed out. Laughing babies regularly remind us of the extraordinary in the mundane because for them it is still extraordinary. Carr and Greeves endorse the idea that comedians are childlike in their appreciation of the world and their questioning attitude. They say that 'a good joke can offer even the stuffiest of adults the opportunity to throw open an internal window on to the fresh, freewheeling creativity of childish imagination'.

Our tiny comedians have another advantage: they are happy

and can easily express their pure, uninhibited joy. As James Sully perceptively pointed out, five-month-old babies laugh with the sheer joy of being alive (Sully, 1902). A colleague from my Ph.D. days, Dr Anna Ashworth, regularly sends me video updates on her baby boy. After the most recent video of him giggling in his kitchen high chair as she entertained him, she jokingly queried if I ever get bored of laughing baby videos, and we speculated about their enduring appeal. She admitted that as a parent she is a totally biased observer of her own son. But her observations are something we would all recognise to be true:

> Seeing joy and happiness in the little human that you love more than anything in the world… when they're happy, you're happy. It is totally pure. Babies have no inhibitions so they can show their joy. It's beautiful.

Grandma and the Birth of Culture

Becoming a grandmother is wonderful. One moment you're just a mother. The next you are all-wise and prehistoric.

— Pam Brown, Australian poet

Culture is everything humans do collectively that we might have done differently. You speak this language and worship that god; I speak another and worship Terry Pratchett. As well as laws, language, beliefs, customs and morals, culture is jokes, memes, games, stories and slang. Social scientists sometimes say cultures are our learned behaviours. Cultural transmission of knowledge can grow and grow over generations, helping a species thrive in its habitat. In our more dangerous prehistory, cultural knowledge could easily be a matter of life and death, and as nothing was written down, culture could be thought of as the information stored in the heads of its surviving members. Recent research shows our collective wisdom and our long-lived elders have played a central role in our evolutionary success. And it gets better than that. The combination of long-lived grandmothers, large social groups and helpless babies might have been the perfect storm to kick-start our incredible intelligence.

Grandparents, especially grandmothers, have long been an invaluable source of childcare and support for mothers and babies. Ethnographers find grandmothers caring for their daughters' offspring in many societies, often spending more time than fathers as a substitute primary caregiver. But the role of grandmothers is much more far-reaching. For many decades anthropologist Kristen Hawkes and colleagues have been studying the division of labour in the Hadza hunter-gatherer community in northern Tanzania. Her earliest study on 'Hardworking Hadza Grandmothers' was revolutionary (Hawkes, O'Connell, & Jones, 1989). Hawkes tracked groups of women as they went out to forage for buried tubers and ripe berries. Groups consisted of women of all ages, some still carrying nursing infants, a range of young children and a few young men acting as protection. Digging for tubers is hard physical work that takes up to six hours a day. Hawkes was surprised to find not only that older women were more skilled, but they worked longer hours with greater yields. This contrasted with earlier studies of the !Kung people of the Kalhari, where foraging takes up less than two hours per day and skill peaks in middle adulthood. !Kung grandmothers spend much more time babysitting (Lee, 1979).

Hadza and !Kung grandmothers made different choices depending on their environment, but in both cases it benefited their daughters and grandchildren. This helped Hawkes and her colleagues to see the role of grandmothers in a new light. Further field study and computer models of evolution led them to propose the grandmother hypothesis, which states that it profits women to stop having children and support their grandchildren instead. The longer grandma lives, the more grandchildren and great-grandchildren she can care for, increasing the likelihood of her genes, especially those for longevity, surviving another generation (Kim, Coxworth & Hawkes, 2012). This can explain the menopause and why humans live so long, since male children can inherit those longevity benefits too. The hypothesis can also explain early weaning in humans, as this allows relatives to care for the babies and means mothers can get pregnant sooner and have more babies.

In hominins the grandmother effect is unique to the human lineage – no other female primates live past their childbearing age. Interestingly, it also happens in orcas but not in elephants. Both live in social groups but, crucially, baby orcas stay in their mother's pod, while an elephant's children move to a different group. So grandmother orcas can invest in their grandchildren but elephants cannot. A study of villages in rural Gambia found toddlers with a maternal grandmother were twice as likely to survive than those without. In contrast, the presence or absence of a father made no difference (Sear & Mace, 2008). As Kristen Hawkes sees it, 'Grandmothering gave us the kind of upbringing that made us more dependent on each other socially and prone to engage each other's attention.' When grandmothers help mothers, it helps everyone.

We might also expect positive evolutionary pressures on human intelligence to interact with longevity. Older members of communities are an invaluable library of wisdom and knowing how not to die. A recent study finds exactly this. Anthropologist Sally Street compared many different primate groups and concluded that 'the evolution of large brains, sociality, and long lifespans has promoted reliance on culture, with reliance on culture in turn driving further increases in brain volume, cognitive abilities, and lifespans' (Street, Navarrete, Reader & Laland, 2017). A long life is packed with experience, and wisdom equals intelligence plus experience. Thanks to cultural transmission, wisdom can be shared to the benefit of others, especially one's offspring.

Babies join this party too. Our culture and cleverness present challenges for reproduction. Our big brains and reliance on learning rather than instinct means human babies are born vulnerable and hard to keep alive, but this turns out to have evolutionary benefits. Steve Piantadosi and Celeste Kidd collaborated on a computational model of baby rearing. They concluded that humanity rose to the challenge of taking care of our babies and that it was a key factor driving the explosion in our intelligence. Helpless babies need clever parents. Clever parents need bigger brains. Bigger brains and fixed birth canals means giving birth to underdeveloped babies. These even more helpless babies need even cleverer parents, and so the cycle continues (Piantadosi & Kidd, 2016).

This is wonderful, but it did make life difficult for baby hominins. As our brains expanded and our culture accelerated, babies arrived less and less prepared for the world. A complex culture raises the problem of how wisdom is shared and how learning occurs: babies have lots to learn and no one can teach them. When their parents and grandparents were not labouring to provide food, they were stressed with the challenges of keeping their baby alive. Moreover, the things you could try and teach a baby are not things a baby would understand, as the gulf between their perspective and ours is so wide. Babies do learn from us, but it does not happen in any obvious way and it looks nothing like teaching.

Teaching is a very WEIRD way to learn. The present author and most readers of this book are WEIRD. We are Western and Educated, from Industrialised, Rich and Democratic nations. We are the anomaly and a lot of the cultural assumptions we make are not universal. Anthropologists study diverse and remote communities around the world in part to understand our own culture's blind spots. David Lancy believes that teaching is one of these. In *The Anthropology of Childhood*, he points out that the explicit instruction of babies and young children is rare in non-WEIRD countries. He states that 'nowhere in the entire ethnographic record have I found any instance of a parent and child building a block tower together or anything else whose purpose is to entertain while also instructing the child' (Lancy, 2015). He believes that children learn through observation, imitation, play and make-believe.

Across time and geography babies and young children have acquired their cultures, so, clearly, culture can be learned without teaching. This is because culture is not a set of facts. One of the most thoughtful philosophers of education, A. N. Whitehead, felt that 'culture is activity of thought and receptiveness to beauty and humane feeling. Scraps of information have nothing to do with it' (Whitehead, 1967). Whitehead was not thinking about babies, but Colywn Trevarthen sees no reason why this does not apply to them. He believes that 'meaning is discovered in playful collaborative friendships, and that its discovery is motivated by pleasure in dynamically responsive company' and 'human beings have a specially adapted capacity for sympathy of brain activity that drives cultural learning' (Trevarthen, 2005).

Cultural learning in babies is an emotional and empathic experience. In Trevarthen's view, pride and shame are the most important emotions for babies. This probably sounds surprising, but it comes down to the fact these are strongly interpersonal emotions. By pride, Trevarthen has in mind babies' outgoing tendencies, such as their clownishness and their delight in our attention and praise. Shame is the opposite; it is related to babies' timidity and frustration with their failures in front of others. Their emotions are strongly embodied too. Babies do not just feel their reactions to carers – they act them out. This helps the baby be in sympathy with carers. Sympathy derives from a Greek word meaning 'moving and feeling with' and Trevarthen sees this activity as a more holistic version of the eye-to-eye synchrony that we encountered earlier.

Babies are trying to work out the intentions of others and they are doing it from several months of age. It is a large leap from my perspective to yours, from first person to third person. The traditional view is that babies begin as egocentric beings who cannot achieve this transition before 18 months old. First, by playing jointly with an adult, they discover that the adult can pay attention to different things to them. Second, they come to see that they themselves can be an object of adult attention, creating a sense of self. The first of these abilities, called joint attention, arises at around one year of age and the second follows at around 18 months. The 'mirror test of self-recognition' is supposedly a triumphant demonstration of this. An experimenter surreptitiously puts a red dot of make-up on a baby's forehead and sees how they respond to themselves in the mirror. At around 18 months old, babies will touch their own foreheads (Amsterdam, 1972). This is an important landmark and, interestingly, chimpanzees also pass this test (Gallup, 1970) but human babies are aware of your attention much earlier than this.

In peekaboo, mutual eye gaze and other direct interactions, babies notice when you are attending to them. Vasi Reddy calls this the second-person perspective. Your baby is aware of 'you'. It is present from a few months old, and mirrors help us see this more clearly. In a study on infant 'coyness', Reddy documented how two- to three-month-old babies would smile and turn away from a social partner. They would also turn away from their own image in a mirror. In both cases, the coyness helps them regulate the intensity of a strange experience (Reddy, 2000). Darwin noted the fascination of his four-month-old son when shown a mirror. It is fascinating precisely because it odd.

I have a wonderful video of exactly this on my website, sent by a family from Warsaw, Poland. Baby Frederic is on his tummy in a giraffe-covered babygro, seeing himself in the mirror for the first time. He keeps stopping and starting, alternately waiting for the other baby to interact with him or surprised when it seems to interrupt him. He is not consciously aware that this charming stranger is literally mirroring everything he does. He is aware this interaction is not normal, but fortunately he finds it fun. He perceives that it is odd because it breaks the conventions of turn-taking, which is built into all human interaction: parents start doing it with their babies from the very beginning. Turn-taking is a subtle but ubiquitous feature of the world that even a four-month-old might have picked up on.

Babies are highly observant. Lancy is right that even in the West we do not spend much time playing with babies. But babies spend a lot of time watching us and they have a sophisticated ability to work out our intentions by carefully watching our activities. Understanding the intentions of others involves knowing they have goals and being able to make sense of them. Anyone with a pet cat knows this is not completely straightforward. Cats clearly do have motives, but most of the time these are a mystery to their owners. A baby can understand our goals even when we fail to achieve them. Experiments show that babies understand the intention when someone tries to put food into a pan and misses, or operates a switch with their head only because their hands were full (Gergely, Bekkering & Király, 2002). Babies are surprised if a ball moving towards a goal continues to jump unnecessarily when an obstacle is removed (Csibra, Bíró, Koós, & Gergely, 2003).

The scientists behind those studies are Hungarian infant psychologists Gergely Csibra and György Gergely. They call this a 'teleological stance'. They believe babies have an innate bias to interpret actions as goal-directed, which helps them understand the people around them (Gergely & Csibra, 2003). Gergely and Csibra have since gone further and suggested babies know when we are trying to teach them things and come predisposed to believe adults. They believe parents and children have a natural master and apprentice relationship, which operates even in young babies. They see these abilities as built in by evolution to help babies keep up with the challenge of learning and generalising (Csibra & Gergely, 2009).

David Lancy, the anthropologist, sees babies as little anthropologists, observing others in order to infer their intentions. Csibra and Gergely, the cognitive scientists, see babies as little learners, naturally predisposed to discerning goals and recognising when they are being taught. Csibra and Gergely admit it is an open question whether natural pedagogy is universal across cultures, but they think Lancy is being too narrow in his definition of instruction. Both sides agree babies are doing most of the work, and that they are quick and competent learners from early on. This has important implications for our concept of culture.

Babies spend most of their time with mothers and grandmothers, and most of what they learn comes from interaction and observation. A lot of what is going on around them is activity directed towards their care. In our ancestral home in the African savannah, providing for human babies took teamwork. Grandma and older siblings helped mothers care for the babies. Foraging and food preparation were communal activities, and babies were ever-present members of that group. Fathers might have mattered, but not too much.

This is clear when you assemble the evidence, but it is surprising how slow we have been to see it. Only in the last ten years has the story been mapped out, largely due to the work of evolutionary anthropologist Sarah Hrdy. In her 2010 book *Mothers and Others* (Hrdy, 2010), she presents this new version of our prehistory, arguing that the true cradle of our species is the hearth, not the hunt. The central figure is not man the hunter, but woman the mother and grandma the babysitter.

Chapter Ten: The Sound of Happy

Without music, life would be a mistake.
— Friedrich Nietzsche, philosopher (1844–1900)

I like music, but I am not musical. As a small boy, my violin playing was so bad that I got sacked by my violin teacher. She said my arms were too long and I ought to consider a different instrument, but we both knew that was a lie. After three or four years of screechy anguish I had made no progress whatsoever. It was a relief all around that the torture could stop. A few years later I remember marvelling when a friend who played in an orchestra told me she had taught herself to play the violin one summer holiday. Whenever I get forced to sing a song at karaoke, even the person who has jokingly insisted and insisted, despite my many protests, will admit, 'Caspar with music is a mistake.' So it was surreal and terrifying to find myself collaborating with a professor of music psychology and Grammy Award-winning musician to create a song that would make babies happy.

Rock Your Body

When I started my current job at Goldsmiths, University of London, I gave a talk about my research. Afterwards my new colleague, Professor Lauren Stewart, came up to me for a chat and suggested we collaborate on something. Lauren's area of speciality is the psychology of music. She had been at Goldsmiths for 10 years and started a revolutionary graduate programme called Music, Mind and Brain, which takes students with music or psychology backgrounds and teaches them the neuroscience of music. Lauren had recently become interested in how babies respond to music. Music is laden with emotion and so it would be fascinating to learn more about its effect on young babies. I readily agreed, but we could not find a suitable project straight away.

Goldsmiths has an amazing reputation for arts and creativity. For years our creative departments have been training future artists of all kinds, and the end-of-year student art shows are always breathtaking. The art department can count 25 Turner Prize nominees and seven winners among their illustrious alumni, including Damien Hirst and film director Steve McQueen, who has both a Turner Prize and an Oscar to his name. His career started as a result of his 1993 film *Bear*, made for his Goldsmiths graduation. In music, Goldsmiths gave a start to Sex Pistols manager Malcolm McLaren and 1990s pop acts Blur and Placebo. More recently, multi-award-winning rapper and poet Kate Tempest was a graduate of the English department. Even the two token science departments, psychology and computing, are filled with artists and musicians.

I agreed to collaborate with Lauren despite a keen awareness of my own musical limitations. First, this was exactly the kind of thing one is supposed to do at Goldsmiths. Second, I reasoned I would only have to be as musical as a small baby and even I could manage that. In addition, I had helped on one baby music project before. When I was investigating babies' time perception at Birkbeck, our research assistant, Sinead Rocha, had started her Ph.D. on babies' sense of rhythm. I have no sense of rhythm either, but I managed to assist effectively with that.

Sinead's project is an excellent place to start when thinking about babies and music, because rhythm and movement are central to the origin of human music. In Sinead's experiment, she played them 45-second bursts of music with different tempos, ranging from a frantic 'Weird Al' Yankovic song (200 beats per minute) through Little Richard (171 bpm) and Jennifer Lopez (133 bpm), and down to the bump and grind of Justin Timberlake's R&B hit 'Rock Your Body' (100 bpm). Babies were given a set of bells and were encouraged to shake them in time with the music, either accompanied by Sinead or by seeing an animated video of shaking bells. My job was to hide behind a curtain and run the computers.

Sinead found the younger babies could not adjust to the beat of the music but older babies could. Babies enjoyed it when Sinead accompanied them and older babies reduced head-nodding and other movements as they put more effort into ringing the bells although, curiously, a social partner made no difference to their accuracy (Rocha & Mareschal, 2017).

Sinead's next experiment was simple but ingenious. She invited lots of babies to bang away on a lovely big drum. She found that babies' natural rhythm improved with age, which is to be expected as they become more coordinated. More interestingly, the babies of taller mothers drummed more slowly. Taller people have longer, slower strides so babies' natural rhythm seems to derive from being carried around (Rocha, Southgate & Mareschal, 2017).

Babies ain't got much rhythm, but they love dancing or drumming from as soon as they can move. It's estimated that babies spend up to 40% of their time awake making repetitive movements as they gradually learn to choreograph their actions. Give them a rattle to shake or pans to bang and they are even happier. As I mentioned, my mother had me entertaining myself by tap dancing in my cot from a few months old. It certainly was not very musical but, like all babies making noise, my joy was because I was doing it myself. But music and dancing are more than just engagement with sound or movement. They are engagement with other people.

Dancing often gets overlooked when thinking about the origin and meaning of music, but dancing was there from the beginning, and not just for babies. This is the view of Guido Orgs, who has the office next door to mine. Guido is a former professional dancer who moved into psychology to study the neuroscience of dance, movement and something called neuroaesthetics. Guido has worked with choreographers and brain-imaging experts to investigate how dancing connects us with other people. When I ask him to explain where dance and music come from, he emphasises the social aspects: 'Dance and music really are the same thing. The thing that they share evolutionarily is people doing stuff together. Groups of people coordinating their movements to produce something. This has effects on those that do it because they create a group identity, which may well be the basis of culture.'

Guido's research has shown how moving in synchrony with other people strengthens our sense of belonging to our group. He found that 'how closely you couple your movement with another person is the best predictor of how much you like that person, and how much you connect to the group' (von Zimmermann, Vicary, Sperling, Orgs & Richardson, 2018). Moving together brings us together and is also reflected in greater conformity to the group, which is why soldiers spend a lot of time marching and tribes have their war dances. When we move together, we signal our collective strength to outsiders. The Maori war dance, the haka, is the classic example. Adopted by New Zealand's All Blacks rugby team, who perform it before each international match, it aims not just to intimidate the opposition but to unify and inspire the team and their supporters. The loud chorus of supporters at a football match has a similar effect. Every time we clap or cheer a person or their performance, we are signalling our support through collective action.

Evolutionary theories have a tension between communal collaboration and individual competition, with competition often seen as the more important factor. Evolution picks single winners rather than teams, selecting 'selfish genes' rather than social groups, although in mate selection you are looking for the ultimate collaborator. Darwin thought human music and dance could be courtship rituals as they are in birds, a means for competing males to signal physical and mental fitness to choosy females. The evidence is surprisingly thin on the ground. Historically there have been more male composers and musicians but this is primarily due to social restrictions. Physical symmetry is a good indicator of genetic fitness, and researchers find that it can be judged in dancing (W. M. Brown et al., 2005). But we are not always up all night to get lucky. Singing and dancing undoubtedly make us happy for their own sake. Babies have no interest in making love or fighting wars, but they undoubtedly enjoy music, even Justin Timberlake.

Robin Dunbar suspects that in the story of song and dance, sexual selection plays second fiddle to the community chorus (Dunbar, 2012). He believes communal singing and dancing were important social mechanisms as group sizes increased in our branch of the primate family tree. They are the next step up from laughter. Music can be shared with larger groups and, like laughter, it triggers the release of endorphins. In fact, Dunbar thinks laughter was 'a precursor to musical chorusing' and that there is a 'natural sequence running from grooming to laughter to music and finally to language' (Dunbar, 2012).

Music aims to move us. One interesting definition of music is that it is embodied expressive movement that entrains others (Cross & Morley, 2008). As I sit here writing this, Vivaldi's *Four Seasons*, a series of four violin concertos, is playing in the background. It has moved through 'Spring', where the violins imitate the songs of birds and the joyful allegro evokes dancing. Now it has progressed to 'Summer', which starts slowly with us languishing in the sun with cuckoos and turtledoves in the air. But tension builds as a summer storm approaches and bursts. You cannot hear the impossibly fast violins without being aware of their frantic movement. It gets into my own body. My heart rate is undoubtedly elevated and I feel like moving. But more than that, I feel the seasons.

Baby Opera

For all sorts of reasons opera – even comic opera – is usually no laughing matter.

— Tom Sutcliffe, *Believing in Opera,* 1997

Not long after Lauren Stewart and I had discussed our possible collaboration, she had a phone call from C&G Baby Club, a website owned by a food manufacturer, which provides advice on pregnancy and the care of babies and young children. They wanted her help to create 'a song scientifically proven to make babies happy'. This was almost too good to be true, so we decided to meet them. Going into the meeting we were wary. Brands and advertisers have a poor track record when it comes to using science. But I had a very positive experience doing sleep research with Pampers in Brazil. So we met with C&G Baby Club and their advertising agency BTEC to discuss their ideas.

It turned out the inspiration had come from dogs. A few weeks previously, Ciara O'Meara, who was working for BTEC, had been in New York, where avant-garde artist and composer

Laurie Anderson had performed a concert for an audience of dogs. The concert had taken place at midnight in Times Square on a freezing winter's night. Laurie Anderson had played her violin, resampling the frequencies for canine ears. The dogs seemed to enjoy the experience, joining in with barks and howls. Ciara reasoned that if people can make serious music for dogs, why not for babies? The press, naturally, had been unable to resist the concert either, which doubtless had not escaped Ciara's attention.

Lauren and I were intrigued by the challenge and curious to find out what, if anything, had already been done on this topic. In my baby laughter survey I had asked parents what nursery rhymes and silly sounds appealed to their babies. We found, to no great surprise, that babies like raspberries and songs where you tickle them. Lauren's previous research was potentially more useful, as she had looked at 'earworms' – songs that get stuck in your head (Jakubowski, Finkel, Stewart & Müllensiefen, 2017), although we all agreed early on that the song should be catchy, not contagious. Baby songs inevitably get put on repeat and we didn't want to drive parents crazy. We agreed with C&G Baby Club to go away and do more background research while they began their search for a suitable composer.

We discovered surprisingly little research on babies' musical preferences. This was encouraging, as it meant this was a worthwhile project from a scientific point of view. Plenty of research has looked at adults' emotional responses to music, but research with babies is more piecemeal and eclectic, no doubt reflecting the difficulty of asking them what they like.

We already know babies can remember the soap-opera themes and other music they hear in the womb, and one entertaining study found that newborn babies prefer Bach to Aerosmith (Flohr, Atkins, Bower & Aldridge, 2000). The most systematic work has been conducted by Laurel Trainor at McMaster University in Ontario, Canada. She has found that young babies have clear preferences for consonance over dissonance and can remember the tempo and timbre of music they've heard before. Babies prefer the female voice, but like it even more when it takes on the qualities of infant-directed speech. This is the high-energy sing-song tone we all naturally adopt when talking to babies.

Babies can enjoy Mozart, but it will not magically enhance their brains. This persistent myth goes back to a study by Rauscher, Shaw and Ky (1993). They found that college students received the equivalent to a nine-IQ-point boost in a spatial-reasoning task after listening to Mozart's Sonata for Two Pianos in D major (K448) for 10 minutes. This launched a raft of baby Mozart products, but over time it became clear that the effect is small and not related to classical music. One study with 8,000 10-year-olds found they did better when listening to Goldsmiths alumnae Blur than to Mozart (Schellenberg & Hallam, 2005).

When you look around, there is not too much serious music for babies. Most music written specifically for babies is incredibly and deliberately soporific. The most famous lullaby of all, 'Wiegenlied', Op. 49, No. 4 by Johannes Brahms was composed in 1868 for an old flame on the birth of her child. Now it can be heard in thousands of music boxes and baby mobiles. Back in the 1920s, Czech opera composer Leos Janáček tried his hand at nursery rhymes. As well as being a prolific composer, he was interested in folklore and fairy tales, transcribing and adapting many folk songs, as well as producing large choral arrangements of dozens of Czech nursery rhymes. I do not know anyone who has tried these on babies, but they scare the hell out of me. Musician Michael Janisch recorded a whole album of *Jazz for Babies* in 2013. This, too, was very slow and designed to soothe them, not make them happy. Upbeat baby music usually sounds frankly deranged, although I am a big fan of Caspar Babypants, the current baby-friendly band of former rock star Chris Ballew.

With a lack of decent options, babies take matters into their own hands and find preferences in their parents' music collection. For many years I have asked parents visiting my lab what music their babies like. The variety and eclecticism have been bewildering. Babies like a little bit of everything, from Sonic Youth to Taylor Swift. They seem just as likely to pick heavy metal as country and western, pop, punk, hip-hop or classical music. Some little traditionalists even like nursery rhymes. The one pattern is a lack of pattern. Parents are often surprised by the songs that catch their babies' attention. There is no doubt that their babies do have favourites that they recognise and enjoy. It is usually individual songs rather than a style or an artist.

There is considerable depth to their appreciation too. You may have seen the viral videos of babies bursting into tears when hearing emotional music. In one classic, Canadian 10-month-old Marie-Lynne starts out smiling as her mum sings a bluesy song called 'My Heart Can't Tell You No'. But she wells up with tears as the emotion builds. Meanwhile, there is a whole genre of babies reacting to chart-topping opera singer Andrea Bocelli singing an operatic lullaby to Elmo on *Sesame Street*. It is remarkable how these babies are moved by what they hear. We were not setting out to make sad music, but this did make me think about baby opera.

Ask any professional musician the secret of good music and they will tell you that, above all else, music is about emotion. This is particularly true of opera, where the main instrument is the human voice and the main topic the human condition. Through music and drama, story and spectacle, opera aims to explore the highs and lows of life. Anger, joy, love, grief, jealousy and despair are all portrayed in exuberant spectacle. Richard Mantle, director of Opera North, calls it 'the art form that comes closest to expressing pure emotion'. Writer George Bernard Shaw said, 'Opera is when a soprano and a tenor want to make love but are prevented from doing so by a baritone.' Opera is deliberately intense and emotionally manipulative, although, as arts broadcaster Tom Sutcliffe observes, opera does not do comedy well. The pressure is too great and the stakes are too high.

Opera is technically, logistically and economically forbidding. Many fans of opera are unapologetic that it is the most extreme example of human art. Oliver Mears, director of opera at the Royal Opera in London thinks that 'opera is important because it is totally unfeasible'. He adds that 'in scale and cost it is the most excessive of all art forms, and in the totality of its artistic claims, is the most ambitious'. It is surprising then to learn not only that people make opera for babies, but that baby opera might have been the birth of all human art.

Musical Rumpus have been making operas for audiences of babies since 2011. Supported by the Spitalfields Music charity, their shows have been seen by around 15,000 babies in east London and beyond. I knew about them, but for a long time I had no idea what was involved. When I stumbled into the world of baby music myself, I decided it was time to find out. I know nothing about opera, so I took along my friend Sam Wass who, prior to becoming a baby scientist, was an opera director in Berlin. The last time I had been to anything resembling opera was a school trip to see Gilbert and Sullivan's *Pirates of Penzance* when I was twelve. My two abiding memories were that yes, indeed, comic opera is no laughing matter and that despite it being incredibly loud, I fell asleep. Therefore, even though it was opera for babies, I felt a bit intimidated and was glad Sam was there for moral support and to poke me if I looked drowsy.

Sam and I joined the tiny audience for Musical Rumpus's show, *Fogonogo*, an opera about a volcano. It was the eighth show the company have created and the seventh collaboration between composer Sam Glazer and writer and director Zoe Palmer. Just like grown-up opera, baby opera is a full multimedia experience, with set, staging, costumes and orchestra, albeit on a much smaller scale, as the budgets and the subsidies are as diminutive as the audience. The cast consists of just two singers – we saw a performance by Lucy Knight, a soprano, and Peter Braithwaite, a baritone. The orchestra on this occasion had two musicians: Sam Glazer played the cello, accompanied by Rosie Bergonzi, a percussionist. The venue was modest too: one panelled-off corner of the public library in Stratford, east London. Buggies were parked, and babies and their carers all found places to sit. The audience was small in number – around 20 babies, although previous shows have had as many as 50 babies, and then it really is a rumpus.

The numbers are usually kept low because the shows are intimate and interactive. In the show we saw, babies were seated in circle around some blue mats representing the sea, with small orange platforms as islands. From the start the performers were down on the babies' level, moving gently, and sensitive to their reactions. The babies are mostly content to sit and watch, but there are always several infant actors wandering into the performance and handing props to the performers. But even the babies content to stay sitting with mummy or daddy are not left out; the performers take care to connect with every little person in the audience. The babies are part of the show: Zoe calls them 'our gurgling, wriggling, crawling, chorus' and their responses are incorporated into the performance. It means no two shows are the same, and this can be quite daunting for classically trained musicians. Zoe told me about working on a baby show with jazz singers in New York. They 'got it' much faster, happy to improvise around their infant accompaniment.

Fogonogo starts slowly, but the intensity builds. This is a show about a volcano, after all. Sam Glazer is very conscious that baby opera should explore the full range of emotions. Over the hundreds of shows he has done, he has become more confident that the music should not be unrelentingly happy. It should be sad. It should be scary. The babies will respond. They will engage. As Andrea Bocelli says, 'To sing opera, one needs two things: the voice and the passion – and above all, the passion.' Peter and Lucy both get to show off the power of their voices and the music becomes increasingly dramatic, even slightly frightening at times. By my count they are singing in at least four different languages: English, French, Italian and Volcano. The babies lap it up. Many are active participants; others are quietly transfixed. Zoe tells me that, in her experience, tears are very rare. For all of them, the music provides the thread through the performance, holding their attention and inviting them into the action.

American writer Ellen Dissanayake believes that something not too different from Musical Rumpus could have been the origin of music, art and even love. She thinks music and other arts evolved in tandem with our need for intimacy and belonging. In a wonderful book entitled *Art and Intimacy* she provides a deeply humanistic perspective on the evolution of art and culture that puts mothers and babies centre stage. 'It is not surprising that societies all over the world have developed these nodes of culture that we call ceremonies or rituals, which do for their members what mothers naturally do for their babies: engage their interest, involve them in a shared rhythmic pulse, and thereby instil feelings of closeness and communion.' (Dissanayake, 2000).

In an earlier book, Dissanayake had proposed the notion of *Homo Aestheticus* (Dissanayake, 1994). She thinks art makes us feel good and feel bigger than ourselves. Art aims 'to recognise an extra-ordinary as opposed to an ordinary dimension to experience; to act deliberately in response to uncertainty'. It was a counter-revolutionary idea. Rather than looking for explanations of art and aesthetics in psychology or philosophy, she considered its evolutionary benefit. With a background in ethology and 15 years living in Sri Lanka, Nigeria, and Papua New Guinea, she felt she had escaped the narrow Eurocentric perspective of most art theorists, who take their meanings from contemporary European culture and its phases and fashions over the last few centuries. She thinks modern theorists' obsession with the meaning of words blinds them to a deep history of 5 million years of social living and preliterate culture. As a result, she gets very angry with all the relativism of postmodernism and literary theory, which claims that art gets its power because it is a signifier of nothing beside itself. Dissanayake does not stand for this: 'Nothing? Fire is hot. Hunger is bad. Babies are good.'

Art and Intimacy takes things further. It argues that the arts are not tools of sexual competition but expressions of empathy and community. The book was born out of a year Dissanayake spent in Edinburgh at Colwyn Trevarthen's lab learning about the 'primary intersubjectivity' created as mothers synchronise with their babies. Dissanayake proposes that the arts extend this to larger groups. She dismisses the sex-obsessed perspective of most evolutionary psychologists, who, she notes, are mostly male. If music and art are tools of courtship, this is a minor, secondary role. The main evolutionary value of art, music and story is as shared experience. And, just as a mother's attunement with her infant is beneficial for the baby's well-being, art is good for our psychological well-being.

In Dissanayake's account, the origin of art is social, not symbolic. It is found in activity, not imagery. As a highly social species we have a capacity for mutual engagement and for kinship and belonging. Even before we had language, it is likely that we sought and shared meaning by other means, and this is art. The dynamic, interactive nature of music serves this purpose well. We would have been able to sing before we could speak. Dissanayake thinks mothers' musical engagement with infants is much more than the 'soporific bliss' of lullabies. It captures, holds and sustains the infants' attention and explores reciprocity and the full range of emotional states. Anxiety, fear and anger all have life-preserving functions. The songs of mothers provide infants with a real experience of these darker feelings, balancing them with joy, surprise and love.

The songs, ceremonies and rituals of our ancient ancestors created community. So David Pountney, former head of Welsh National Opera, is on to something when he says that 'opera is the embodiment of an essential human instinct: telling stories through music. It links modern, liberal intellectual and artistic culture with our primitive ritualistic origins.' And yet, amazingly, baby opera brings us even closer to that ancient truth. Just as the feigned tickle of a baby might have been humanity's first ever joke, a mother's emotional songs to her baby might have been our first artwork.

'The Happy Song'

Bring! Bring! on the bicycle
Beep! Beep! in the car
Ping! Ping! a submarine

Phew! Phew! helicopter
A choo-choo train,
An aeroplane,
A 'whee', down the slide.

I just adore-dore-dore
You every day more
Wherever we are.

— 'The Happy Song', Imogen Heap, 2016

To find a composer for our happy/science/baby song, C&G Baby Club brought in music consultant Liz Williams. Liz prepared a list of popular musicians who might be up to such an unusual job. Top of her shortlist was Imogen Heap. Imogen is a multi-instrumentalist, singer, songwriter, engineer and producer. She was already writing songs in her teens and had signed her first recording deal before she was 18. As well as five albums of her own music, she has collaborated with dozens of artists from Jeff Beck to Ariana Grande. Imogen is also a music geek who likes the technological and innovative aspects of the business. She has been an electronic and computer music whiz since her teens, and is the inventor of electronic gloves that create music as they are moved through space and gesture. She has two Grammy Awards, both for music engineering: one for her own album, *Ellipse*, and one as a producer and engineer on Taylor Swift's massive hit album, *1989*. When Liz approached her to join our project, Imogen had just finished writing the music for the stage production of *Harry Potter and the Cursed Child.*

The other big reason Imogen was asked and why she accepted was that she had a baby daughter of her own, Scout, who was around 18 months old at the time. The previous year Imogen had composed a song, 'Tiny Human', about Scout. That song was an honest and personal response to the first few months of Scout's existence. Scout had been a very unsettled baby and, like most first-time parents, Imogen and her partner Michael felt completely unprepared for life after their tiny human 'came crashing in on that day'. The song confronts the physically and emotionally exhausting challenges of a baby who, it seemed, cried for three months non-stop. The lyrics to 'Tiny Human' ask 'How long can one live without sleep?' and admits that this is 'the hardest thing I've ever done'.

Our song was a different kind of challenge, an opportunity to create a happy song for babies rather than about a baby, while still appealing to parents. Like us, Imogen had noticed that 'there are very few "baby songs" that don't make you want to eat your own hands off' (Heap, 2017).

With Imogen on board, we met up to give her some guidance

based on existing research. Curiously, most of what is known about babies' musical preference comes from Canada – the labs of Sandra Trehub at the University of Toronto and Laurel Trainor at McMaster University in Hamilton, Ontario. Thanks to many decades of research from Trehub and Trainor, we know babies can tell the difference between happy major keys and sad minor keys. They like songs with a simple and repetitive main melody with musical devices like drum rolls, key changes and rising pitch glides to provide opportunities for anticipation and surprise (Trehub & Trainor, 1998).

The ideal person to sing to a baby is their mother and, generally, female voices are preferred over male. Most remarkably of all, babies can tell if you mean it or not. In one very cool study Laurel Trainor discovered that babies preferred versions of songs recorded in the presence of an actual baby over versions where the singer just imagined they were performing to a baby (Trainor, 1996). We recommended Imogen recorded the song with Scout in the studio. Next, as you might expect, fast songs sound happier than slow ones. But we recommended Imogen to make the song even faster than she would imagine. Babies' heart rates are much faster than ours. A 12-month-old's resting heart rate is about 50% faster than that of an adult. What sounds fast to us could sound like a waltz to a baby. If you want a good idea of a song that would appeal to babies, you cannot do much better than 'Happy' by Pharrell Williams. At 160 beats per minute it is certainly fast enough. It has a clear, repetitive melody and lyrics. There are long glides on happyyyyyyyyyyyyy and some nice moments of anticipation and surprise. The prominent clapping makes a difference too; babies (and adults) respond positively to physical cues that get them moving in time with the music. For example, one study found babies smiling more when they moved with the music (Zentner & Eerola, 2010).

We would be happy if we had even a fraction of the success of Pharrell Williams. We did have something that he did not: a small army of baby music consultants who would help us determine what babies liked. Imogen had her daughter, Scout, to help her with the composition and, with the help of C&G, we recruited families who would come to the lab to see their babies' reactions. We decided that Imogen would create us a selection of 20-second-long mini-songs we could play to babies in the lab. She and Scout went away to create four short melodies for us to test in the lab, two fast and two slow. For each of these she would create two versions, with and without simple sung lyrics.

A few weeks later Imogen sent us the eight candidate songs and, one after another, 26 babies between six and 12 months came to our lab with their mums to give us their opinions. We would know which song the mums liked because we could ask them. We also asked the mums to tell us what they thought their babies preferred best. Mothers are the experts on their own babies, so it would be foolish to ignore their wisdom. But we wanted more objective measures, so we filmed the babies and 'blind-coded' their responses. My two student assistants, Omer and Kaveesha, watched all the videos with the sound turned off so they did not know which song was which. They counted all the laughs, smiles and dancing. Amazingly, most of the mums and 20 out of the 26 babies had a clear preference for one melody. In line with our predictions, this was a faster melody. Even more amazingly, this was the tune that had evolved from something Scout had been humming. Is making music is her genes?

Now we had a winning melody, Imogen (and Scout) set about turning it into a full-length song. At this point a few more considerations came into play. First, we all wondered what noises babies found funny. Around 2,500 parents from the C&G Baby Club and Imogen's fan club voted on silly sounds that made their babies happy. The top 10 sounds included 'boo!', raspberries, sneezing, animal sounds and baby laughter. Second, we know babies respond better to plosive vocal sounds like 'pa' and 'ba' compared to sonorant sounds like 'la' or 'wa'. Imogen very cleverly worked many of these elements into the song. Third, it should be sweet, silly and social. It ought to be something that parents could enjoy themselves and share with their children. Happiness is a shared emotion and the success of many nursery rhymes is that they are interactive. Most importantly of all, the song needed a theme, lyrics and structure. But a two-time Grammy winner does not need advice from scientists on songwriting. Imogen carefully crafted the lyrics to tell a joyous tale of how we love our little babies wherever we are – from the sky to the ocean, on a bike or on a rocket. Cunningly, the transport theme permitted lots of plosives like 'beep, beep' and lots of opportunity for interaction between parent and baby.

Once Imogen was happy with 'The Happy Song', our baby music consultants came back to the lab and listened to two slightly different versions: a fast version at 163 beats per minute and an even faster one that was 168 beats per minute. We gave the parents a copy of the lyrics and encouraged them to get their babies dancing. To help with this, we set up a baby bouncer in the lab. Interestingly, most babies preferred the slightly slower version, because it gave mums and babies a little more time to respond to the lyrics. We found the chorus was the most effective part of the song and we used the babies' reactions to determine which lyrics and sound effects worked better or worse.

After one final round of tweaks from Imogen, we went for a different kind of test. We assembled our babies in one room and played them the song all together. It was perhaps a silly thing to do, but as Imogen and I sat on the sofa in front of a colourful and chaotic room full of parents and babies and pressed play, we were cautiously optimistic. If you have ever met an excited toddler or young baby, you will know two-and-a-half minutes is a long time to hold the attention of even one child, let alone two dozen. When 'The Happy Song' played we were met by a sea of entranced little faces. This was not very scientific as tests go, but it convinced me we had a hit on our hands.

It also gave the film crew some nice footage. Our sponsors, C&G Baby Club, wanted to document the process, so they had hired a hotshot young director, Michael J. Ferns, and a crew from Pretzel Films to follow us around. They filmed lots of interviews with parents, footage of us testing babies and of

Imogen creating the song. They edited this down to a short video that you can find on YouTube if you search for 'The Happy Song – Making Of'. But Michael and his team had a second goal: they had to make a music video for the song. For this they hit on the wonderful idea of asking some of the families to film themselves enjoying the song at home. One other thing we know about music is that it grows on you. To get the best reactions, it was good to let the babies have lots of listens. Filming happy babies at home also fitted the theme of the song and the theme of the project.

On its release, the song quickly reached number one in the iTunes children's charts, and over the next two years the video collected 14 million views, a sign we did something right. In the comments we found plenty of evidence it works for babies, parents and plenty of random teenagers who stumbled on it by accident. We've received thanks from parents all around the world. I recently heard of a 'lifehack' spreading in a new mothers' Facebook group, recommending you ask, 'Hey Alexa, play "The Happy Song".'

By happy coincidence, Lauren got to do a special case study of her own on 'The Happy Song'. One month after it was released, she gave birth to her second child. Lauren said, 'Megan must have heard the song such a lot in the womb as we played it over and over making decisions about it.' Though it was only when Megan got to around fix or six months and was more active that Lauren started using the song. 'I remember she was sitting at the kitchen table as I was cutting vegetables and she was about to cry. I put on "The Happy Song" and it completely transformed her. After that I'd say I used it strategically. Which I guess is as we intended.'

Hello Baby!

Here is an experiment to try next time you meet a baby: try talking normally. It is very difficult, isn't it? Yes, it is! Oh yes, it is!

When we talk to babies we naturally switch to a high-energy, sing-song tone. We use simple words and short sentences. We sound happy and excited. Our pitch rises at the end of the sentence. This is known as infant-directed speech or IDS for short. It used to be called 'motherese' or 'parentese', but IDS is the preferred term now because fathers, grandparents and most other adults do it when talking to babies. Moreover, the characteristics of IDS seem to be common across many languages. Listen to IDS in Mandarin and you would know it is aimed at a baby even if you understand nothing that is said. This is another part of the puzzle linking music, language and laughter.

The universal nature of IDS has been long suspected but only recently demonstrated, thanks to a study by Elise Piazza and colleagues at Princeton Babylab (Piazza, Iordan & Lew-Williams, 2017). First, they invited 12 English-speaking mothers of eight- to 12-month-olds to the lab and recorded them talking to their babies and then to an adult. The recordings were converted into 'vocal fingerprints' using a standard statistical method. This produces a unique frequency profile for a given speaker that can reliably discriminate one speaker from another based on timbre. Timbre describes the quality of a voice or a musical instrument. The difference between a violin and a trumpet playing the same note is a difference in timbre.

Piazza and her team used a computer classification algorithm to compare adult- and infant-directed speech. This showed that all the mothers altered the timbre of their voice in the same way when talking to babies. The authors ran several controls to check this was not just a result of mothers speaking in a higher pitch to babies. But the real test came when a further 12 mothers were recorded speaking nine different languages including Spanish, Russian and Cantonese. The algorithm picked up the same differences between their adult- and infant-directed speech. Piazza describes the change as a 'cue mothers implicitly use to support babies' language learning'.

The exact purpose of IDS is not known. One theory is that it helps babies learn. The sing-song quality of IDS makes words clearer and easier for babies to discriminate. Patricia Kuhl and a large international team analysed the difference between IDS and adult-directed speech in English, Russian and Swedish. In all languages IDS increased the acoustic separation of the key vowel sounds 'ee', 'aa' and 'ooh' (Kuhl et al., 1997). This exaggerates the differences between words like 'big', 'bag' and 'bug'. This benefits a baby learning a new language, but it might be a side effect of trying to catch their attention. IDS has the acoustic features of happy adult-directed speech. It might sound the way it does because we are happy to see our babies and smiling as we talk to them, which in turn attracts their attention. Infant-directed speech is not culturally universal, as there are some groups where parents do not address young babies. Often in these cases, such as the Kaluli in Papua New Guinea and Ganda in Uganda, the babies still get a lot of social contact in their daily life. Mothers carry their babies everywhere, usually strapped facing outwards, so they are part of whatever is going on.

A lot of our earliest conversations with babies continue the gentle dance that starts during nursing. Mothers whispering sweet nothings or singing lullabies are unconsciously regulating the babies' state of arousal. Curiously, when we enjoy sad music, it promotes the release of the breastfeeding hormone prolactin. Meanwhile, research has shown that premature babies in intensive care make more vocalisations in response to hearing adults' speech. If adults stop responding, infants notice and stop. Testing five-month-old infants with this procedure also found they ceased vocalising. The more in tune these infants were to their caregiver's behaviour at five months, the better their language comprehension at 13 months (Goldstein, Schwade & Bornstein, 2009).

Early on, the tone and tempo of a parent's words matter more than their content or meaning. Most phrases in baby talk, nursery rhymes and lullabies are divided into the same three- to five-second bursts as adult speech and music. The babies respond to the rhythm and melody and it is always a conversation. We leave gaps for our infants to answer us and they do. One delightful study by Kimbrough Oller (Oller et al., 2013) eavesdropped on three- to four-month-old infants who were 'chatting' to themselves in their cribs. They found that the infants expressed a full range of emotions in their growls and gurgles. By six months, babies have built a repertoire of vocal expressions. As well as crying and laughing, they can squeal, squeak and babble. They also manage something called a 'bilabial trill', a soggy 'brr-brr-brr' sound produced by blowing through closed lips.

Crying, laughter, singing and speech form a natural progression in our evolutionary story. Millions of years ago our vocal production started with primal screams of fright, fear, longing and need. Then came laughter and other positive exclamations expressing playfulness, delight and surprise. These are more social and more complex to produce, needing increased control of expression and emotion. Next came singing and language, which needed the anatomical changes that set us apart from other apes. We must have delicate control over our lungs, independent of breathing, to let us stop or sustain airflow to our voice boxes. We must be able to shape and modulate the noises we can make. Our ribcage had already changed shape with walking upright around 2 million years ago but, judging by the fossil record, the most important physical changes required for speech and singing happened around half a million years ago. Most noticeably, the hyoid bone in our necks is lower to make way for a larger vocal tract and a lower larynx, while changes in the shape of our ear canals tuned them to the frequencies of human speech. The pathway of the hypoglossal nerve grew larger, indicating a far greater control over the tongue. The same happened for the thoracic nerve, which controls the diaphragm and chest muscles (Dunbar, 2014).

Singing and language upgrade our voices, our brains and our lives. Once language takes off it can carry us to the stars, as we will see in the next two chapters. But we cannot start from language and work backwards. It is important to understand where it came from and what drove it forward.

Evolution never plans anything. It gets where it goes by chance and opportunism. Dunbar's theory that laughter and musical chorusing helped promote group cohesion is great for explaining the emotional expressiveness of the human voice. Small groups of adult primates could vocally groom each with other calls not much more complex than those of chimpanzees. Likewise, Dissanayake's theory of the origin of art gives important roles to mothers, infants and music in the birth of art. But neither theory give a mechanism that drives us towards the rich structure of music or the symbolic power of words. This might have come from nursery rhymes.

Ancient motherese and lullabies needed to communicate more than just emotion. Anthropologist Dean Falk thinks the first important role for IDS was not to learn language but to know that mother was nearby. In her view, motherese existed before language as an important type of protospeech that turned into music and language (Falk, 2004). Unlike other primates, our larger, more helpless babies cannot cling to our fur. Often a hominin mother would need to put her baby down to forage, prepare food or attend to older children. Falk thinks each mother invented her own patterns of calls that their babies recognised and used this as a means of 'keeping in touch'. Think back to those babies calmed by hearing the familiar soap-opera theme tune.

Once established, prelinguistic vocal communication between mother and infant could build in complexity. Individual mothers needed versatile and distinctive vocal calls to calm their own babies. Only mummy will do. Additionally, there would be strong selection pressures to communicate intent to toddlers. It is easy to imagine that an urgent 'No!' was the first ever human word. Thus, mothers need memory capacity to create and recall their own calls and a growing range of commands. Falk believes evolution built this capacity to help mothers care for their infants and this incidentally opened it to other uses. The campfire choruses of adults could become more complex, hunters and gathers could exchange information. By explaining how the symbolic and syntactic features of language and music could first emerge, Falk's theory sets an important ball rolling.

Most likely, the evolution of music and language happened in parallel. At their start they were so entwined that, rather than talking about protospeech or protomusic, some people prefer to talk about 'musilanguage' (Brown, 2017). In those earliest stages, the important aspects were emotion, prosody and structure. We have seen the importance of emotion. Prosody is the pattern of placing stress on appropriate syllables:

ROCK-a-bye BA-by ON the tree TOP
WHEN the wind BLOWS the CRA-dle will ROCK

Prosody marks the beat and provides the organisation of the phrase that lets several singers keep in synchrony. In speech, prosody can change the meaning of the word or the intent of a sentence.

Mary had a little LAMB	(not a little goat)
Mary had a LITTLE lamb	(not a great big one)
Mary had A little lamb	(just the one lamb)
Mary HAD a little lamb	(but not any more)
MARY had a little lamb	(It was Mary's lamb, not Jack's or Jill's)

Prosody can turn nouns into verbs or statements into questions. More subtle variations can convey emotions like excitement, anger or sadness. Complex linear structures can emerge with simple rules of grouping, embedding and repetition.

The wheels on the bus go round and round,
Round and round, round and round.
The wheels on the bus go round and round
All day long.

The people on the bus go up and down,
Up and down, up and down.
The people on the bus go up and down
All day long. (Verna Wills, 1939)

This lets you build up long songs others can follow or join and that you can remember. Importantly, these features can emerge long before you have any words and can provide a pathway to language. To sing the same song again you need some representation of it in your head, even if you are only humming. That representation can be the foundation for words, grammar and music. In Brown's theory, musilanguage develops further and diverges into music and language.

For her doctoral thesis at the University of Edinburgh, Elena Longhi looked in depth at baby songs and nursery rhymes (Longhi, 2003). She videoed mothers singing to their babies at home in English and Gaelic. Then she analysed them in depth to understand what was going on. She compares mothers to orchestral conductors. Mothers signal the rhythm and tempo through their prosody, like a conductor signalling the beat. They understand that music is movement and convey this with their bodies while looking for the synchronised response in their offspring because, like conductors, they are attending to their babies, who are part of the performance. They modulate their performance and the babies respond, bringing the pair of them into harmony. Mothers know the differences in performance between energising play-songs and soothing lullabies and use different tempos to create different moods. They know what is appropriate when and, like conductors, their ultimate goal is to direct the emotional state of their audience.

As these fun games get played, babies are learning the basics of music and language, but that was never the primary goal of happy songs or happy talk. We sing and chat to our babies to let them know they are *our* babies. By happy coincidence, while this is happening, they will teach themselves language.

Chapter Eleven: Happy Talk

Baby being told
'Stop' finds it hilarious
Giggles, waits—giggles

— #2207 from Calvin Olsen's Ten Thousand Haiku project (tenthousandhaiku.com)

We can only speculate on what language was like half a million years ago but by 50,000 years ago we have a pretty good idea. By then humans had fire, clothes, art and houses. They had spread across the whole world and their bodies and brains were anatomically identical to ours. Our ancestors had reached behavioural modernity. They looked like us, acted like us and thought like us. If you ignore our better nutrition, clever technology and complex culture, then, to a first approximation, they were us. Their languages are lost but they were undoubtedly as rich and as expressive as our own. Borrow a time machine to bring a baby of that era 50,000 years forward to the present day and they would cope just fine.

Languages change rapidly but the essence of language learning stays the same. Every baby in the past 50,000 years has had to tune in to the sounds of their mother tongue and practise their pronunciation. They have had to discover the magic of words, learning how arbitrary sounds can stand for objects and ideas. They have had to pick out the words and rules of their local language and map them onto their experience of the world. They had help from their parents and from their genes, but they were doing most of the work themselves. Babies learn language through conversation, observation and constant practice. They are highly motivated because very early on they discover that language lets them communicate with us, sharing their thoughts, feelings and intentions.

The biggest challenge for twenty-first-century babies might be that they have too much to talk about. Babies today live in a busy world full of people, places, objects and events. WEIRD babies have more varied lives than their ancient ancestors. They visit more places and meet many more people. In one trip through town a baby might see more people than a hunter-gatherer would encounter in a lifetime. Our babies have more toys and more time to play with them. They hear more songs and music. They have television and tablets to entertain them.

Modern life can leave babies overstimulated and under-socialised. There is plenty to talk about but there is not always someone to talk to. Babies have ways of dealing with too much information, but they depend upon us to be the other half of their conversations. Studies show there are large variations between families in the language environment they create for their children. There can be big differences in the amount of social contact babies receive, the number of words they hear or that are spoken directly to them, and in the complexity and content of their parents' own language. In this chapter we look at what is required to learn language and which differences make a difference.

The Tower of Babble

Māma, mama, mamá, ma, mama, mamă, maa, mama, haha and mamī.

— The word for 'mama' in the 10 most widely spoken languages in the world.

When I think about baby language learners, an image that often comes to my mind is of an eight-month-old girl who came to our lab a few years ago. Let's call her Barbara. Her mother was Swiss French and spoke to Barbara in French. Her father was Czech and spoke to her in Czech. Her parents spoke to each other in German, as that was their most fluent common language. They had recently moved to London, so much of daily life outside the home was in English. They also had a Spanish au pair, whom they encouraged to speak to Barbara in Spanish. On a typical day Barbara heard five different languages. She might not become fluent in all of them, but knowing multiple languages is no problem for a baby. In fact, monolinguals are currently a global minority, with only 40% of the world's population knowing only one language. Lots of babies grow up multilingual.

We are born with a head start on our mother tongue. Babies

have heard a muffled version of it in the womb and picked up a few clues. At just one day old, baby Barbara would prefer the sound of her mother's voice to that of a stranger. If you filtered her mother's voice to make it sound muffled and distorted, the way it was in the womb, she would prefer that even more. Studies show newborn French babies prefer the sound of French over Russian. Interestingly, they also prefer English over Japanese but have no preference between English and Dutch (Nazzi, Bertoncini & Mehler, 1998). This suggests that babies are picking up the broad patterns of their language, which lets them notice when they hear a language from the same family.

Babies are born ready to tackle any language on the planet. As an English speaker I have lost the ability to hear the difference between Hindi speech sounds /Ta/ and /ta/ or between the click-like sounds <xa> and <ca> found in Zulu. If I was Japanese, I would have trouble with English /ra/ versus /la/. Newborn babies arrive able to tell all these sounds apart – and more. These sounds are called phonemes and they are the building blocks of words. Spoken language is a messy business but, roughly speaking, phonemes are the consonants and vowels of that language. English has about 24 consonant sounds and 20 vowels (compare the different sound of 'a' in the words bat, ball, baby, ma and mama). French and German are similar to English but there is dramatic variation. Modern Arabic has just three vowels, while the !Kung language has 141 phonemes, thanks to its use of click consonants. Tonal languages like Mandarin make things interesting by letting changes in pitch alter meaning. Foreigners learning Mandarin often get challenged by the sentence 'Mā má mǎ mà ma'. The different accents mark rising and falling pitches, and the sentence translates as 'Mum is bothered by the horse's scolding – yes?' This may be nonsense, but it is clear and unambiguous to native speakers. Babies are born able to hear all these contrasts, but by the end of their first year they tune in to the sounds of languages they will use (Werker & Tees, 2003).

Speaking is tough. Psycholinguist Peter MacNeilage calls speech an 'invisible miracle'. He estimates that to speak fluently at full speed we must coordinate 40 different muscles and orchestrate about 225 muscle movements every second (MacNeilage, 2008). It is no wonder babies take around a year to say their first clear word. They need a lot of practice. From around two months of age there are 'goos', 'gahs' and a whole range of other random squawks and squeaks. The 'oohs' are the start of vowels, the vocal sounds created by air flowing evenly through the vocal tract. Changing the position of the tongue in the mouth and the shape of the lips changes the vowel. English has so many vowels because it allows diphthongs, which slide from one vowel sound to another as in 'wait' or 'loud'. Consonants are more complex still. They are created when the airflow is interrupted in some way. These arrive as babbling begins at around four months, but are still being worked on two years later.

Babbling is an essential stepping stone to speech. Like musicians practising endless scales and arpeggios before graduating to melodies, babies are getting into the flow of speech. By six months babbling starts to have recognisable syllables. The first consonants to arrive are b, d, m, n and w, and babies practise them one at a time. Parents eavesdropping on babies put to bed while still wide awake will hear 'mamamamama' and 'dadadadadada' coming through the baby monitor. The words /ma/ and /pa/ are an interesting special case. They are found with minor variations in hundreds of languages across the globe. Some researchers argue that these words get reinvented many times, as parents pick these sounds out from babies' limited early repertoire. Linguists Pierre Bancel and Alain de l'Etang argue that /ma/ and /pa/ are too widespread and consistent for this to have happened by chance, and must instead be words inherited from an ancient common ancestor. They are so resilient because the 'mmmm' and 'aaaaah' sounds are so easy for babies say and because the words are so important (Bancel & de l'Etang, 2013). 'Mama' is not always a baby's first word, but it is one of humanity's and is undoubtedly one of the oldest words in existence.

Early babble seems monotonous, but even in a song of one note there is a lot for babies to learn. They are learning about changing tempo and stress, and about which vocal actions make which sounds. They are also learning to keep going. Talking is like walking – you need to string a whole sequence of steps together and you need a *lot* of practice. Deaf babies babble in sign language (Petitto & Marentette, 1991). As babbling progresses, babies mix it up, talking a delightful nonsense that sounds like a private language. They string together a wider variety of syllables. Babies' babbles capture some aspects of their mother tongue, particularly intonation. But their 'words' are mostly not recognisable. We can usually tell a French babbler from a British babbler from a Chinese one (Petitto & Marentette, 1991). It is almost as if they are imitating their idea of what they hear around them. Or maybe it is freestyle jazz?

To be fair to babies, even with infant-directed speech, adults can be hard to follow. We do not notice this for our own language, but speakers of foreign languages sound as if they are speaking fast and speaking indistinctly. This is sometimes called the 'gabbling foreigner illusion' (Cutler, 2012). Weallspeakfastanddonotleavemany pausesbetweenwordswhenspeaking. If you look at the waveform of recorded speech, you see that the pauses do not line up nicely with the intervals between words. This makes life difficult if you are trying to learn that language. It is hard to pick out words if you have no idea what they might be or where one ends and another begins.

In the late 1990s three American researchers, Jenny Saffran, Dick Aslin and Elissa Newport, realised this must be a problem for babies and wondered how they solved it. They decided that babies did it with statistics. Suppose you are a baby. You will hear lots of phrases like 'Youwannajuice?', 'Youwannabottle?' or 'Youwannacuddle?' and 'Areyousleepy?', 'Areyouhungry?', 'Areyoumummyslittlemonkey?' Hearing variations like these, you might start to think 'Youwanna' and 'Areyou' are blocks and that the gaps come after. Combine lots of examples like this and you start to notice that some syllables clump together, which helps you segment out the words. When someone says 'Hellobaby', the baby hears 'Hello baby' not 'Hell obey bee'.

This was a reasonable idea, and Saffran and colleagues came up with a clever way to test it (Saffran, Aslin & Newport, 1996). They presented eight-month-old infants with a computer-synthesised stream of syllables like so:

> ...tupirobidakutupiropadotibidakugolabutupiropadotigol-abubidaku...

The computer kept reading for three minutes with no pauses or variations in tempo and emphasis. The sequence was made from four nonsense words – tupiro, padoti, bidaku, golabu – randomly repeated. To see if the babies noticed this after the recording stopped, the researchers played them examples that were 'words', like 'tupiro, golabu' and other examples were 'part-words', with the end of one word and the beginning of another, such as 'piropa, kugola' and some 'non-words', which had the same syllables but in a completely new order 'dapiku, tilado'. The results were clear. The babies, who we know love novelty, paid less attention to the familiar words than the other novel combinations.

This kind of statistical learning helps babies get their language learning underway. It allows them to segment speech into words before they even know what words are, building language from the ground up. You can do it too. If you listen to that computer language or a foreign language for long enough, you start to perceive the words. My colleague Bob French came up with a computer model that would learn in this way. Its full name is Truncated Recursive Autoassociative Chunk Extractor but we just call it TRACX (French, Addyman & Mareschal, 2011). The details of exactly what it does are not too important, except to say that it is a neural network that learns a lot like the brain.

We used TRACX to see if Saffran et al.'s idea scales up to real-world languages. First, we confirmed it could solve the simplified artificial grammar tasks researchers had used. Then we found a database of infant-directed speech, which included 9,800 phrases like 'Look at the doggie' or 'Who's on the telephone?' We coded these phonetically with no spaces between the words and let TRACX 'listen' to the whole set. After several run-throughs, it was correctly dividing phonemes into words. We also found it had no issue with an artificial language problem we called 'equal probabilities', which confused other computer models. This led to a nice, testable prediction that if our model was realistic then babies ought to be able to learn the equal probabilities language too.

Barbara was one of the babies who came to the lab to test that prediction. Like Saffran et al., we set up a computer to read out our made-up language while the babies sat and listened. In our language there were six words – feego, feerou, neipau, neikoi, duhlu, duhtai – and the starting syllable was the same for three pairs of the words. This made it a harder task than the original studies and this was why some other computer models failed. The babies had no problems: they could discriminate between words and part-words from our made-up language. We also were not concerned that Barbara was already multilingual. Our model was perfectly happy learning two different languages simultaneously. Classic studies of bilingual infants find they acquire words just as rapidly as monolinguals (Pearson, Fernández & Oller, 1993).

For babies, being bilingual seems be an advantage. There is a lot of literature that claims bilingual adults have an advantage in several important non-linguistic abilities such as executive control and working memory (Adesope et al., 2010), although some researchers dispute this, saying there has been a bias towards publishing only the positive results (de Bruin, Treccani, & Della Sala, 2015). But early in life the advantage seems clearer. Agnes Kovács and Jacques Mehler compared monolingual and bilingual seven-month-olds and found that the bilinguals showed an advantage in tests of executive control where babies had switch from one task to another (Kovács & Mehler, 2009). Natalie Brito and Rachel Barr found a memory advantage in six-month-old bilinguals (Brito & Barr, 2014). Curiously, in another study they found that bilinguals were better than monolinguals and trilinguals (Brito, Sebastián-Gallés, & Barr, 2015). However, the trilinguals do no worse than monolinguals and they have the undeniable advantage of speaking two more languages. If parents ask me if they should be exposing their baby to two, three, four or more languages I nod enthusiastically.

The First Words

In the beginning God created the heaven and the earth.

— Old Testament, Genesis 1:1

In the beginning was the Word.

— New Testament, John 1:1

Words define us. Words shape our thoughts and let us communicate them to others. One of the 12 apostles, John, was fond of saying little baby Jesus was the 'Word of God'. Without getting too deep into theology, John thought Jesus was the bringer of God's law and was God transformed into something humans might understand – namely words. I think it must be an interesting theological question whether Jesus's first word was 'mama' or 'dada', although scholars overlook it. The Gospels were written many decades after the fact, so no one could find Holy Mama Mary and ask her. She would undoubtedly remember. The first laugh, the first step and the first word are all indelible memories.

A baby's first word is a small step and a giant leap forward. It is obviously a great delight to parents and an important achievement – to be able to understand that arbitrary sounds stand for things out in the world is the start of symbolic thought. But the progress from a single word to fluent conversation is the longest race a baby runs. Within weeks of a baby's first step they are running around, unsteady but effective. Early word-learning is slow and painful by comparison. Every footstep is much like another, but every word is different. That is kind of the point of words. The first spoken word arrives anywhere from six months to a year, and it can then take another six months or more for the next handful of words.

What are the first words and why is progress so slow? The first question helps answer the second. Weirdly, until recently no one had tried investigating it. Twila Tardif, from the University of Michigan, and colleagues noticed most research on word learning was about object naming and focused on toddlers with about 100 words in their vocabulary. Instead they looked systematically at the first 10 words babies speak, comparing large groups of English, Mandarin and Cantonese speakers (Tardif et al., 2008).

Many of our earliest words are about people, not things. Mummy and daddy words were the most common and half of all the words referred to people, more so in the Chinese groups, where even young children are supposed to use correct kinship terms (auntie, uncle, and so on). Short exclamation words like 'hi', 'bye', 'uh-oh' and 'yum yum' were the next most common, followed by nouns and verbs. Early nouns were usually the names for small objects, usually ones the baby could handle themselves, like balls, bottles or food items rather than large objects like chairs. These were more common among English speakers while action verbs like 'hit' and 'grab' were prominent in Mandarin and Cantonese.

Tardif's survey shows how words serve many purposes and present babies with multiple challenges. Some words specify individuals like mummy and daddy, others are more general labels, like dogs or cups, and others, like verbs and exclamations, pass comment on the world without there being anything you can grab or point to. For any given word it is not obvious what type of purpose it serves, and so, when learning their first words, babies are in effect solving several different mysteries simultaneously. We underestimate their progress because babies understand many words before they can use them.

When I was learning Dutch I thought I was doing pretty well because I could read a newspaper, but whenever I tried to talk all I could manage were short basic sentences with terrible, mangled pronunciation. Babies are in the same boat. My mother tells me my first word was 'duck'. Putting me to bed each night she would say goodnight to each of the animals on a chart on my wall. 'Goodnight, cow!', 'Goodnight, sheep!'. After 'Goodnight, duck!' I made a strangled 'grurk' noise she generously interpreted as 'duck'. I did it several more times, which made her believe it was not an accident, but for a long time I am sure she was the only person who knew what I was on about. Children carry on mispronouncing words for years, especially in sentences. For many years I was Uncle Pasta because my nephew Tycho had trouble with the repeated 'c' sounds in Uncle Caspar.

Videos of babies' first words shared by excited new parents usually have the same problem: if you are not the doting parent it sounds a lot like gibberish. As a child of about seven or eight, I remember listening to cassette recordings of 'conversations' my parents had with me and my sister when we were babies. They were incomprehensible and hilarious. When their son was born, Massachusetts Institute of Technology (MIT) engineering professor Deb Roy and his wife took this to a whole new level. They recorded sound and video from their whole house all day, every day for the first three years of his life. They ended up with 230,000 hours of recording. Using some clever computer code, Professor Roy and his research team sifted out the interesting footage and laboriously transcribed every single word his son said, from 'mama' at nine months up to 'goodness' and 'popsicle' around his second birthday. Using this multimedia library of about 8 million words of conversation, they were able to track the emergence of 679 unique words and how they were learned (Roy, Frank, DeCamp, Miller & Roy, 2015).

Professor Roy calls this the Human Speechome Project in metaphorical comparison to the Human Genome Project, which mapped the full sequence of human DNA. The Speechome dataset is an amazingly rich resource that confirms many common ideas about early word learning. Roy Junior showed that short, simple words came first. 'Mama' was followed by words like 'car', 'cat', 'no' and 'yes'. Duck was word seven. The recordings revealed that all words took a lot of practice. In Deb Roy's TED talk on the topic, 'The Birth of a Word', he plays a montage of how an indistinct 'gaga' gradually transforms into the word 'water' over many, many occasions. Thanks to the accompanying videos, the researchers can tell those early gagas really do mean water – an adult may have just offered the baby a drink or put him in the bath.

The Speechome dataset has a 'shark's fin' profile – the learning of new words starts slowly before increasing to a sharp point around 18 months before dropping off again. Roy's son learned nine words in the first three months of the project, from 'mama' at nine months to 'hey' just before his first birthday. From 12 to 15 months he learned 32 including 'book', 'bus', 'dog' and 'wow'. From 15 to 18 months he learned 214 more, including 'bunny', 'bed', 'god' and 'yuck'. But between 18 and 21 months it was 369, or about four new words a day, including delightful words like 'igloo', 'delicious' and 'explosion'. From there, word learning dropped off to just 54 words between 21 and 24 months. These included longer four-syllable words like 'motorcycle', 'helicopter' and abstract concepts like 'beautiful'. However, the drop-off is probably an illusion; two-year-olds are learning to understand new words just as fast. The words they learn are not as common, so they will not appear in conversation as regularly.

The language explosion is real and, once started, it keeps going. By age five children may have an active vocabulary of about 2,000 words they use regularly. They understand five times that number. Precise counting is complicated by the fact that words have different tenses, senses and meanings. For example, the *Oxford English Dictionary* gives over 400 different meanings for the word 'set'. The big questions in infancy concern the internal or external factors that drive successful language learning. Does something change in babies' brains to speed up language learning, and what difference do parents and preschools make? Obviously the Speechome dataset cannot answer these questions conclusively. It is the data of just one child in a rich family with highly educated parents who were highly motivated to provide the best learning environment they could.

One reason for the explosion is that learning helps learning. As pronunciation improves, babies can practise their newest words. 'Écoute*z et répétez*,' as the Pimsleur language cassettes used to say. With each new word a baby learns, other words are easier to isolate and understand. Think how useful it is to understand the phrase 'look at the...' or recognise your own name so you know when someone is talking to you. Babies do even better. They can learn new words by a process called fast mapping. Let's imagine you take a baby to an exciting new place like an aquarium. You hold them up to see in the first big tank, which is full of fish and weeds and, 'Look, a crab!' The baby has seen fish and plants before and knows their names. He leaps to the conclusion that the unknown creature and the unknown name go together (Horst & Samuelson, 2008).

Babies can do better still. Suppose the aquarium has lots of unfamiliar creatures. In the first tank, the parent tells the baby to look at the crab, the seahorse and the cuttlefish. In the next tank she tells the baby that there is a clownfish, a nudibranch and a crab. The tank after that there might be a seahorse, a clownfish and an anemone. They are rushing around and she doesn't point out any of the individual creatures. Nonetheless, when they get back round to the first tank the baby correctly points out and names all three creatures, solving the problem by realising that the word 'seahorse' only fits one type of creature across the tanks they saw. Linda Smith and Chen Yu ran a version of this task and found that babies learned new object-word pairings by keeping track of these kind of statistical co-occurrences (Smith & Yu, 2008).

Philosophers love to point out that word learning is even harder than this. In his 1960 book, *Word and Object*, Willard Quine imagines visiting a remote tribe and trying to learn their language. A rabbit jumps out in front of you and your guide exclaims, 'Gavagai!' You might assume this means 'rabbit' but, logically enough, it could also mean 'floppy ears', 'mmm, tasty' or even 'look at that'. Most word-learning situations come with ambiguity like this and we make assumptions in order to communicate. Sure enough, baby scientists found that babies have a bias to apply a new word as a name to whole object (Hollich, Golinkoff & Hirsh-Pasek, 2007). What is often overlooked is that concrete nouns like 'rabbit' are easy in comparison to verbs or abstract ideas, which make up the majority of our speech (Recchia & Jones, 2012). I went through the first 50 words Deb Roy's son learned and found that only half were names or nouns. The rest were abstract terms you could not point to, like 'bump', 'down', 'go', 'mine' and 'hi'. And my three favourite examples of infant word learning, 'yes', 'no' and 'gone'. You can literally never point directly to 'gone'. But babies learn these words with few problems, although it is hard to know exactly when they understand the concepts behind them.

It is interesting to know what we can do to help infants learn language. One simple thing is to spend more time talking to them. A hugely influential study of early language learning claimed there was a large gap in the number of words heard by richer and poorer children in their first three years of life (Hart & Risley, 1995). In a heroic effort, Betty Hart and Todd Risley recorded and transcribed samples of the home speech environment of 42 families in Kansas every month as their children grew from nine months to three years. They concluded that children from impoverished families did worse because they heard about 10 million fewer words per year. This '30 million word gap' made many headlines, but subsequent studies found, not surprisingly, that quality matters as much as quantity (Pan, Rowe, Singer & Snow, 2005). The Speechome dataset supports this. Roy's son heard just 6 million words a year in the home, suggesting that total words are not the key factor.

Intriguingly, Roy and his team discovered that distinctiveness makes a massive difference to how easy it is to learn words. Words like 'bath', 'kick' and 'peekaboo' are easy to learn because they are tied to a particular setting or activity (Roy et al., 2015). This might be why bilingual babies have no problem with 'Mummy' language or 'Daddy' language or 'at home' and 'outside' languages. The context is key, which also supports Jerome Bruner's idea that language learning happens in context. Babies learn words in the places they use them, and variety and consistency both matter. Games and nursery rhymes help learning because they are both repetitive and idiosyncratic. Roy's son learned lots of words associated with nursery rhymes. He probably had no occasion to use words like twinkle, merrily, itsy, bitsy, dickory and dock outside of nursery rhymes, but he learned them just the same. Poet Dylan Thomas, talking about nursery rhymes, said:

> Out of them came the gusts and grunts and hiccups and heehaws of the common fun of the earth; and what the words meant was, in its own way, often deliciously funny enough, so much funnier to me, at that almost forgotten time, the shape and shade and size and noise of words as they hummed, strummed, jugged and galloped along.
>
> (Thomas, 1961)

It is unlikely Thomas accurately remembered his own early life. Nonetheless, he is completely correct.

Nim Bites Noam

Colorless green ideas sleep furiously.

— Noam Chomsky

Give orange me give eat orange me eat orange give me eat orange give me you.

— Nim Chimpsky

Noam Chomsky is one of the intellectual giants of the twentieth century. He has written about 100 books and has almost as many honorary degrees and awards. He has spent his career as a professor of linguistics at MIT in Boston but he wears many hats – linguist, philosopher, anarchist, historian, social activist and political theorist. He is well known to first-year psychology students as 'the man who killed behaviourism'. It's surprising, therefore, that his most famous sentence is perfect nonsense. But that's the point. Chomsky's nonsense sentence first appeared in his 1955 Ph.D. thesis and crops up in many later papers and books. The sentence has three interesting features. Firstly, it is completely meaningless. Secondly, it is perfectly grammatical. Thirdly, until Chomsky wrote it down, it had never existed. For Chomsky, this illustrated that grammar and meaning were independent of each other and that language was infinitely flexible and yet constrained by rules. It follows, Chomsky thought, that language and grammar are impossible to learn and must be innate.

Behaviourists thought the opposite. They believed language was a skill we acquire through practice. In his 1957 book *Verbal Behavior*, B. F. Skinner argued that babies learn language thanks to the praise we give them when they get words right. A reasonable idea, but Chomsky was having none of it. In 1959 he wrote an extended review of Skinner's book, attacking the idea that humans learn language like lab animals working for a reward. His attack was scathing and deadly. Reflecting on Chomsky's review a decade later, the editor of Skinner's book called it 'ungenerous to a fault; condescending, unforgiving, obtuse, and ill-humored' (MacCorquodale, 1970). Chomsky's review was unclear and unfair, but it was highly effective. As we now teach our undergraduates, Chomsky challenged a simple view of how language might be learned. This helped launch a cognitive revolution and the idea that the contents of our thoughts matter more than the actions they produce – cognition before behaviour. However, the grumpy and confrontational attitude of Chomsky and his supporters did not do the field any favours.

Nim Chimpsky is famous for his lack of intellectual achievements and for his tragic life, as depicted in the 2011 documentary *Project Nim*. As his name suggests, Nim was a chimpanzee. He was named 'in honour of' Noam Chomsky, although it not clear who was being honoured and who was being mocked. Nim was an unwilling foot soldier in the war over human linguistic uniqueness. At the start of the project, in 1973, the scientist in charge, Herbert Terrace, was a former student of B. F. Skinner and was confident Nim would learn American Sign Language and prove Noam's theories wrong. Four years later, Terrace had changed his mind and abandoned Nim, who ended his life as a test subject in a pharmaceutical research laboratory.

Project Nim followed Project Washoe. Washoe was a female chimpanzee, originally captured as a baby in 1965, intended to be part of the US space programme, but in 1967 she was adopted by Allen and Beatrix Gardner at the University of Nevada, Reno. They raised her in their backyard, treating her as part of their family and much like a human child. She had her own bed and toys. She had clothes, a toothbrush and went on family outings. All communication happened in sign language; no one spoke English in front of her. Washoe was happy, playful and a quick learner. She built up a vocabulary of 350 words, including PEEKABOO, HUG, TICKLE and BABY.

Although Nim was also raised in a human family, his training could not have been more different. None of the families he stayed with used sign language and he was taught to a rigid schedule in three-hour blocks. Lessons took place in a bare two-metre-by-two-metre concrete cell 'to avoid distractions'. Over the four years of the project he had 60 different teachers. Like Skinner's rats and pigeons mentioned in Chapter 5, he was rewarded for using the correct signs.

Nim learned between 25 and 125 signs, depending on who was counting. Everyone agreed he never learned anything resembling language. Terrace decided Nim was merely mimicking his teachers. He thought Nim interrupted them more than children would and was not using grammar. Rules of grammar include information that word order is important. 'Noam bites Nim' has a very different meaning to 'Nim bites Noam'. Nim did not form many long sentences, but when he did they were usually strings of demands for food with little evidence of grammar (Terrace, Petitto, Sanders & Bever, 1979).

When Terrace's results were published they were taken up by Chomsky's cheerleaders as an excuse to dismiss all ape language experiments as examples of the 'Clever Hans effect'. Hans was a horse who appeared to be able to count and do simple addition. However, psychologist Oskar Pfungst showed that he could only do it if he could see his trainer. Hans was using subtle cues in the trainer's body language to know when he had the right answer. Nim's test sessions were not 'double-blind' and the experimenter always knew what answer they wanted from Nim. Having been trained with bribery, Nim became highly adept at working out what this was. It was clever, but it wasn't language. Terrace described Nim as a 'brilliant beggar'.

Other ape language researchers were well aware of the Clever Hans effect and included double-blind tests in their research. However, Nim's failure hit the headlines and Terrace's bad experimental method killed a lot of funding for ape language research. Many researchers tried to counter the damage done by the failure of Project Nim. They pointed to Nim's impoverished learning environment and Terrace's lack of understanding of American Sign Language. Linguist William Stokoe had compiled the official dictionary of ASL and reviewed videos of Nim and apes from Project Washoe (which studied other apes apart from Washoe). He explained that the interruptions Terrace saw were a standard part of the language and concluded 'there can be little doubt that chimpanzees have well-developed abilities to communicate using signs' (Stokoe, 1983). Terrace also never even visited Project Washoe, convinced his experiments were the final word on ape language.

Washoe and other apes learned far more like young children. There was plenty of evidence they could learn spontaneously without any need for reward. When Roger Fouts took over Project Washoe, a baby chimp was brought in for Washoe to adopt after she had lost two babies of her own. Loulis learned signs from his mother. Later, another star ape linguist, a bonobo called Kanzi, learned to use a symbolic keyboard as a baby by watching scientists struggling to teach his adoptive mother, Matata. More amazingly, Kanzi was multilingual. Over the course of several decades Kanzi built up a vocabulary of hundreds of symbols using his keyboard and understood nearly 2,000 words in English. Kanzi also had a few words of 'gorilla sign language' that he had picked up from watching videos of Koko, a famous gorilla who communicated using sign language. Koko was bilingual too. She had a vocabulary of 1,000 signs and understood about 3,000 words of English.

It is doubtful that anything would convince Chomsky to change his mind. He takes a very dogmatic attitude to language and has tended to ignore any evidence against his position or from outside linguistics. He was not interested in how babies learned language or in how language might have evolved. In Chomsky's view language is very specific module in the brain that appeared as a single mutation. It switches on as babies start to speak. They must learn a few special parameters relevant to their mother language but, essentially, all languages share a deep structure that can be revealed by linguistic analysis. Exactly what this 'universal grammar' is has kept changing as Chomsky adjusts his theory to accommodate differences between real languages (Chomsky, 1995). Gorillas and chimps are dismissed as incapable of learning language because they lack the magic language acquisition device to make it happen.

After 40 years Chomsky's theories are fading from dominance. One important fact has been the methodical research of Sue Savage-Rumbaugh, who worked with Kanzi to debunk all the criticisms of previous ape language learning work. It is now widely accepted that Kanzi can use his symbolic keyboard to communicate with abilities comparable to a three-year-old child (Savage-Rumbaugh & Lewin, 1994). Next, the genetic story for language does not support Chomsky's position. No language gene has been found to fit his theory. One candidate gene, FOXP2, is definitely involved in language but has changed only gradually over the last few million years (Atkinson et al., 2018). Meanwhile, missionary-turned-linguist Daniel Everett has shown the language of the Amazonian Pirahã people does not fit the predictions of Chomsky's universal grammar (Everett, 2009).

Pirahã does not have the property of 'recursion', which in the latest versions of Chomsky's theories is the most central property of language (Fitch, Hauser & Chomsky, 2005). In Chomsky's theory, recursion is what lets us unpack and understand sentences like 'The cat the dog the mouse bit chased ran away.' This sentence may be grammatically accurate but it is very difficult to understand. Of course, almost no sentences in English are like this. Much more common are right-branching sentences like, 'This is the rat that ate the malt that lay in the house that Jack built.' Not only are they easily understood, but they only require a simpler mechanism called iteration. Recently, cognitive scientists Morten Christiansen and Nick Chater have argued you can throw away recursion completely (Christiansen & Chater, 2016). This simplifies the story of language. It provides a consistent, integrated theory of language that restores an important role to childhood learning and gradual evolution. It is early days for their theory and plenty of linguists in the Chomsky camp disagree, but Christiansen and Chater may do for Chomsky what Chomsky did for Skinner.

Here I admit to my own bias. Two decades ago I read Roger Fouts's account of working with Washoe, *Next of Kin*. More a memoir than a monograph, it recounts how Washoe and her family became his family. Fouts regularly had to give up scientific research to fight for Washoe's freedom. The book is packed with examples of Washoe charging around and commenting on the world like a gleeful child.

> By early 1969 my three-year-old chimpanzee sister was not just acting like my two-year-old son, she was talking like him as well. At 7 a.m. Washoe would greet me with a flurry of signs – ROGER HURRY, COME HUG, FEED ME, GIMME CLOTHES, PLEASE OUT, OPEN DOOR – that were a gestural version of what I heard from two-year-old Joshua every morning. (Fouts & Mills, 1997)

The same month I read a book called *Children Talk About the Mind*, which sampled thousands of everyday conversations from a group of toddlers (Bartsch & Wellman, 1995). The verbal life of toddlers is a running commentary on the world mixed with charming demands like 'Shoe me!', 'Sock me!', 'Juice me!' The parallels between the language abilities of apes and babies were impossible to miss.

It was a life-changing experience for me. I was still working in banking and had not even thought about going back to university to study psychology, let alone become a baby psychologist. Nonetheless, I laboriously typed up long passages from both books and posted them on my web page. Washoe and Nim Chimpsky are nowhere near as clever as you, me or Noam Chomsky, but along with Koko, Kanzi and other talking apes they have told us in their own words that this is a matter of degree. Only in a limited sense did any of these apes learn language, but almost all of them learned to communicate. They are important to our understanding of the evolution of language, but Chomsky's dogma meant their achievements were rejected and mocked. I feel confident that Nim Chimpsky will have the final laugh.

Chapter Twelve: Yes, No, Maybe, Baby

For over a decade I have had silly-coloured hair. Usually it's turquoise, sometimes dark blue, occasionally purple, pink or red. It has become a feature. If I try to go back to my usual mousy brown, friends and colleagues complain my hair is the wrong colour. It is bright blue in my passport photo, so perhaps they have a point. In that time, I have met a *lot* of babies and toddlers. And here's the weird thing: as far as I can tell, not a single baby under two years old has ever noticed. Or if they noticed, they did not care. Over two and it is the *first* thing they notice, and it is hilarious. This long-running experiment is just one example of how of sense and nonsense build our picture of the world. This chapter is about how that happens. Although it starts with a digression into very serious philosophy.

Language Games

If people never did silly things, nothing intelligent would ever get done.

— Ludwig Wittgenstein, philosopher (1889–1951)

Everyone who met Frank Ramsey agreed he was a phenomenal genius. In the few short years before his death in 1930 aged 26, he made profound and lasting contributions to philosophy, economics and mathematics. There's a whole branch of mathematics known as Ramsey Theory. When he arrived to study at Cambridge University his genius was already recognised, not least by Ramsey himself. Although he was charming, he could also be arrogant and intense. Early in his time at Cambridge, perhaps to get rid of him, a tutor handed him a book of German grammar, an English-to-German dictionary and an abstruse work of philosophy in German by philosopher Ernst Mach. Ten days later Ramsey came back having learned German and with several profound queries. In 1923, word reached Cambridge from Austria that Ludwig Wittgenstein had finally put his thoughts on paper. Ramsey, who had just graduated top of the year in mathematics, was dispatched to Austria to translate the book into English.

Wittgenstein was even more intense and brilliant than Ramsey. Before the First World War he had spent several years in Cambridge hounding the eminent philosophers Bertrand Russell and G. E. Moore over matters of mathematical logic, returning to Austria in 1914 to fight. During the war he wrote his first masterpiece – *Tractatus Logico-Philosophicus.* With Ramsey's help it was translated into English and is neatly summarised by its famous opening and closing statements:

1. The world is everything that is the case.

7. Whereof one cannot speak, thereof one must remain silent.

The bits in the middle were a sequence of terse, numbered statements. In just 75 pages, *Tractatus Logico-Philosophicus* proposed that thought consists of statements in language that correspond to facts about the world, and that philosophy consists of nothing more than the analysis of the logical form of these thoughts and sentences. If this all sounds a bit too neat and tidy to you, then you are a better philosopher than early Wittgenstein and you might prefer late Wittgenstein.

Just before the war, Wittgenstein's father died and he inherited a share of the fortune that in today's money would have been more than £70 million. This made Wittgenstein very depressed. He renounced the inheritance, returning it to his sister. He spent the decade after the war earning his own money as a primary-school teacher and a gardener in remote parts of Austria. In 1929 Ramsey and the economist John Maynard Keynes persuaded Wittgenstein to return to philosophy and to Cambridge. Collecting him from Cambridge Station, Maynard Keynes famously wrote to his wife: 'God has arrived. Met him on the 5.15 train.' Wittgenstein spent the next two decades teaching, thinking and writing extensively. He was never quite satisfied with his own work and only two books were published in his lifetime, the *Tractatus* and a children's phonetic dictionary in German.

Wittgenstein's second masterpiece, *Philosophical Investigations*, was published shortly after his death. It argues against his previous point of view. He claims there cannot be an internal private language of thought and, consequently, all language is in some sense public. The meanings of words are a set of socially agreed and transacted usages and these always depend on context. Wittgenstein illustrates this with two different ideas. He imagines a simple builders' language with words for blocks and slabs. It is basic and won't mean much outside the building site, but it gets the job done. Next he considers how difficult it is to give a definition of the word 'game'. Any definition must cover the word's usage as understood when referring to a game of chess, of football, of solitaire, or of catch. No such definition is forthcoming, yet we understand how to use the word without knowing any perfect definition of it. All of which is a roundabout way of saying ideas matter more than words and ideas rely on social conventions and have an inescapable fuzziness about them.

John Dewey had reached a similar opinion several decades earlier when he observed that 'language does express thought, but not primarily, nor, at first, even consciously. The primary motive for language is to influence (through the expression of desire, emotion and thought) the activity of others; its secondary use is to enter into more intimate sociable relations with them' (p.179, Dewey 1910). This is evident to anyone who meets a young child. They already have strong opinions on lots of things long before they can put them into words. Every toddler throwing a tantrum when you do not let them have your smartphone or your food is expressing a clear desire.

Unfortunately, since Wittgenstein's time digital computers have been invented, which makes the computational metaphor of thought seductive. To make matters worse, at a foundational level brains are computational. The brain is made of neurons, which operate according to known laws of physics and chemistry. As a result, many people think that thought involves juggling a set of symbols, like mathematicians solving equations or computers shifting bits. Certainly, we do some of this, though often relying on tricks and mnemonics to keep track of things – counting on our fingers or muttering under our breath. We privilege the written word and verbal argument. It is almost impossible to communicate without them, but the core of thought is more amorphous. Recalling the beginning of Genesis and the Book of John, it seemed as if 'God' had disproved the Bible. Words did not come first. Language is part of our game, but the game itself is more important. This is hard to follow, but it gets easier when you think about babies.

Same Difference?

A weasel is weasily recognised.
A stoat is stoatally different.

— Traditional rule of thumb

When I started my Ph.D. in 2005 the first book I bought was *The Big Book of Concepts* by Greg Murphy (2002). I was charmed and delighted by the title. I imagined that every Ph.D. student would be handed a book like that, a large almanac of ideas. Your first task would be to pick out the concept you were going to investigate and then set to work. In fact, *The Big Book of Concepts* is nothing like that. It is about the science of category learning, about how we acquire our concepts. Even someone starting a doctorate in philosophy would not be expected to start out by reading a big book of concepts. Yet I wondered if they should. Understanding the structure of concepts and the process by which they are acquired is part of the foundation of an understanding of thought itself. This was the topic of my doctorate, so I am biased, but concept formation is central to cognition and babies do it remarkably well.

We encountered part of this process in the section on 'Categories and doggeries' in Chapter Seven. We saw that by five months old babies were learning just the kind of messy, real-world concepts that got Wittgenstein so excited. The category of cats does not depend on knowing a word 'cat'. Young babies have some version of this category. Dogs probably do too. Cats certainly do, or there would not be kittens. These categories are less well defined than they first appear. In fact, this fuzziness is often how we recognise that a category is a category: they work by family resemblance. Members of a category are more like each other than like things outside the category.

A second category of categories is based on single defining features, such as the category of red things, shapes with four sides, objects larger than a house. These categories are more abstract. These rule-based categories do not, on the face of it, look like categories. The set of red things could include tomatoes and telephone boxes. Wittgenstein showed that there is still always some inescapable fuzziness: for example, 'redness' is a fuzzy category, as is the 'size of a house'. But the ability to ignore the differences between the individual objects and focus in on what makes them the same is the foundation of abstract thought.

This is what I looked at in my Ph.D. I decided to find out when babies first understand the concepts of 'same' and 'different'. To do this I showed babies pairs of photographs in a standard habituation experiment. One baby would see pairs of same objects – two rubber ducks, then two cowboy boots, then two mugs of tea, and so on. Each time the objects were completely unrelated to the ones before and the pictures changed when the babies got bored and looked away. When they were completely bored, I showed them a new pair of mismatched objects, such as a lipstick and an eight ball. For a second group of babies we reversed things, so they saw mismatching pairs during the boredom phase and only saw matched pairs at test. The results were clear. At eight months old babies spotted what was going on in both cases, but four-month-olds were oblivious (Addyman & Mareschal, 2010).

To check that the babies were learning an abstract rule, we ran a second experiment asking the same question in a very different way. This time pairs of geometric shapes would disappear behind an occluder. If there were two blue squares or two yellow circles they would reappear on the left. If there was a circle and a square they reappeared on the right. Again, eight-month-old babies figured it out, but four-month-olds did not. The eight-month-olds even succeeded in generalising what they had learned about pairs of squares and circles to stars and hearts. I was very pleased with my first experiment, and once I received my doctorate I celebrated by having stars, hearts, a cowboy boot, a lipstick, a rubber duck, a mug of tea, a tap and an eight ball tattooed on my left arm.

The baby science establishment was underwhelmed by our experiments. One journal rejected our paper for publication because similar things had been found before. My supervisor and I knew this. We knew that pigeons, chimps, macaque monkeys and even honeybees can pass same-difference tests (Wasserman & Young, 2010). A key feature of our study was to be easily comparable to the studies published involving animals. It demonstrated that babies were like animals in the way they acquired the concepts, just a lot faster. Macaque monkeys take around 20,000 trials to figure out a version of the picture task. The eight-month-olds in our study picked it up with about a dozen examples. The animal researchers liked our experiment and so, rather bizarrely, my first baby experiment was published in a journal called *Animal Cognition*. I even got a nice letter about it from Ed Wasserman, the leading expert on animal concept-learning, which cheered me up after the indifference of the infantologists.

Conceptually speaking, same–different is a big deal. Wasserman calls it 'the keel and backbone of thought and reasoning' (Wasserman & Young, 2010). My collaborator Bob French wrote a book on *The Subtlety of Sameness*, which argued that recognising sameness is what drives our ability to make analogies (French, 1995). This was why we thought it was important to study it directly. Baby scientists were focused on a different question. In 1999, Gary Marcus and colleagues caused a big splash with a study in which babies spotted the difference between strings of syllables with an AAB pattern and ones with a CDC pattern. The babies generalised, so if they had heard examples like 'li na li', they understood that 'wo fe wo' has the same pattern (Marcus, Vijayan, Bandi Rao, Vishton & Ausubel, 1999). Many variations on this experiment followed. My favourite, by Jenny Saffran, involved babies seeing the AAB pattern with breeds of dogs and cats. Babies first saw three dogs in a row: malamute – malamute – elkhound, and recognised the pattern when they saw: husky – husky – Labrador (Saffran, Pollak, Seibel & Shkolnik, 2007).

It is easy to see how same–different underpins this ability. A malamute is the same as another malamute and different from an elkhound. But a lot of the discussion of the Marcus study skipped over the subtleties of sameness to focus on rules and symbols. These experiments were taken as proof the mind operates by manipulating mental symbols. This would be a big deal, because symbols need not have any relationship to the things they symbolise. Words are the classic example. The word 'dog' does not look or sound like a dog. This makes words and other symbols very powerful. You can say things like 'All dogs like sausages', then 'Spot is a dog' and deduce 'Spot likes sausages'.

A lot of work on the foundations of logic by Bertrand Russell and others had shown that, even if you ignore the meanings of the words themselves, a small set of rules, called axioms, can build all of maths (barring a few weird exceptions). This is called formal logic because it involves the form of expressions, not their contents. Alan Turing went further and showed that all systems of computation are equivalent to a simple, idealised computer called a universal Turing machine (Turing, 1937). These heavyweight logical ideas, combined with Chomsky's claims that language needed its own universal grammar, set the scene for many decades of the symbolic approach to thought and cognition. Marcus et al.'s experiment seemed to support this symbolic approach. Marcus even wrote a book called *The Algebraic Mind* (Marcus, 2003).

However, the symbolic approach overlooks the subtlety of sameness. The word 'dog' is a symbol, but what about the *idea* of a dog? It would be foolish if the idea of dog was symbolic. That would throw away all the things you know about dogs and would fail to summarise their inherent doggyness. An idea stripped of all its features would not help you recognise a new dog. Almost every time you think about dog you care about its features – the idea of 'dog' is inextricably linked to ideas of furriness, friendliness and wagginess. You cannot avoid the problem that doggyness is a real thing. Dividing it into properties like furriness, wet-nosed, friendly just shifts the issue to what those symbols represent. You encounter something called the symbol-grounding problem. How can a system of symbols make contact with the real world? Each time you try to redefine an idea in terms of its properties, you need to define them too. It seems like symbols all the way down.

A solution that works for dogs, cats and similar categories is that the idea of dog is somewhat dog-shaped. It resembles a dog because this is what it's standing in for. The idea of a dog is more than a symbol of a dog: it is an icon or a map. And to quote the Polish philosopher Alfred Korzybski, 'A map is not the territory it represents, but, if correct, it has a similar structure to the territory, which accounts for its usefulness' (p.58, Korzybski, 1933). This works nicely for things we can see and point to. But can it work for abstract concepts like same, different, truth, justice, beauty or philosophy? It certainly works for a lot of them. Our ideas of beauty or love are undoubtedly tied up with our personal experiences. Shakespeare's idea of love is not separate from his personal experience. One can bet that aspects of Romeo are based on his own teenage years, and Juliet is based on a schoolyard crush. Likewise, our definitions of thoughts and ideas are often presented in analogical form. Even our most abstract reasoning fits this model, as hugely influential mathematician Henri Poincaré famously said: 'Mathematics is the art of giving the same name to different things.' Russell and Turing escaped the symbol-grounding problem in maths by putting axioms at the base of their system. Are there also axioms of thought?

Susan Carey at Harvard suggests something like this in her book *The Origin of Concepts* (Carey, 2009). Carey builds on the physical core knowledge of Elizabeth Spelke, suggesting babies also have core concepts. Carey believes we need some built-in ideas to get us started, because 'one cannot capture concepts such as goal, agent, object, or approximately 10 in terms of primitives such as locations, paths of motion, shapes, and colors' (Carey, 2009). Unfortunately, *The Origin of Concepts* does not explain the origin of concepts. It says babies have innate primitive concepts, just like Konrad Lorenz's geese have an innate ability to imprint on mother goose. Like imprinting, Carey does not think babies' core concepts are learned and that instead they are built in by evolution. My problem with this is how did evolution learn them? Presumably by incremental improvement, so why cannot babies learn the same way?

At present scientists do not have a full origin story for concepts. But it is on the horizon and babies will help us get there. Evolution might do some of the work by creating learning mechanisms tuned for concepts. This is the ambition of Bayesian learning. Josh Tenenbaum at Massachusetts Institute of Technology (MIT) and his research team have been building computer models that aim to achieve this (Tenenbaum, Kemp, Griffiths & Goodman, 2011). In addition, a recent trend in the philosophy of cognitive science is realising that symbols suck for thinking and that instead concepts are likely to be like maps or icons First, plenty of neuroscientific evidence shows that brains are full of maps. Humans and rats have mental maps they use for navigation and for lots of the basic systems for time and quantity. Second, thanks to Karl Friston's work, cognitive neuroscience is moving away from the metaphor of the brain as a computer and thinking instead of it as a statistical prediction engine (Williams & Colling, 2018).

Carey and I agree that all concepts have iconicity, not just the dog-like ones. We differ on whether core concepts like 'same' and 'different' are also learnable in the way we learn about dogs, cats and mathematics. However, it is fair to say the jury is still out. Even for something as simple as same–different we do not fully understand how the brain does it. Although my friend Jean-Rémy Hochmann recently took us one step further. Working in Carey's Harvard lab, he tested seven- and 12-month-old babies with a method called 'delayed match to sample' that had been widely used by animal researchers. They found that babies find it easier to learn 'same' than 'different'. In essence, 'different' is not-same, so 'same' comes first. (Hochmann, Mody & Carey, 2016). Curiously, my own experiment with coloured shapes had found the opposite, with 'different' being learned faster. I am not entirely sure why this is, but I suspect my experiment will turn out to be anomalous. Hochmann's model is simpler and fits nicely with our intuition. Sameness is a highly salient and fundamental relationship; difference is usually defined as the absence of sameness.

When I came to write up my thesis I opened with a funny Ogden Nash poem called 'The Purist' about a 'conscientious scientist'. The punchline of the poem is that when hearing that his wife has been eaten by an alligator, the scientist pedantically corrects the messenger that it must have been a crocodile. The joke revolves around the sameness and difference between alligators and crocodiles. They are so similar you need rules to tell them apart (one useful rule of thumb is that if you are in Africa they are crocodiles). Ogden Nash is poking fun at pedantic scientists missing the bigger picture. This is a useful analogy for our focus on thought being algebraic. Karl Friston's work suggests that the driving force is to stay alive. You only concern yourself with differences between crocodiles and alligators after you have escaped. If you look closely, thought it is always messy. Neat logical rules are the exception, not the rule.

No! No! No!

The oldest, shortest words – yes and no – are those which require the most thought.

— Maybe or maybe not Pythagoras of Samos, sixth century BC

My friend Claire and her children are currently staying with me. Sascha-Jack is now 15 months old and the two biggest abstract concepts in SJ's world are 'yes' and 'no'. SJ is very talkative but still at the stage where most things seem to be a private language that conveys their desires without using that many words we adults recognise. 'Yes' is one such example; SJ does not use the word as such, preferring to make do with 'More!' The word mainly applies to food, but with the boundless energy and enthusiasm of a toddler, there are lots of things SJ wants more of – strawberries, silly games, Peppa Pig, dangling upside down. Laughter and smiles, of course, are also useful indicators of how wonderful these things are, but 'more' is a better label for the concept when trying to communicate with the adult in charge of providing more. Often we adults do not get the message, so SJ adds some flapping and waving to emphasise the urgency or importance of more fruit or more tickles.

Likewise, SJ is not yet using the words 'no' or 'not' but has a very clear sliding scale for their application. A turn of the head or other physical rejection works very well to politely turn down another spoonful of porridge. The next step up is an exasperated whole-body freeze with jaw clenched and hands curled into fists. This is the negative response to more serious injustices, like being deprived of a remote control or being carried away from the cooker. A full howl with flushed red face is for such inhumanities as not being allowed a glass of red wine or being deprived of a smartphone or Peppa Pig, and when the witching hour strikes this extremely emphatic 'no' is also deployed for, well, pretty much anything.

Parents dealing with these Dionysian 'yeses' and Titanic 'noes' probably will not have much time to think what Pythagoras was talking about two-and-a-half millennia ago. I am more at liberty to speculate, and I like to think the great philosopher and mathematician was anticipating the theories of Karl Friston. I think the heart of the matter is that 'yes' and 'no' express our desires and state our intended actions. This is certainly how Sascha-Jack and other babies use them, and that gives a good clue to their ancient origins. These are the oldest words because they express our primal wants, good and bad. SJ's affirmations and denials are visceral and predictive; they use the whole body to declare this is the future they want or do not want. This echoes Friston's perspective that internal states exist to act on the world. Our decisions matter to us. 'Yes' and 'no' require the most thought because they represent choices we usually cannot take back.

'Yes' and 'no' are both big concepts, but 'no' is more interesting, more important and more ancient. A shouted 'No!' undoubtedly had its origins in the alarm calls of our tree-dwelling ancestors. It is an especially handy thing for parents to shout at infants in case of emergency. Babies first respond to 'No!' at around six months, when they will freeze momentarily if they hear it. Interestingly, just as 'different' starts out as 'not same', 'yes' might start as 'not no'. Canadian psychologists Viktoria Kettner and Jeremy Carpendale studied the early use of 'yes' and 'no' and observed that many early yeses are primarily a 'lack of no': babies going along with being fed, being washed and so on (Kettner & Carpendale, 2013). Each yes or no decision is a binary choice, but logically and linguistically 'yes' has less force than 'no'. A response of 'yes' just affirms the preceding statement or question, while 'no' is totally transformative. Interestingly, this is true for computers too. In some sense the logical operation AND is a judgement of sameness and OR represents a choice, but it has been proved that you also need NOT to construct all possible logical expressions, reaching a state called functional completeness.

Kettner and Carpendale were investigating the active, embodied nature of yes and no. They were interested in a surprising inconsistency. Babies' gestural versions of yes and no appear later than pointing, which emerges around 12 months. Shaking the head for 'no' is first seen around 13 to 15 months, with nodding coming later at 16 to 18 months. The shaking gesture may come from twisting the head to avoid food and nodding from chomping down to obtain it. If so, we might expect babies to use them to sooner.

It was unsung baby psychologist Charles Darwin who first speculated about the origins of nodding and shaking in *The Expression of Emotions* (Darwin, 1872). He knew the gestures were widespread but not universal across cultures and might derive from babies' reactions to food. He wrote 'with infants, the first act of denial consists in refusing food; and I repeatedly noticed with my own infants, that they did so by withdrawing their heads laterally' (p.273). Infants may also tip their heads back, which he knew to be the gesture in Greece, Turkey and Bulgaria. Conversely, 'in accepting or taking food, there is only a single movement forward, a single nod implies an affirmation' (p.273).

If this is the case, why do nodding and shaking get learned relatively late? The answer is that young babies get by fine without them. Crying and other physical reactions signal 'no' highly effectively. Laughter, smiles and simple indifference signal 'yes'. Delightfully, one parent in Kettner and Carpendale's paper describes their baby giving a 'yes wiggle' when they got their way.

Language learning also reflects the greater importance and complexity of 'no'. The Stanford University Wordbank database shows 'no' is learned earlier than 'yes' in all languages for which there is data (Frank, Braginsky, Yurovsky, & Marchman, 2017). This is entirely understandable, given how many times a parent has to say 'no' every day and in how many ways. Soonja Choi has identified nine different ways we use negation. She showed that these categories are present in English, French and Korean, and in each case children acquire them in a similar order (Choi, 1988). In English, the grammar of negation isn't simple, with contractions like won't and don't, and changes in word order. As a result, the word 'no' often gets used to cover many of these cases, as children are learning the full concept. As in:

No cookies (zero cookies)
No cookies (no, [I don't want carrots, I want] cookies)
No dog (not a dog)
No eat (I won't eat)
No working (not working)
No do it (I can't do it)
No me (it wasn't me).

It used to be thought that this type of baby talk was highly ungrammatical, but psycholinguist Kenneth Drozd argues otherwise, as the title of his paper helpfully explains: 'Child English pre-sentential negation as metalinguistic exclamatory sentence negation' (Drozd, 1995). Amazingly, this gobbledegook was an improvement on the alternative theory of 'nonanaphoric preclausal negation'. In plain English, he believes that in most cases babies are using the word 'no' conversationally in the same way adults might use idioms like 'nonsense' or 'poppycock'.

Babies grasp concepts better than the language they are expressed in. One lovely study found that toddlers understand negatives better when they are useful. It makes sense to them to say a cup is not a jug but weird to say it is not a table (De Villiers & Flusberg, 1975). More recent research suggests toddlers understand the principle of negations but are often creative in their use because they haven't mastered the complexities of grammar (Cameron-Faulkner, Lieven & Theakston, 2007) – like my own attempts to speak Dutch. Unsure of the correct negatives, I would invent my own phrases.

Frowns and winces showed me I wasn't getting it right, but my meaning was usually understood.

It is also a mistake to think adults' use of negatives follows the laws of formal logic. In many experiments Nick Chater and Mike Oaksford find Bayesian networks and probabilistic reasoning account for human performance on classical logical problems. They call this Bayesian Rationality (Oaksford & Chater, 2007). Curiously, the foundations of this approach build on something called the Ramsey Test, proposed by Frank Ramsey (Ramsey, 1931). The details and implications of Oaksford and Chater's arguments are far outside our current scope. But they imply that humans rarely use classical logic, preferring probability.

You might think this would be beyond babies, but there is evidence that infants are rational Bayesians. We already saw babies reasoning about the probabilities of red and white ping-pong balls (Xu & Kushnir, 2013) in the chapter on surprise. Some equally ingenious experiments by Ernő Téglás, Luca Bonatti and colleagues demonstrate similar probabilistic reasoning in a whole raft of conditions (Téglás et al., 2011). Their latest experiment investigated logical negation and is perhaps inspired by the classic Usborne picture book *That's Not My Dinosaur*. In their experiment, 12- and 19-month-old infants see two objects, a dinosaur and flower (Cesana-Arlotti et al., 2018). The objects are carefully created so the spikes on the back of the dinosaur look exactly like the petals on the flower. If you hide either of them in a shallow cup, the bit that pokes out looks identical. In one version of the study, babies see the flower and dinosaur sitting side by side. A screen pops up and hides them both, before a cup scoops one up and is placed next to screen. The screen drops to reveal just the flower. This lets babies deduce that in the cup is 'not flower', therefore 'dinosaur'. The screen and flower get removed, leaving just the cup and its contents. Finally, the cup is lowered away to reveal either the logically deduced dinosaur or an impossible flower. All the babies have their 'expectations violated' by the missing dinosaur and look longer.

The jury is still out on how babies do these things. All Chater and Oaksford's experiments were done with adults and they do not have a developmental version of their theory that explains how we get there. The word-learning databases and infant reasoning experiment do seem to present a story consistent with Bayesian Rationality, but word learning is a very messy business and the reasoning experiments have multiple interpretations. Not surprisingly, Bayesian brain enthusiasts Fei Xu and Josh Tenenbaum are strongly optimistic that babies will prove to be Bayesian. By contrast, algebraic brain advocate Gary Marcus is highly sceptical (Marcus & Davis, 2013). Téglás and Bonatti seem to have a foot in both camps, liking Bayesian explanations for their probability experiments and formal logic for their dinosaurs. The most remarkable thing is that this debate cannot be settled by logic alone. We need experiments like these to understand the foundations of our thought. We have already seen babies outwitting Descartes; now they have Wittgenstein in their sights.

Magic, Mischief and Mayhem

No man is exempt from saying silly things; the mischief is to say them deliberately.

— Michel de Montaigne, *The Complete Essays*, 1580

I could easily imagine my colleague Gustav Kuhn performing some illusions with cups and dinosaurs. He is psychologist and magician. He does a version of the famous cup and ball trick with a lemon that baffles me. In his research Gustav uses magic tricks to study perception, attention and, of course, the psychology of magic. Magic tricks work by playing with our perception, our attention and our expectations. As I have said before, violation of expectation studies resemble magic tricks. Gustav and I have discussed what tricks we try on babies in the InfantLab at Goldsmiths. Most regular magic tricks do not impress babies too much. They are not going to be enthralled by a card trick. They will love an appearing dove or white rabbit but won't appreciate that it appeared from completely thin air. And I would not recommend sawing mummy in half.

Adults watching magic shows know we are being fooled even if we do not understand how. Babies in VoE (violation of expectation) experiments have no reason to suspect trickery. In fact, Csibra and Gergely's theory of natural pedagogy, mentioned in Chapter Nine, says young children are innately trusting of information received from adults (Csibra & Gergely, 2009). But it turns out that babies can appreciate the difference between jokes, mistakes and fibs. They know the difference between real and pretend. They know a toy hippo is not a real hippo. But they also know a toy hippo makes a perfectly good horse, car and telephone. Especially telephones, since we will not give them phones of their own. This afternoon my 15-month-old house guest Sascha-Jack has played telephone with a toy car, my watch and every remote control in the house. They do not get my actual phone any more, as I learned quite quickly that I never get it back. This is clear proof of their keen awareness of the difference between pretend and reality.

What you or I might call lies and make-believe, philosophers prefer to call counterfactuals. Philosophers love counterfactuals, which is not surprising, seeing as most of philosophy is itself an exercise in counterfactual thinking. Babies love counterfactuals too. Babies cannot get enough of pretending, teasing and silly games. Alison Gopnik points out that it might seem odd that young children, who have so much to learn about the real world, spend so much time in pretend play. They do so for much the same reasons as philosophers. To reason effectively about the world you need to be able to consider alternative viewpoints, adopting, then adapting them: to plan for the future you must take an alternative and pursue it several steps beyond the starting point (Weisberg & Gopnik, 2013). Pretend play is training in this ability.

Educational theories say that good learning is about improving your reasoning abilities, not about absorbing endless facts. This is no less true for the under-twos, and pretend play is building these skills. All young mammals play but only humans are practising counterfactual 'what if' reasoning. This helps us distinguish babies' pretend play from kittens 'hunting' and puppies 'fighting'.

Toddlers practise grown-up skills too. It is delightfully cute to see the serious concentration that can go into playing shop, playing with cars and playing parent to their dolls and teddies. But the real lessons learned are in improved planning, reasoning, executive control and perspective taking. Pretend play also increases babies' confidence in reality. In adults, psychosis is both terrifying and debilitating, and the biggest difference between imagination and psychosis is knowing the difference.

Important to all of this is babies' awareness of the difference between joking, pretending or being wrong. I will come the social side of pretend play and false beliefs in the next chapter. But how do babies know if we are making mischief? Are we confusing them if we say they are a stinky little monster or pretend to steal their ice cream? Elena Hoicka at the University of Bristol has studied babies' understanding of humour and pretence. The headline from her research is that we can carry on being silly and sarcastic with our babies. In one clever experiment two-and-a-half-year-olds could tell the difference between a foreigner making mistakes and a native language user making jokes (Hoicka & Akhtar, 2011). They understand joking and pretending and know the difference between silly or sincere (Hoicka & Gattis, 2011). This also influenced their actions. Toddlers were more likely to use a toy chicken as a hat when a parent was pretending it was one than if the parent was joking about it (Hoicka & Martin, 2016).

Exactly how joking, lying and make-believe link to babies' cognitive development is still a very open question. But in one promising study with toddlers, Rana Esseily and colleagues at

Université Paris Nanterre showed that 'getting the joke' is a good indicator of learning about the world (Esseily et al., 2016). They showed 18-month-olds a task with a serious and a funny version. In the serious version an experimenter used a rake to pull a rubber duck towards them to play with it. Babies were not very good at copying the action, with only 25% retrieving the duck. The silly version was identical, except once the experimenter got the duck, she smiled at the infant and threw the duck on the floor. Babies in this version divided into those who did or did not laugh. Just 19% of the non-laughing babies retrieved the duck with the rake. But 15 out of 16 (93%) babies who laughed succeeded in retrieving the toy. Get the joke, get the duck.

These findings are very exciting. As Elena says, it seems that 'knowing how to joke is good for maintaining relationships, thinking outside the box, and enjoying life. Pretending helps children to practise new skills and learn new information.' But it is still early days. Even in adults we do not understand how creativity, intelligence and cognitive control connect up with each other (Benedek, Jauk, Sommer, Arendasy & Neubauer, 2014). Joking and pretending are a central part of a baby's day and are likely to have a central role in the story of creativity and intelligence. The interplay of cognitive control points to another surprising element of this picture – tantrums.

Tantrums are not fun for anyone involved, but they are a natural and inescapable of part of being a toddler. Every parent will have their war stories – sandwiches that should have been triangles, not squares; not wanting socks; not wanting these socks; and 1,001 attempts to avoid bedtime. Very little academic research has looked at tantrums because who would willingly engage with these unreasonable little monsters? Worse still, much of the advice literature problematises tantrums or focuses on the battle of wills. I don't like the phrase 'Your baby is testing their boundaries' or, worse still, 'Your baby is testing your boundaries'. It implies that babies are Machiavellian, scheming over every little bit of power they can obtain. This is not how they experience it at all. Unpleasant though they are, tantrums may be an important part of our intellectual development. They escalate quickly into the absurd and illogical, but there is something very deliberate at their start. Tantrums are counterfactuals. A toddler wants something they do not have but strongly desire. A tantrum imagines an alternative world in vivid fashion and although those desires get out of control, their causes are entirely understandable.

Professor Michael Potegal of University of Minnesota Medical School is one of the few brave, masochistic scholars to have studied tantrums in detail. He analysed detailed parental surveys from 335 children to discover the components and time-course of tantrums (Potegal & Davidson, 2003; Potegal, Kosorok, & Davidson, 2003). He finds that tantrums are built out of fast-acting anger and slowly accumulating distress. Anger is a sharp, intense emotion that builds quickly with different levels of intensity but can dissipate quickly. Potegal found that tantrums that reach a peak quickly also finish quickly. Distress is a more diffuse sense of sadness that builds more slowly and is a harder emotional state for children to escape. Anger is one of Jaak Panksepp's key biological drives, but the toddler tantrum has more than animal rage. Anger is an energy for toddlers: they are driven towards their desires. In other circumstances we recognise persistence as a positive thing, and cast in positive terms anger can be thought of an 'approach emotion'. It is an extension of toddlers' insatiable curiosity and determination.

Unfortunately, toddlers' desires are often doomed. Lacking knowledge or mastery of the world, they will embark on impossible tasks or make impossible demands. Why can't they drive the car or have that shiny kitchen knife? Unless energies are redirected, their own anger distresses them and meltdown ensues. So how should we handle tantrums? The first step is to keep calm: parental anger and frustration will undoubtedly make things worse. Tantrums are natural side effect of our imagination and counterfactual reasoning abilities. Do not try and make them into learning opportunities, as being reasonable does not help the situation. When a toddler is having a tantrum, asking questions just makes things worse. It just intensifies the focus on the thwarted goal and creates an 'anger trap' that lets distress take hold. Professor Potegal advises the best course of action is diplomatic neutrality.

Parents should be reassured they only have to put up with wilful disobedience for another 20 years or so. They may lament the absurdity of many toddler tantrums, but most adult arguments are just as bad. They start over the most inconsequential things and escalate beyond what is healthy or rational for either party. Our wars are even worse. The 'terrible twos' is harsh branding of late infancy, because at around the same age we see the emergence of many wonderful traits such empathy and concern. Accompanying toddlers' awareness of their own distress is a greatly increased sensitivity to the emotions of others. This age sees a blossoming of their ability to see themselves as a separate individual and recognise the same thing in others. This is the topic of my final chapter.

Chapter Thirteen: Friends

You cannot make a friend. You can only be a friend.

— Anon, paraphrasing Ralph Waldo Emerson, American writer (1803–32)

It must be nice being a baby. Everywhere you go everyone is pleased to see you. The whole world is your friend. Your mummy, your daddy, granddad and granny, all the adults you ever meet have a smile and friendly word for you. Older children are magic creatures you hero worship and who are mostly kind and benevolent, pleased to have someone looking up to them. But there is something different in the first meetings of equals, baby's first friends. Apart from the special case of twins or higher multiples, first friendships mostly begin between one and two years old. Before that babies are not equipped to interact with each other. Plonk a pair of under-ones down next to each other and they will play happily but separately. It is in the second year of life that babies can acknowledge a peer and move on to playing together and genuine friendship. Maybe this is when we can stop calling them a baby, because they move beyond the constant dependency on their caregiver to begin having a life of their own.

Looking Inwards and Outwards

The first time her 12-month-old daughter blew raspberries in her dinner, my sister could not help laughing. So Mirabelle did it again – and again, and again. The second time my sister didn't laugh quite as much and by the 10th time there was nothing funny left. She did not want to show her annoyance, because her laughter had started the game. The first raspberry was a spontaneous bit of exploration. It was the reaction that caused the deliberate repetitions. Mirabelle had become aware of her power to make her mummy laugh. This is a revelation that hits all babies at some point around this time and it delights them. Giggly games of any kind are fun, but there is little to compare to the giddy joy of a toddler who realises they have an audience. It also marks an early awareness of the self in relation to others.

Our sense of self builds slowly. It is constructed out of our relationships. As we saw in Chapter Nine, Vasi Reddy and Colwyn Trevarthen think this is already happening at six months in the early teasing games that babies and parents play with each other (Reddy, 2001). This is a gradual process that takes off in the second year of life. The first time children realise they can make you laugh is a handy milestone for their ability to look inwards on themselves as an individual and outwards to others as 'others'. If life is a performance, then the first time we consciously take the stage is usually around the time of our first birthday. Before this we are too artless, too helpless, too oblivious to act intentionally for the entertainment of others. Maybe it even happens at our first birthday party, an occasion where we are centre stage in a scene set for us to be the star. When children realise they have the power to make us laugh, it opens up a whole new dimension. Now they become clowns who play to the crowd.

The other side of this coin is shyness. Once infants are more aware of themselves in relation to others, they show considerable shyness. This is more than the coyness Vasi Reddy recognised in very young infants. Coyness was a withdrawal from a face-to-face interaction that was overstimulating. Clinginess is often similar. A different, more internally driven form of shyness appears between 12 and 18 months. Now babies are recognisably embarrassed and self-conscious on encountering unfamiliar people, both strangers and friends they have not seen for some time. They retreat to a parent or act with extreme wariness, keeping a distance between themselves and the unfamiliar person.

Clowning and shyness seem like they might map onto the adult traits of extraversion and introversion, labels we apply to our friends with ease and to ourselves with caveats. Extraverts are outgoing, energetic and enthusiastic. They get charged up by interaction with others. Introverts are reserved, deliberate and shy. They need time alone to recharge after social interaction. Karl Jung divided people into those who look inwards and outwards. But the extraversion–introversion dichotomy was popularised by highly controversial and highly prolific psychologist Hans Eysenck, who linked them to a biological process he called 'arousal'.

He thought introverts were physiologically overstimulated and so needed solitude to reduce their arousal. Extraverts were understimulated and so needed energy from external stimulation to raise their arousal (Eysenck, 1967). Modern psychology does find some biological basis for introversion and extraversion and recognises they are two ends of a spectrum. Most people are somewhere in the middle and could show elements of both, depending on circumstance (DeYoung, 2010). When he was not on stage, Jimi Hendrix was a classic introvert. Eysenck himself was shy and introverted but nevertheless loved the limelight, writing popular books and taking every opportunity to appear on television.

Extraversion is just one dimension of personality. The most widely accepted model has four other such dimensions. The Big Five are openness to new experience, conscientiousness, extraversion, anxiety and neuroticism, often going by the acronym OCEAN. Here is not the place to delve into the complexities of adult personality except to say that binary labels are a simplistic way to describe humans. You should never let a personality test define you, as all measures can change across situations and over life. One remarkable 63-year-long study found essentially zero correlation between personality measured at age 14 and later at 77 (Harris, Brett, Johnson & Deary, 2016).

It does not make sense to use adult personality dimensions with babies, so instead we talk about infant temperament. The main measure is Mary Rothbart's Revised Infant Behaviour Questionnaire (IBQ-R), which I used with my sleepy babies study in Brazil (Gartstein & Rothbart, 2003). It identifies three dimensions called surgency/extraversion, negative affectivity, and orienting/regulation, based on parental judgements of how infants respond to everyday situations. The names alone should give the clue that infant 'personality' measures are a little weird. Taking these in reverse order, 'orienting' refers to babies' ability to stay focused on things. Babies high in this aspect of temperament can be easily soothed and enjoy it when parents read them books, play music or rock and hug them. It does not correspond or directly predict any aspect of adult personality. 'Negative affect' is a measure of how easily a baby can become distressed; it identifies babies who are tearful and clingy and it maps onto the OCEAN dimension called neuroticism. The 'extraversion' dimension identifies babies who are full of beans by asking questions about things like how much the baby squirms around during changes or when being put in a car seat. These babies are usually very interested in new surroundings and quite vocal. It identifies babies who laugh in the bath or when being thrown in the air.

Infant extraversion maps quite well onto adult extraversion, even though none of the relevant questions in the IBQ-R ask about how such babies respond to other people. Instead the questionnaire focuses on the more biological aspects, which Eysenck might have called arousal. It seems that extravert babies are energetic and outgoing because they are seeking stimulation. In addition, traits like shyness fall within the negative affect dimension. Early in life it is hard to separate babies' social fear from their other fears. This paints a picture where happy-go-lucky babies become extraverted adults and cautious babies become introverts. But babies' sociability does not emerge just from innate biological factors. Babies can be even more changeable than adults. Studies comparing temperament at one year and two years old find just a 30% correlation between scores (Casalin, Luyten, Vliegen & Meurs, 2012). Psychologists often consider this a high correlation, but it means it is hard to predict what type of toddler your baby becomes. To be fair, one year of life is half a lifetime for a two-year-old.

The development of friendship goes hand in hand with the development of the sense of self and strengthening imagination. Some delightfully ingenious experiments investigated this in the 1990s, using the mirror test I mentioned in Chapter Nine (Asendorpf, Baudonnière, & Warkentin, 1996; Asendorpf & Baudonnière, 1993). The ability to recognise oneself in a mirror develops at around 18 months. Prior to that our level of self-awareness is more limited. Infants in this test get a blob of red make-up placed on their face in such a way that they do not notice. They are then placed in front of a mirror. Eighteen-month-olds who pass the test will touch the dot on their face. Researchers argue it takes some imagination to see yourself from the outside. The clever part of the studies of Asendorpf and colleagues was that they also looked at how these children would imitate a play partner. The results were very clear: only toddlers who passed the mirror test engaged in extended imitation. It is likely that friendship and sense of self both develop as children increase their ability to form secondary representations – counterfactuals and other ideas about ideas. Babies only form real friendships after they develop imagination and pretend play.

Knowing Me, Knowing You

You know that I know you know, but I want you to know that I know you know I know you know I know. It's important for you to know that, you know?

— Jarod Kintz, *There Are Two Typos Of People In This World*, 2010

Imagine the scene: you witness two puppets, Amy and Becky, clapping in synchrony and hopping in synchrony, then laughing together. Amy leaves the room but remains watching through the window. Another puppet, Claire, arrives and you and Amy both witness Becky deliberately hitting Claire, knocking her to the floor. Now Claire leaves and Amy comes back in. In the final scene one of two things happens: either Amy and Becky laugh and wiggle in synchrony as before, or Becky does this on her own while Amy ignores her. Although this is quite long-winded to describe, we could take in the scene with ease and would likely construct a narrative. If Amy is silent, we imagine she does not approve of her friend's violence. If Amy and Becky both laugh, we are surprised and decide that they both don't like Claire. When You-Jung Choi and Yuyan Luo from the University of Missouri presented these scenes to 13-month-old babies, they found a similar pattern. Babies looked longer at the callous, laughing friend. For another a group of babies the scenes played out similarly, except that Amy did not witness the hitting incident. This reversed the results. Babies were more surprised by the silent friend. In a final control condition, the hitting was accidental and babies showed no difference in their reactions (Choi & Luo, 2015). In short, babies kept track of what Amy had seen and adjusted their expectations accordingly. Already at 13 months old they seem to possess a 'theory of mind' they use to understand the actions and intentions of others.

Theory of mind is also known as mentalising, mind-reading, folk psychology or common-sense psychology. It is the capacity people most often think is at the heart of psychology. Psychologists at parties are often asked, 'Do you know what I am thinking?' My preferred answer is, 'No, but I know how you are thinking.' Although, when it comes to mentalising, we are not entirely sure how people do it or even what they are doing. Apologies if that sounds confusing, but this is a confusing topic. Theory of mind appears to be our mental representation of what someone else's mental representations are. As the quote at the top of this section makes clear, that can be a little like trying to see the back of your own head.

People have been thinking about thinking for millennia, but it was not until four decades ago, when we wondered about the inner life of chimps, that the problem of theory of mind was thrown into focus. The phrase 'theory of mind' and the complexity of the problem became apparent thanks to a paper asking if chimpanzees have the same mentalising abilities as we do (Premack & Woodruff, 1978). In that experiment a human-reared chimp called Sarah was shown videos of her trainer, Keith Kennel, trying to solve various puzzles. Sarah had to infer his mental state. Half the puzzles involved Keith trying to get bananas that were out of reach, echoing some classic experiments by German psychologist Wolfgang Kölher (1925), and in others he was locked in a cage or feeling cold. In almost all cases Sarah picked out a photo showing the correct solution: a box for him to stand on to reach the banana, a picture of keys for the cage, or even a lighted wick to relight an apparently faulty heater. Premack and Woodruff decided Sarah could infer mental states in Keith and that she and other chimps had a theory of mind.

This was a controversial conclusion. Looking back 30 years later, Derek Penn and Daniel Povinelli concluded there was no evidence that 'non-human animals possess anything remotely resembling a "theory of mind"' despite 'decades of effort by some of our brightest human and non-human minds' (p.731, Penn & Povinelli, 2007). Premack and Woodruff's conclusion also sparked a controversy about mental representations in general. Not because it challenged the by then unfashionable tenets of behaviourism, but because it is indirect evidence. We can be confident about our own internal mental states because we can experience them and talk about them. But that is not so easy for chimps and children. One big problem is how humans might have acquired the mind-reading trick. Scottish infancy researcher Alan Leslie summarised the issue succinctly, noting that 'it is hard to see how perceptual evidence could ever force an adult, let alone a young child, to invent the idea of unobservable mental states' (p.422, Leslie, 1987). If you did not have mental states yourself, you would never infer them in others. But if so, where did theory of mind come from and what supports it? How does a baby learn about beliefs, wants and other invisible desires?

Alan Leslie's answer was that pretence creates the capacity for theory of mind. Counterfactuals are a powerful cognitive tool in themselves. But Leslie sees imagination as the source of meta-representation – the ability to think about thinking. Believing this yellow object is a banana is very different from pretending that the same banana is a telephone. The first belief is very tightly bound to experience in the world; the second requires a decoupling mechanism that is the beginning of an ability to represent mental states. At that point I can like bananas, I can know that I like bananas and I can even imagine that you do not. When confronted with some weird person who, whenever they are given the choice between bananas and broccoli always picks broccoli, you know which food to offer them. Which is exactly what Alison Gopnik found in one experiment with 18-month-olds, although she used cheese-flavoured goldfish crackers, which babies love even more than bananas (Repacholi & Gopnik, 1997). Subsequent experiments did not replicate when they tested 18-month-olds but did show it at age two and a half (Ruffman, Aitken, Wilson, Puri & Taumoepeau, 2018).

Pointing is another fascinating skill that helps us see how babies develop the ability to understand someone else's perspective. As adults we take pointing completely for granted, overlooking the fact it is a culturally laden gesture. No other animals use pointing in the wild, although human-reared chimps can pick up the rudiments. Dogs can learn too, although most of them will just stare at your hand. Meanwhile, some remote tribes prefer to point with their chins. Babies will start pointing at around 12 months, and understand adult pointing around the same time. It used to be thought that babies started with 'imperative' pointing, using the gesture to demand out-of-reach objects before graduating to 'declarative' pointing, which indicates something of joint interest (Tomasello, Carpenter, & Liszkowski, 2007).

But while I was at Birkbeck BabyLab some of my colleagues, led by Vicky Southgate, set out to show otherwise. In one study infants pointed more to demand information when paired with a knowledgeable rather than a 'stupid' adult. The knowledgeable adult had previously been good at labelling familiar objects, but the stupid person had mislabelled a banana as a shoe and a cup as an apple (Begus & Southgate, 2012). In a second study infants learned more about new objects they had actively chosen by pointing (Begus, Gliga & Southgate, 2014). Southgate believes that all infant pointing is 'interrogative', with infants using pointing to request information, an account that fits in well with natural pedagogy, an idea we encountered in Chapter Nine (Southgate, van Maanen & Csibra, 2007). I also think these experiments help point to the correct explanation of theory of mind.

Like many theories about babies, there are two main options – nature and nurture. Theory of mind is an excellent candidate as the work of nature. It is a uniquely human skill that confers a strong evolutionary benefit. On top of this, autism seems to be a condition where theory of mind is selectively impaired. During his Ph.D., psychologist Simon Baron-Cohen showed that children with autism were bad at a theory of mind task called the Sally-Anne task, where the 'Anne' puppet moves a marble from one hiding place to another without the 'Sally' puppet seeing. The child is then asked where Sally will look for the marble (Baron-Cohen, Leslie, & Frith, 1985). It is a complex task and children get asked verbally complex questions about it. Children who are developing in the typical way do not pass the test until they are three to four years old, but many children with autism fail it much later, despite otherwise advanced mental abilities. This led Baron-Cohen and his supervisors, Alan Leslie and Uta Frith, to propose there was a theory of mind module in the brain that was impaired in autism (Leslie, 1992).

Thirty years later we view autism very differently. It is not the result of a faulty theory of mind module, but the result of a complex interaction of genes and environment. More importantly, psychiatry is starting to see autism as an example of neurodiversity – not as a disease or a disorder to be 'cured', but as a difference or disability to be accommodated and celebrated (Baron-Cohen, 2017).

Explanations for theory of mind have evolved too. No brain area has been found to house a theory of mind module and we no longer believe a specialist module would help with understanding other minds. Firstly, a module is essentially a black box divided from the rest of the brain by its specialist role; it is connected but strictly demarcated. But the goal of mentalising is to evoke the experience of another person. Knowing that your friend is reaching for a glass of juice because they are thirsty is a lot easier if you can draw on your own experience of thirst. Knowing they will jump if they spill their ice-cold drink on themselves is obvious if you can place yourself in their position and almost impossible otherwise. This seems like you are climbing in the black box alongside the other person, which defeats the point of having the box. Secondly, this whole approach to beliefs and desires as things we can label – in our own heads or in others' – is another example of the 'private language' of thought, which Wittgenstein rejected (Carpendale & Lewis, 2004).

Fortunately, there is an alternative called simulation theory that solves these problems. It says we understand other people because we imagine them as if they were us (Gallese & Goldman, 1998). Simulation is a bit like method acting, where actors immerse themselves in a character: similarly, we predict what others are going to do by pretending to be them and in the process make direct use of our own experience and imagination. This keeps Wittgenstein happy and fits very nicely with the anti-symbolic approach to concepts that we encountered in the last chapter (Williams & Colling, 2018). It also seems more parsimonious. Why not simply recruit my own decision-making system to understand other people's decisions rather than having a specialist module? The biggest selling point of simulation theory is that it fits with what we know about how our brains work.

Simulation theory got a big boost with the discovery of mirror neurons by Giacomo Rizzolatti and colleagues (Gallese et al., 1996; Rizzolatti et al., 1996). These are neurons in the pre-motor system that are activated both when planning an action or observing someone else do so. This is exactly what you would want in order to imagine or simulate you or someone else doing something. For example, the mirror system could help babies understand that their own pointing is equivalent to similar actions by their carer. This is incredibly useful because the first-person point of view looks different from the third-person. If we go back to the Machiavellian chimpanzees from Chapter Six, their dramas and their resolutions were highly physical and emotional in a way that fits well with simulation theory and mirror systems. Penn and Provinelli may be right that chimps do not have an equivalent to our theory of mind but they are sensitive to each other's mental states in a way that, thanks to simulation theory, provides an evolutionary pathway towards our abilities.

Not all the details of simulation theory have been worked out, and some psychologists think apes and babies have no mentalising abilities whatsoever (Burge, 2018). But I feel confident that the theory is along the right lines. There is not time to get into all the details here, but one very recent proposal by Katerina Fotopoulou and Manos Tsakiris claims that babies' earliest sense of self and our ability to mentally represent ourselves and others are tied together by simulation (Fotopoulou & Tsakiris, 2017). The core of self is a combination of the feeling of being an embodied individual but also recognising our similarity to others. They think 'the most minimal aspects of selfhood, namely the feeling of being an embodied, agentive subject, are fundamentally shaped by embodied interactions with other people in early infancy' (p.6, Fotopoulou & Tsakiris). Their proposal also draws on predictive coding and the free-energy principle, and it has met with the approval of Karl Friston, who says it 'fits comfortably with the notion of a mirror neuron system providing predictions of both my own behavior and yours' (Friston, 2017). Parents and carers are the most important people shaping this early identity, but the skill exists so we can interact with the wider world.

The quote at the top of this section was deliberately confusing to suggest that multiple levels of reference can be bewildering. In reality, knowing other minds is made easier because perspective-taking is enactive and embodied, not symbolic. All the dramatic arts are built on the premise that we don't require constant internal monologues to understand why characters act the way they do. Take the classic double bluff in old detective movies where the private eye pretends to have a gun in his coat pocket. We know he is pretending, but the bad guy doesn't. Perhaps it is just a banana? We watch the baddie trying to work out if the detective is bluffing. We know the hero knows his opponent is weighing this up and must act to fool him. On top of that we also know they are both actors pretending to pretend. We do this not with a theory-of-mind computer but by putting ourselves in the detective's shoes. That is why your heart is racing. Simulation theory lets us understand these dramas, both real and fictional. But it does not tell us one thing: are we the good guys or the bad guys?

Kind and Just

Hello babies, welcome to Earth. It's hot in the summer and cold in the winter. It's round and wet and crowded. At the outside, babies, you've got about a hundred years here. There's only one

rule that I know of, babies:
'God damn it, you've got to be kind.'
— Kurt Vonnegut Jr, *God Bless You, Mr Rosewater*, 1965

As my *Joys of Toys* collaborator Nathalia Gjersoe memorably said, 'If you have any experience of babies you'd be forgiven for thinking of them as entirely selfish, self-oriented little beasts with scant regard for others' (Gjersoe, 2013). She was, of course, joking to raise a serious point. Kindness and justice, also known as empathy and morality, take us considerably further than theory of mind. They are separable traits – an emotionless robot could have a pretty good theory of mind and even an understanding of right and wrong – but still lack empathy. Arguably this is the case for the few humans with antisocial personality disorder – what was known historically as sociopathy/psychopathy. Donald Trump, with his poor impulse control, anger-management issues and lack of moral compass keeps getting portrayed as big orange baby. But this deeply unfair to babies. Babies do have a strong moral sense and natural empathy, and it is a surprising and challenging thing to explain.

It is often said that morals reside in the head while empathy happens in the heart. But morality and empathy are entangled concepts. Religious figures like Jesus and Gautama Buddha are defined by their wisdom and their compassion, and philosophers debate whether you can have one without the other. Developmental psychology can bring a very valuable perspective to this debate. When researchers study this subject in babies, the headlines always emphasise the moral dimension –

'moral babies' sounds paradoxical while 'empathic babies' sounds tautological. We easily imagine a baby showing concern for someone who is upset but not judging whether something is fair.

This fits with a loose definition of morality given by Jean Decety and Jason Cowell, who say 'a central focus of morality is the judgment of the rightness or wrongness of acts or behaviors that knowingly cause harm to people' (p.527, Decety & Cowell, 2014). They feel that 'empathy' is too vague a term to be useful. They feel it should be divided into three separate behaviours – emotional sharing, empathic concern, and perspective-taking. In simple language these are the differences between 'I feel', 'I care' and 'I understand'. Emotional sharing is the foundation of this system. One nice aspect of the embodied self-awareness of simulation theory is that it gives you this aspect of empathy 'for free'. And this leads easily enough into empathic concern. If you can feel someone else's pain, it makes sense to help them. Of course, in order to help, you must understand what is wrong and may need to be selfless in the process. Empathic concern builds from family and in-group concern, leading it to be parochial, divisive and potentially immoral (Decety & Cowell, 2014) Overcoming selfish desires and tribal biases requires self-control and knowledge. This helps us draw the lines between empathy and morality. These may be beyond young babies. But not just babies, as Jesus was fond of pointing out.

Babies are certainly capable of emotional sharing. From the womb onwards they respond to their mother's emotional state and the bond they have with their parents is a two-way street (Trevarthen, 2005), but their concern spreads wider still. Newborn babies cry when they hear other young babies crying but not if they hear the cry of an older baby or an infant chimpanzee. This could be an early sign of empathy, or perhaps newborn cries are a very distressing stimulus. Opinion is currently divided (Ruffman, Lorimer & Scarf, 2017). There is no doubt babies become increasingly emotionally affected by other people as they get older, and try to comfort people who are suffering (Roth-Hanania, Davidov & Zahn-Waxler, 2011). These little saints are impossibly cute – they give gentle strokes and offer upset individuals their bottles or toys. In dire circumstances they'll even offer up their security blankets. The beginnings of understanding are there – 'This helps me when I am sad, perhaps it will help you too.' Another nice study with identical and non-identical twins tracked a large increase in concern and prosocial behaviour (friendly, helpful behaviour) over time in both groups (Zahn-Waxler, Robinson & Emde, 1992). Genetic effects were small, suggesting there is no 'gene for empathy'. Carolyn Zahn-Waxler of the University of Wisconsin-Madison, who was behind both of those studies, believes that we learn to be nice.

Babies can also teach us empathy. Recall the 'closely observed infants' from Chapter Nine who form part of psychotherapeutic training. The goal was for therapists to gain insight about adult emotional reactions – their clients' and their own – by seeing the processes start in babies. Amazingly, in Canada something similar happens in schools. For two decades babies have been visiting primary-school classrooms to teach children how to be kind as part of the 'Roots of Empathy' programme, founded in Toronto in 1996 by Mary Gordon. A baby (wearing a tiny 'Teacher' t-shirt) and their parent comes to class nine times through the year. Children learn from direct interaction with the babies and from reflecting on the experience. Gordon originally devised it to teach children parenting and family skills, but the idea of teaching young children 'how to be parents' met with resistance (Gordon, 2005). Besides, the benefits seemed wider. Seeing the babies respond to them directly changed the children's own understanding of empathy. Studies of the programme have shown that it increases prosocial behaviour and reduces bullying (Schonert-Reichl, Smith, Zaidman-Zait & Hertzman, 2012). The programme now operates across Canada and has spread to 12 other countries.

When one puppet hits the other in the experiment by Choi and Luo (2015), we interpret the babies' reactions as surprise when the witness, Alice, stays friendly with the aggressor, Becky. However, the babies do not react when the hit was accidental. They are not just keeping track of who saw what, but apparently making a moral judgement. This is consistent with studies showing that babies as young as six months old make lists of who is naughty and nice. One early study was run by Kiley Hamlin and colleagues at Yale Infant Cognition Center (Hamlin, Wynn & Bloom, 2007), although the drama in their study was more subdued. The characters were coloured shapes with googly eyes stuck on them and the participants were six- and 10-month-olds. The babies saw a red circle trying and failing to climb a steep hill, then a yellow triangle came along and helped the circle to the top. The scene began again, but this time a blue square came and pushed the circle back down. At the end the babies were given a chance to reach for the helpful triangle or the hindering square. All 12 younger babies and 14 out of 16 older babies picked the helpful shape. Lots of careful controls and counterbalancing ruled out more mundane explanations, such as babies preferring yellow or getting cues from parents or experimenters.

It is not all rosy in babyland. Describing this study in the *New York Times*, one of the experimenters, Paul Bloom, writes that sometimes babies gave the naughty shape a smack before opting to play with the nice shape (Bloom, 2010). Later experiments showed that babies – like adults – divide people into 'us' and 'them', favouring the in-crowd. Neha Mahajan and Karen Wynn (2012) gave babies a choice of two pairs of mittens and then confronted them with two puppets, one who shared their preference and one who expressed disapproval. Fourteen out of 16 babies preferred the puppet who shared their fashion sense. In an even more elaborate experiment babies were more keen on enemies being treated badly than friends being treated well (Hamlin et al., 2013). A strange pattern occurred with the twins in Zahn-Waxler's study. Identical twins who were more responsive to each other became less empathic to outsiders. In contrast, non-identicals who were more prosocial towards each other became more prosocial to outsiders too. It is not clear why, but it is possible the identical twins had a narrower view of what it meant to be 'like me'.

Mostly though, toddlers are 'indiscriminate altruists' who want to help everyone. This is the view of Felix Warneken, a German psychologist currently based at the University of Michigan, who has studied infant helping in many ingenious and adorable experiments (Warneken, 2018). The first things you notice when meeting Felix are that he is smiling and that he is really tall. I am just under six foot and I have to tilt my neck uncomfortably to talk to him. To the 18-month-olds in his study he is a big friendly giant. Yet they consider him sufficiently 'like me' that they want to help him out. In the experiments Felix plays the part of a clumsy oaf who is always dropping pens or bumping into doors. The toddlers watch him trying ineffectually to pick up the pen or negotiate a closed cupboard with an armful of books. Watching the videos of Felix's experiments, you can see the babies do not entirely believe his incompetence but take pity and help him out anyhow (Warneken & Tomasello, 2006). I remember the first time I ever saw Felix present this work. It showed very plainly that babies are good people. It also taught me that a good conference presentation should include videos of cute babies being cute.

Other experiments took the form of cooperative games, such as a long tube with handles at each end that needs two people to open it, or a large disc that could bounce balls if two people worked together. Toddlers quickly get the hang of these games. Interestingly, chimpanzees could perform some of the helping tasks but totally failed these cooperation games (Warneken, Chen & Tomasello, 2006). Felix believes successful cooperation is a game with two challenges. First you need to know how to play the game and you need to know who to play it with. He calls these the problems of 'creating and distributing benefit' (Warneken, 2018). Biologists and game theorists know that the evolution of cooperation requires a careful balance to avoid being taken for chump by freeloaders. Humans have these skills and chimpanzees do not. Rules of fairness and reciprocity create the moral dimension to direct our empathic urges effectively. Best of all, helping makes toddlers happy. Recent research looking at their body language found they showed pride when they were able to help an adult (Hepach, Vaish & Tomasello, 2017).

Paul Bloom agrees up to a point. His last two books have been called *Just Babies* (2014) and *Against Empathy* (Bloom, 2016), and his position has evolved quite dramatically in that time. The first book was a strong defence of the innate empathy and morality of babies. But it set forth a challenge to understand how those can be effective beyond the family and the tribal in-group. The second book takes up the challenge and concludes that empathy is the enemy within. Empathy is too 'narrow-minded, parochial, and innumerate'. Instead, Bloom argues for rational compassion. There is not space to get into Bloom's arguments here, and maybe they do not apply to babies, as he concedes 'perhaps empathy is like milk. Adults don't need it; we do fine without. But babies need milk to grow' (p.165, Bloom, 2016). I prefer the view of the Buddha, for whom the goal was to increase your empathy to such an extent that it encompasses everyone. This is easier said than done (but I suggest you meditate on it). Meanwhile, for babies, we should return to the simpler challenge of how to be a friend.

We're Friends, Right?

Think for a moment about your best friend. How did you become friends and why are you best friends? We all have different answers to how we found our friends, but why we stay friends is remarkably similar. Debra Oswald and colleagues have identified four factors that sustain successful adult friendships – positivity, supportiveness, openness and interaction (Oswald, Clark & Kelly, 2004). You want your best friends to be good for you and to be there for you. You also want them to accept you in a way that lets you be you. Friends do not have to agree on everything or share all the same interests, but there must be space for intimacy and you need to support each other's sense of identity. And this only works when the relationship is reciprocal. Oswald's research applies from '17 to 70' but the foundations of baby friendships are not much different.

Babies make friends through play. It is not until two years old that they can play nicely together for extended periods, but friendships can begin much earlier. In the mid-1920s Viennese psychologist Charlotte Bühler went to New York and ran some experiments where she plonked pairs of babies (six to twelve months) together in cots and saw what happened. She divided the babies into three types – socially dependent, socially independent and socially blind (Bühler, 1931). These distinctions were mostly ignored and the idea that young babies are only capable of 'parallel play' came to dominate (Green, 1933). If you put two unfamiliar babies under 18 months together they will largely ignore one another and do their own thing, but they almost always acknowledge a fellow baby. I see this every time there are two new babies in my lab. They see each other and share a moment of recognition – 'you're like me'. They play individually but always with an awareness of each other. For babies who see each other regularly, friendships and favouritism start to emerge from around one year of age.

Within the psychoanalytic tradition, babies' precocious social skills were recognised much earlier. Esther Bick was a Ph.D. student of Bühler, and in her thesis work she delved a lot deeper into the complex emotional life of infants. As we encountered in Chapter Nine, Bick and John Bowlby introduced infant observation as part of psychoanalytic training at the Tavistock Clinic. Since then, members of the Tavistock have upped the ante, running 'Babies in Groups' sessions, where groups of four eight-month-old babies are set up in a fixed circle of baby walkers and left to interact. The babies start having a 'conversation', complete with complex and sophisticated social dynamics. The sessions only run for five to ten minutes, but will include hundreds of bids for attention and changes of focus. The babies take turns to 'hold the floor' and go through complex cycles of high and low engagement with the group (Bradley, Selby & Urwin, 2012). A friend whose daughter took part in one of these sessions described it as one of the most remarkable things she had ever witnessed.

If we pay attention, we discover that young children are surprisingly competent social actors. William Corsaro, author of the highly influential textbook *The Sociology of Childhood* (Corsaro, 1997) spent lots of time in nursery schools observing how children negotiate their first friendships. He compares a nursery school to an adults' cocktail party, with clusters of participants involved in different activities. Children circulate and negotiate entry into new groups. Just as adults rarely make direct bids to join a new group, children do not make direct requests to join in games. They wait for an opportunity to enter the flow of the game and there can be 'access rituals' for new participants. The games involve plenty of pretend play with identifiable roles, such as two children agreeing they were both 'mothers', while a third was their child. The children in most of Corsaro's studies were three years old and upwards and were articulate enough to ask each other, 'We're friends, right?' (Corsaro, 1979).

Younger, preverbal children can be social butterflies too. Observations of toddlers in nursery and day care commonly find greeting rituals at the start of the nursery day where friends and carers are recognised and acknowledged. Even children under one year old in the 'baby room' are pleased to see their friends. These daily greetings are an important part of the friend-making process (Engdahl, 2012). Babies can still seem socially blind, often ignoring another infant crying right next to them. But this is affected by their social bonds – they are three times as likely to respond to crying of a friend. Babies who cry more themselves are more likely respond sympathetically, suggesting an empathic 'like-me' reaction (Howes & Farver, 1987). Early friendship is about building up those similarities to each other. By 14 months, babies can imitate each other during play. If one baby bangs a block on something, the other baby joins in simultaneously. As they get older this changes into complementary play: now they take turns and more complex games are possible where toys get passed back and forth, and games can have a 'follow the leader' structure (Eckerman, Davis & Didow, 1989).

Playtime is still precarious. Toddlers have empathy but they lack awareness and self-control – which is why nurseries need so many adult staff. They will hit and bite each other and snatch toys. Arguably this is theory of mind in action: 'That toy must be good or you wouldn't be playing with it.' Joint play provides many such challenges. When one toddler is approached by another, they do not know if their peer is going to share a toy, steal a toy, hug, hit, bite or something else. Nor will they want help from someone else. If you have tried to help a determined but incompetent toddler attempting to stack blocks or post shapes through holes, you will know that your assistance is *not* welcome. They want to do it themselves. Babies playing together want to help each other, but they also want to do everything. As much as anything else, early friendship is about building these skills in give and take (Whaley & Rubenstein, 1994).

When children are not directly interacting with each other, perhaps focused on the adult leading an activity, they are still a social group, and here laughter is their main social currency. Together with my students Lotta Fogelquist, Lenka Levakova and Sarah Rees, I ran a simple study to show this (Addyman, Fogelquist, Levakova & Rees, 2018). In a quiet corner of a nursery, preschoolers watched funny cartoons alone, in pairs or in larger groups of six or eight. Each time we counted their laughs and smiles. The difference between being on your own and having just one other child there was dramatic – smiles increased by a factor of three and there were eight times as many laughs. Children were laughing to share the experience. Importantly, we found the amount of laughter per child was the same in pairs or in large groups. This implies that the increased laughter was a social signal that children used to let each other know their reactions and was not a consequence of them copying each other.

The benefits of preschool are fiercely debated. Proponents say early socialisation has prosocial and cognitive benefits. Critics say it makes children distressed and manipulative. One of my old Birkbeck professors, Jay Belsky, attracted controversy in the 1980s and 1990s by saying that extended day care was bad for under twos. He claimed it made them more aggressive and defiant, and led to problem behaviours at older ages (Belsky, 1990, 2009). Other experts claimed the same data showed that children with more day care were more social, kicking off a fierce new battle in the 'mommy wars'. It was even rumoured Belsky took the job in London to flee the battleground in the United States. I doubt this, as Professor Belsky never seemed like someone who avoided confrontation. His move to Birkbeck did help the debate. Belsky worked with Ted Melhuish and Jacqueline Barnes to assess the Sure Start programme, introduced in 1998 by Britain's Labour government. This demonstrated that high-quality day care is unequivocally good for even young babies and money spent on improving the quality of infant care is one of the best investments a country can make (Melhuish, Belsky & Barnes, 2010).

Sadly, policy-level research does not tell us about the experience of individual toddlers. It is surprisingly difficult to do observational work with this age group. If trained scientists cannot keep up, no wonder toddlers get overwhelmed when they interact with each other. But among those dramas intimacies are shared and identities built. Seeing joy and sadness in another child is an opportunity for the child to gain insight into their own mental and emotional state. Personally, I wish there was more research that examined the joy. The positivity that friends provide in our lives was the first and most important factor in Debra Oswald's study of adult friendship (Oswald, Clark & Kelly, 2004). A huge meta-analysis published in 2015, covering thousands of people from ages six months to 68 years, found that friendship and happiness create a virtuous cycle. Friendship makes us happy; happiness makes us better friends (Ramsey & Gentzler, 2015). Friends are there for us because we are there for them too, and it starts from as soon as we can smile.

Epilogue: Laughing Matters

Babies laugh.
Babies laugh a lot.
They laugh at mummies and at daddies,
They laugh at siblings and at grannies,
They laugh at cats. They laugh at dogs,
They'll laugh while sleeping in their cots,
They laugh at songs and peekaboo,
They laugh way more than me or you,
They laugh while playing on the swings.
Babies laugh at all the things.

— Me, TEDx Bratislava, July 2017

It is a Thursday and I am sitting alone in a small café in Rickmansworth and, like any fan of Douglas Adams, my mind naturally turns how the world could be made a good and happy place. I won't tempt fate by pretending I have The Answer, but if you want a hint, I think babies might know more than they're letting on. I have just come from filming for the BBC documentary called *Babies: Their Wonderful World*. We went through a laughter experiment we had run and then the presenter asked me to explain in a single sentence why laughter matters so much in life. It was an obvious question but tricky to answer on the spot. I cannot remember exactly what I said, but hopefully they will edit it to make me sound wise. I am now trying to think what I should have said.

When it comes to the meaning of life, babies certainly have a more joyful answer than most philosophers. In 2004 I wrote to every professional philosopher in the United Kingdom to ask them all the meaning of life, the universe and everything. If you're interested, I collected the replies as an interlude in my novel, *Help Yourself* (Addyman, 2013). But, spoiler alert, they're a bit disappointing. Out of 644 only 22 replied, and many of them patiently explained this was not a real philosophical question. I even got a philosophical death threat. 'Life is preparation for death. I hope you are well prepared.' The funniest and most optimistic reply came from Michael Rush from the University of Manchester. Michael thought Aristotle was on the right lines in trying to tackle the question 'How should we behave?', but that the best answer is Bill and Ted's sage advice to 'Be excellent to each other, dudes.'

Babies would agree with that. Everywhere they go everyone is excellent to them and, as we saw in the final chapter, they are inclined to be excellent back. They might not have entirely mastered good behaviour, but their hearts are in the right place. Aristotle would also approve of the nature of babies' answers to these important questions. The answer is in actions, not words. Babies show us the meaning of life by how they live. The first two years of life might seem a long way distant from the challenges of the adult world, but babies have dynamism and optimism that puts adults to shame.

In July 2017 I went to Bratislava in Slovakia to give a TEDx talk about happy babies. I titled it 'Life Lessons from Laughing Babies'. It was challenging and fun squashing all the delightful things babies do into a 15-minute presentation. I was quite pleased when I had written a version with 12 bullet points. But the organisers pushed me to go further. What was the essence of the lessons? I boiled down infant wisdom to four words: LOVE, SAME, EUREKA, HAPPY. I was only midway through writing this book at the time. But, here at the end of the journey, I don't think I can condense it any further.

Babies laugh because they are loved. The bond between babies and their parents is the secret of their success. Parents need the love they get from their babies to cope with sleepless nights, endless nappies and all the rest. Babies need their parents for everything, but not least for the love. Babies need emotional support and they need close connection. Freud and other psychoanalysts were right that mothers matter, but they were wrong to fill the early years with so much psychodrama. They missed the importance of the successes babies experience every day and the joys they share with us: joys that can be shared with everyone.

Laughing babies show that we are all the same. Comedian Victor Borge toured the world making people laugh. He understood that laughter can always make a genuine connection even when language and culture are alien. Robert Provine and Robin Dunbar took us further, pointing out that laughter is a central social skill of deep evolutionary importance. We can add that this is especially true for babies. They need to connect with us to learn from us and their laughter is the gold dust they pay us for our attention, an arrangement that reaches its pared-down perfection in peekaboo, the ultimate in infant mirth.

Babies will laugh at surprises of all kinds. Little shrieks of joy are the 'Eureka!' of our little scientists surprising themselves as they push the boundaries of their own knowledge and discover the laws of their universe. They are Bayesian brains wrapped up in Markov blankets. They were the original scientists and, as Alison Gopnik and Karl Friston agree, scientists are big kids, using that same method and trying to capture some of that same delight. You laugh when you get the joke and so does a baby. A laughing baby has often just discovered something new about the world.

And it makes them happy. Returning yet again to Aristotle, he thought pleasure consists of achieving mastery of the world. He was not wrong. When Mihaly Csikszentmihalyi studied the happiest people in life, he discovered that this was their secret. All his insights apply naturally to babies, who are on the boundary of their abilities every day and effortlessly achieve a 'flow state' as they play. Play is their work and they are driven forward by accidental discoveries and helpful nudges from us as they strive to imitate us.

Babies are constantly moving forward, but they are never in such a rush as to miss the magic of right now: knowledge and learning for their own sake. Babies don't chase happiness. They are happy. They are little Zen masters, always present, experiencing the world as fresh and vivid. They live in the moment and make most of it. They wake up happy and take pleasure in simple things, never in a such a rush that they miss the magic of right now. Through laughter they share their happiness with their families, their friends and with the world.

Laughter makes life worth living. It connects us. It consoles us. It elates us. It's contagious. Laughter is the soundtrack to our triumphs and makes the impossible possible. It is the chorus of our shared delights and deepens our love and our joys. When you are happy, make the most of it. Slow down and enjoy life – you will be glad you did. If you are not sure quite how, just ask a baby.

References

AAP Council on Communications and Media. (2016). Media and young minds. *Pediatrics*, 138(5), e20162591.

AAP Council on Communications and Media, & Brown, A. (2011). Media use by children younger than 2 years. *Pediatrics*, 128(5), 1040–1045.

Adam, K., & Oswald, I. (1983). Protein synthesis, bodily renewal and the sleep-wake cycle. *Clinical Science*, 65(6), 561–7.

Adams, D. (1979). *The hitchhiker's guide to the galaxy*. London: Pan Books.

Addyman, C. (2013). *Help yourself*. London: OneMonkey. Available at http://onemonkey.org/help-yourself

Addyman, C., Fogelquist, C., Levakova, L., & Rees, S. (2018). Social facilitation of laughter and smiles in preschool children. *Frontiers in Psychology*

Addyman, C., & Mareschal, D. (2010). The perceptual origins of the abstract same/different concept in human infants. *Animal Cognition*, 13(6), 817–833.

Addyman, C., & Mareschal, D. (2013). Local redundancy governs infants' spontaneous orienting to visual-temporal sequences. *Child Development*, 84(4), 1137–1144.

Addyman, C., Rocha, S., Fautrelle, L., French, R. M., Thomas, E., & Mareschal, D. (2016). Embodiment and the origin of interval timing: Kinematic and electromyographic data. *Experimental Brain Research*, 235(3), 923–930.

Addyman, C., Rocha, S., & Mareschal, D. (2014). Mapping the origins of time: Scalar errors in infant time estimation. *Developmental Psychology*, 50(8), 2030–2035.

Adesope, O. O., Lavin, T., Thompson, T., & Ungerleider, C. (2010). A systematic review and meta-analysis of the cognitive correlates of bilingualism. *Review of Educational Research*, 80(2), 207–245.

Adolph, K. E. (2000). Specificity of learning: Why infants fall over a veritable cliff. *Psychological Science*, 11(4), 290–295.

Adolph, K. E., Cole, W. G., Komati, M., Garciaguirre, J. S., Badaly, D., Lingeman, J. M., Sotsky, R. B. (2012). How do you learn to walk? Thousands of steps and dozens of falls per day. *Psychological Science*, 23(11), 1387–1394.

Ali, A. (2015, June 15). Give children iPads from birth – they're better than books, say scientists. *The Independent*, Retrieved from http://www.independent.co.uk

Amsterdam, B. (1972). Mirror self-image reactions before age two. *Developmental Psychobiology*, 5(4), 297–305.

Asada, M., Hosoda, K., Kuniyoshi, Y., Ishiguro, H., Inui, T., Yoshikawa, Y. & Yoshida, C. (2009). Cognitive developmental robotics: A survey. *IEEE Transactions on Autonomous Mental Development*, 1(1), 1–44.

Asendorpf, J. B., Baudonnière, P.-M., & Warkentin, V. (1996). Self-awareness and other awareness: Mirror self-recognition, social contingency awareness, and synchronic imitation. *Developmental Psychology*, 32(2), 313.

Asendorpf, J. B., & Baudonnière, P. M. (1993). Self-awareness and other-awareness: Mirror self-recognition and synchronic imitation among unfamiliar peers. *Developmental Psychology*, 29(1), 88–95.

Atkinson, E. G., Audesse, A. J., Palacios, J. A., Bobo, D. M., Webb, A. E., Ramachandran, S., & Henn, B. M. (2018). No evidence for recent selection at FOXP2 among diverse human populations. *Cell*, 174(6), 1424–1435

Baillargeon, R., Spelke, E. S., & Wasserman, S. (1985). Object permanence in five-month-old infants. *Cognition*, 20(3), 191–208.

Bancel, P. J., & de l'Etang, A. M. (2013). Brave new words. In C. Lefebvre, B. Comrie & H. Cohen (eds.) *New perspectives on the origins of language* (pp. 333–378). Amsterdam: John Benjamins Publishing.

Baron-Cohen, S. (2017). Editorial perspective: Neurodiversity – A revolutionary concept for autism and psychiatry. *Journal of Child Psychology and Psychiatry*, 58(6), 744–747.

Baron-Cohen, S., Leslie, A. M., & Frith, U. (1985). Does the autistic child have a theory of mind? *Cognition*, 21(1), 37–46.

Bartsch, K., & Wellman, H. M. (1995). *Children talk about the mind*. Oxford: Oxford University Press.

Bedford, R., Saez de Urabain, I. R., Cheung, C. H. M., Karmiloff-Smith, A., & Smith, T. J. (2016). Toddlers' fine motor milestone achievement is associated with early touchscreen scrolling. *Frontiers in Psychology*, 7, 1108.

Begum Ali, J., Spence, C., & Bremner, A. J. (2015). Human infants' ability to perceive touch in external space develops postnatally. *Current Biology*, 25(20), R977–R978.

Begus, K., Gliga, T., & Southgate, V. (2014). Infants learn what they want to learn: Responding to infant pointing leads to superior learning. *PLOS ONE*, 9(10), e108817.

Begus, K., & Southgate, V. (2012). Infant pointing serves an interrogative function. *Developmental Science*, 15(5), 611–617.

Belsky, J. (1990). Parental and nonparental child care and children's socioemotional development: A decade in review. *Journal of Marriage and Family*, 52(4), 885–903.

Belsky, J. (2009). Classroom composition, childcare history and social development: Are childcare effects disappearing or spreading?: Debate. *Social Development*, 18(1), 230–238.

Benedek, M., Jauk, E., Sommer, M., Arendasy, M., & Neubauer, A. C. (2014). Intelligence, creativity, and cognitive control: The common and differential involvement of executive functions in intelligence and creativity. *Intelligence*, 46(1), 73–83.

Berne, E. (1964). *Games people play; the psychology of human relationships*. New Jersey: Grove Press.

Berridge, K. C., & Kringelbach, M. L. (2011). Building a neuroscience of pleasure and well-being. *Psychology of Well-Being: Theory, Research and Practice*, 1(1), 3.

Blakemore, S.-J., Wolpert, D. M., & Frith, C. D. (1998). Central cancellation of self-produced tickle sensation. *Nature Neuroscience*, 1(7), 635–640.

Block, R. A., Hancock, P. A., & Zakay, D. (2010). How cognitive load affects duration judgments: A meta-analytic review. *Acta Psychologica*, 134(3), 330–343.

Bloom, P. (2004). *Descartes' baby: how the science of child development explains what makes us human*. New York: Basic Books.

Bloom, P. (2010, May 9). The moral life of babies. *New York Times, Sunday Magazine*, MM44.

Bloom, P. (2011). *How pleasure works: the new science of why we like what we like*. New York: W. W. Norton.

Bloom, P. (2014). *Just babies: The origins of good and evil.* New York: Broadway Books.

Bloom, P. (2016). *Against empathy: the case for rational compassion.* New York: Ecco Press.

Bowlby, J. (1969). *Attachment and loss*. New York: Basic Books.

Bradley, B., Selby, J., & Urwin, C. (2012). Group life in babies: Opening up perceptions and possibilities. In C. Urwin & J. Sternberg (Eds.), *Infant observation and research*. London: Routledge.

Bremner, A. J., Mareschal, D., Lloyd-Fox, S., & Spence, C. (2008). Spatial localization of touch in the first year of life: early influence of a visual spatial code and the development of remapping across changes in limb position. *Journal of Experimental Psychology: General*, 137(1), 149–62.

Brito, N., & Barr, R. (2014). Flexible memory retrieval in bilingual 6-month-old infants. *Developmental Psychobiology*, 56(5), 1156–1163.

Brito, N., Sebastián-Gallés, N., & Barr, R. (2015). Differences in language exposure and its effects on memory flexibility in monolingual, bilingual, and trilingual infants. *Bilingualism*, 18(4), 670–682.

Brown, S. (2017). A joint prosodic origin of language and music. *Frontiers in Psychology*, 8, 1894.

Brown, W. M., Cronk, L., Grochow, K., Jacobson, A., Liu, C. K., Popović, Z., & Trivers, R. (2005). Dance reveals symmetry especially in young men. *Nature*, 438 (7071), 1148–1150.

Bruner, J. S., & Sherwood, V. (1976). Peekaboo and the learning of rule structures. In J. Bruner, A. Jolly, & K. Sylva (Eds.), *Play: Its role in development and evolution* (pp. 277–285). Harmondsworth: Penguin.

Bryant, G. A., & Aktipis, C. A. (2014). The animal nature of spontaneous human laughter. *Evolution and Human Behavior*, 35(4), 327–335.

Buchen, L. (2010). Neuroscience: In their nurture. *Nature*, 467(7312), 146–148.

Buckley, S. J. (2015). Hormonal physiology of childbearing: Evidence and implications for women, babies, and maternity care. *The Journal of Perinatal Education* (Vol. 24). Washington, D.C.: Childbirth Connection Programs, National Partnership for Women & Families, January 2015.

Bühler, C. (1931). The social behavior of the child. In C. Murchison (Ed.), *A handbook of child psychology*. (pp. 392–431). Worcester, MA: Clark University Press.

Burgdorf, J., & Panksepp, J. (2001). Tickling induces reward in adolescent rats. *Physiology and Behavior*, 72(1–2), 167–173.

Burge, T. (2018). Do infants and nonhuman animals attribute mental states? *Psychological Review*, 125(3), 409–434.

Cameron-Faulkner, T., Lieven, E. V, & Theakston, A. (2007). What part of 'no' do children not understand? *Journal of Child Language*, 33, 251–282.

Campos, J. J., Hiatt, S., Ramsay, D., Henderson, C., & Svejda, M. (1978). The emergence of fear on the visual cliff. In M. Lewis & L. A. Rosenblum (Eds.), *The development of affect* (pp. 149–182). Springer.

Cantor, R. S. (2015). The evolutionary origin of the need to sleep: An inevitable consequence of synaptic neurotransmission? *Frontiers in Synaptic Neuroscience*, 7, 15.

Carey, S. (2009). The origin of concepts. *Behavioral and Brain Sciences* (Vol. 34). Oxford: Oxford University Press.

Carhart-Harris, R. L., & Friston, K. J. (2010). The default-mode, ego-functions and free-energy: A neurobiological account of Freudian ideas. *Brain*, 133(4), 1265–1283.

Carpendale, J. I. M., & Lewis, C. (2004). Constructing an understanding of mind: The development of children's social understanding within social interaction. *Behavioral and Brain Sciences*, 27(01), 79–151.

Carr, J., & Greeves, L. (2006). *The naked jape: Uncovering the hidden world of jokes*. London: Michael Joseph.

Casalin, S., Luyten, P., Vliegen, N., & Meurs, P. (2012). The structure and stability of temperament from infancy to toddlerhood: A one-year prospective study. *Infant Behavior and Development*, 35(1), 94–108.

Cesana-Arlotti, N., Martín, A., Téglás, E., Vorobyova, L., Cetnarski, R., & Bonatti, L. L. (2018). Precursors of logical reasoning in preverbal human infants. *Science*, 359(6381), 1263–1266.

Charles, M. (2012). A laughing party. Retrieved from https://worship.calvin.edu/resources/resource-library/a-laughing-party/

Cheung, C. H. M., Bedford, R., Saez De Urabain, I. R., Karmiloff-

Smith, A., & Smith, T. J. (2017). Daily touchscreen use in infants and toddlers is associated with reduced sleep and delayed sleep onset. *Scientific Reports*, 7, 46104.

Choi, S. (1988). The semantic development of negation: A cross-linguistic longitudinal study. *Journal of Child Language*, 15(3), 517–531.

Choi, Y.-J., & Luo, Y. (2015). 13-month-olds' understanding of social interactions. *Psychological Science*, 26(3), 274–83.

Chomsky, N. (1995). *The minimalist program*. Cambridge, MA: MIT Press.

Christiansen, M. H., & Chater, N. (2016). *Creating Language: Integrating Evolution, Acquisition, and Processing*. Cambridge, MA: MIT Press.

Cohen, L. B. (1972). Attention-getting and attention-holding processes of infant visual preferences. *Child Development*, 43(3), 869–79.

Conde-Agudelo, A., Diaz-Rossello, J. L., & Belizan, J. M. (2003). Kangaroo mother care to reduce morbidity and mortality in low birthweight infants. *Birth*, 30(2), 133–134.

Corsaro, W. A. (1979). 'We're friends, right?': Children's use of access rituals in a nursery school. *Language in Society*, 8(2–3), 315.

Corsaro, W. A. (1997). *The sociology of childhood*. Thousand Oaks, California: Pine Forge Press.

Cowles, H. (2017). Child's play. Retrieved from https://aeon.co/essays/how-the-scientific-method-came-from-watching-children-play

Cross, I., & Morley, I. (2008). The evolution of music: Theories, definitions and the nature of the evidence. In S. Malloch & C. Trevarthen (Eds.), *Communicative musicality* (pp. 61–82). Oxford: Oxford University Press.

Csibra, G., Bíró, S., Koós, O., & Gergely, G. (2003). One-year-old infants use teleological representations of actions productively. *Cognitive Science*, 27(1), 111–133.

Csibra, G., & Gergely, G. (2009). Natural pedagogy. *Trends in Cognitive Sciences*, 13(4), 148–153.

Csikszentmihalyi, M. (1990). *Flow: The psychology of optimal experience*. New York: Harper & Row.

Cutler, A. (2012). *Native listening: Language experience and the recognition of spoken words*. Cambridge, MA: MIT Press.

Darwin, C. (1872). *The expression of the emotions in man and animals*. London: John Murray.

Davila Ross, M., Owren, M. J., & Zimmermann, E. (2009).

Reconstructing the evolution of laughter in great apes and humans. *Current Biology*, 19(13), 1106–1111.

de Bruin, A., Treccani, B., & Della Sala, S. (2015). Cognitive advantage in bilingualism: An example of publication bias? *Psychological Science*, 26(1), 99–107.

Decety, J., & Cowell, J. M. (2014). Friends or foes: Is empathy necessary for moral behavior? *Perspectives on Psychological Science*, 9(5), 525–37.

Dekker, T., Mareschal, D., Sereno, M. I., & Johnson, M. H. (2011). Dorsal and ventral stream activation and object recognition performance in school-age children. *NeuroImage*, 57(3), 659–670.

Denil, M., Agrawal, P., Kulkarni, T. D., Erez, T., Battaglia, P., & de Freitas, N. (2016). Learning to perform physics experiments via deep reinforcement learning. Retrieved from http://arxiv.org/abs/1611.01843

Dennett, D. C. (1991). *Consciousness explained. Theory & psychology* (Vol. 7). New York: Little, Brown and Co.

Dewey, J. (1910). *How we think*. Boston: D. C. Heath & Company.

DeYoung, C. G. (2010). Personality neuroscience and the biology of traits. *Social and Personality Psychology Compass*, 4(12), 1165–1180.

Dissanayake, E. (1994). *Homo aestheticus: Where art comes from and why and what is art for?* Seattle: University of Washington Press.

Dissanayake, E. (2000). *Art and intimacy – How the arts began*. Washington DC: University of Washington Press.

Donald, I., Macvicar, J., & Brown, T. (1958). Investigation of abdominal masses by pulsed ultrasound. *The Lancet*, Jun 7(1(7032)), 1188–95.

Donaldson, O.F. (1994) *Playing by heart: The vision and practice of belonging*. Health Communications

Donate-Bartfield, E., & Passman, R. H. (2004). Relations between children's attachments to their mothers and to security blankets. *Journal of Family Psychology*, 18(3), 453–458.

Drozd, K. F. (1995). Child English pre-sentential negation as metalinguistic exclamatory sentence negation. *Journal of Child Language*, 22(3), 583–610.

Dunbar, R. (2012). On the evolutionary function of song and dance. In N. Bannon (Ed.), *Music, language, and human evolution* (pp. 201–214). Oxford: OUP.

Dunbar, R. I. M. (2012). Bridging the bonding gap: the transition from primates to humans. *Philosophical Transactions of the Royal Society B: Biological Sciences*, 367(1597), 1837–1846.

Dunbar, R. I. M. (2014). *Human evolution: A Pelican introduction*. London: Pelican Books.

Dunbar, R. I. M. (2017). Group size, vocal grooming and the origins of language. *Psychonomic Bulletin & Review*, 24(1), 209–212.

Dunsworth, H. M., Warrener, A. G., Deacon, T., Ellison, P. T., & Pontzer, H. (2012). Metabolic hypothesis for human altriciality. *Proceedings of the National Academy of Sciences of the United States of America*, 109(38), 15212–6.

Eckerman, C. O. C., Davis, C. C. C., & Didow, S. M. (1989). Toddlers' emerging ways of achieving social coordinations with a peer. *Child Development*, 60(2), 440–453.

Einstein, A. (1905). Über die von der molekularkinetischen Theorie der Wärme geforderte Bewegung von in ruhenden Flüssigkeiten suspendierten Teilchen. *Annalen Der Physik*, 322(8), 549–560.

Elman, J. L., Bates, E., Johnson, M. H., Karmiloff-Smith, A., Parisi, D., & Plunkett, K. (1996). *Rethinking innateness: A connectionist perspective on development*. Cambridge, MA: MIT Press.

Engdahl, I. (2012). Doing friendship during the second year of life in a Swedish preschool. *European Early Childhood Education Research Journal*, 20(1), 83–98.

Esseily, R., Rat-Fischer, L., Somogyi, E., O'Regan, K. J., & Fagard, J. (2016). Humour production may enhance observational learning of a new tool-use action in 18-month-old infants. *Cognition & Emotion*, 9931 (May), 1–9.

Everett, D. L. (2009). Pirahã culture and grammar: A response to some criticisms. *Language*, 85(2), 405–442.

Eysenck, H. (1967). *The biological basis of personality*. Springfield, IL: Charles C. Thomas.

Falk, D. (2004). Prelinguistic evolution in early hominins: Whence motherese? *Behavioral and Brain Sciences*, 27(04), 491–541.

Farroni, T., Csibra, G., Simion, F., & Johnson, M. H. (2002). Eye-contact detection in humans from birth. *Proceedings of the National Academy of Sciences of the United States of America*, 99(14), 9602–9605.

Field, T. (2003) *Touch*. Cambridge, MA: MIT Press

Feldman, L. B. (2018). *How emotions are made: The secret life of the brain.* London: Pan Macmillan.

Feldman, R. (2007). Mother-infant synchrony and the development of moral orientation in childhood and adolescence: Direct and indirect mechanisms of developmental continuity. *American Journal of Orthopsychiatry.*

Feldman, R. (2012). Parent–infant synchrony: A biobehavioral model of mutual influences in the formation of affiliative bonds. *Monographs of the Society for Research in Child.*

Feldman, R. (2015). The adaptive human parental brain: Implications for children's social development. *Trends in Neurosciences*, 38(6), 387–399.

Feldman, R., Rosenthal, Z., & Eidelman, A. I. (2014). Maternal-preterm skin-to-skin contact enhances child physiologic organization and cognitive control across the first 10 years of life. *Biological Psychiatry*, 75(1), 56–64.

Feldman, R., Singer, M., & Zagoory, O. (2010). Touch attenuates infants' physiological reactivity to stress. *Developmental Science*, 13(2), 271–278.

Ferber, R. (1985). *Solve your child's sleep problems.* New York: Simon & Schuster.

Ferber, S. G., Feldman, R., & Makhoul, I. R. (2008). The development of maternal touch across the first year of life. *Early Human Development*, 84(6), 363–370.

Fernald, A., & O'Neill, D. K. (1993). Peekaboo across cultures: How mothers and infants play with voices, faces, and expectations. *Parent-Child Play: Descriptions and Implications*, 259–285.

Fiser, J., Chiu, C., & Weliky, M. (2004). Small modulation of ongoing cortical dynamics by sensory input during natural vision. *Nature*, 431 (7008), 573–578.

Fitch, W. T., Hauser, M. D., & Chomsky, N. (2005). The evolution of the language faculty: Clarifications and implications. *Cognition*, 97(2), 179–210.

Flohr, J. W., Atkins, D. A., Bower, T. G. R., & Aldridge, M. A. (2000). Infant music preferences: Implications for child development and music education. In C. Mizener (Ed.), *Annual meeting of the Texas Music Educators Association* (pp. 26–31). San Antonio, Texas: Texas Music Educators Association.

Fosse, M. J., Fosse, R., Hobson, J. A., & Stickgold, R. J. (2003). Dreaming and episodic memory: A functional dissociation? *Journal of Cognitive Neuroscience*, 15(1), 1–9.

Fotopoulou, A., & Tsakiris, M. (2017). Mentalizing homeostasis: The social origins of interoceptive inference-replies to commentaries. *Neuropsychoanalysis*, 19(1), 3–28.

Fouts, R., & Mills, S. (1997). *Next of kin*. London: Michael Joseph.

Fraiberg, S. (1977). *Insights from the blind: Comparative studies of blind and sighted infants*. New York: Basic Books.

Frank, M. C., Braginsky, M., Yurovsky, D., & Marchman, V. A. (2017). Wordbank: An open repository for developmental vocabulary data. *Journal of Child Language*, 44(3), 677–694.

French, R. M. (1995). *The subtlety of sameness: A theory and computer model of analogy-making*. Cambridge, MA: MIT Press.

French, R. M., Addyman, C., & Mareschal, D. (2011). TRACX: A recognition-based connectionist framework for sequence segmentation and chunk extraction. *Psychological Review*, 118(4), 614–36.

French, R. M., Addyman, C., Mareschal, D., & Thomas, E. (2014). GAMIT – A Fading-Gaussian Activation Model of Interval-Timing: Unifying prospective and retrospective time estimation. *Timing & Time Perception*, 1 (December), 1–17.

French, R. M., Mareschal, D., Mermillod, M., & Quinn, P. C. (2004). The role of bottom-up processing in perceptual categorization by 3- to 4-month-old infants: Simulations and data. *Journal of Experimental Psychology: General*, 133(3), 382–97.

Freud, S. (1905). *Jokes and their relation to the unconscious. The standard edition of the complete psychological works of Sigmund Freud, Volume VIII* (1976th ed.). London: The Pelican Freud Library and Penguin Books.

Friedman, W. J. (2001). The development of an intuitive understanding of entropy. *Child Development*, 72(2), 460–473.

Friedman, W. J. (2002). Arrows of time in infancy: The representation of temporal-causal invariances. *Cognitive Psychology*, 44(3), 252–296.

Friston, K. (2010). The free-energy principle: A unified brain theory? *Nature Reviews Neuroscience*, 11(2), 127–138.

Friston, K. (2013). Life as we know it. *Journal of the Royal Society, Interface*, 10(86), 20130475.

Friston, K. J. (2017). Self-evidencing babies: Commentary on 'Mentalizing homeostasis: The social origins of interoceptive inference' by Fotopoulou & Tsakiris. *Neuropsychoanalysis*, 19(1), 43–47.

Gallese, V., Fadiga, L., Fogassi, L., & Rizzolatti, G. (1996). Action recognition in the premotor cortex. *Brain*, 119(2), 593–609.

Gallese, V., & Goldman, A. (1998). Mirror neurons and mind-reading. *Trends in Cognitive Sciences*, 2(12), 493–501.

Gallup, G. G. (1970). Chimpanzees: Self-recognition. *Science*, 167(3914), 86–87.

Gartstein, M. A., & Rothbart, M. K. (2003). Studying infant temperament via the Revised Infant Behavior Questionnaire. *Infant Behavior and Development*, 26(1), 64–86.

Gaskin, I. M. (2010). *Ina May's guide to childbirth.* London: Ebury Publishing.

Gergely, G., Bekkering, H., & Király, I. (2002). Developmental psychology: Rational imitation in preverbal infants. *Nature*, 415(6873), 755–755.

Gergely, G., & Csibra, G. (2003). Teleological reasoning in infancy: the naive theory of rational action. *Trends in Cognitive Sciences*, 7(7), 287–292.

Gerhardt, S. (2004). *Why love matters: How affection shapes a baby's brain* (1st ed.). Hove East Sussex: Brunner-Routledge.

Gibson, E. J., & Walk, R. D. (1960). The 'visual cliff'. *Scientific American*, 202(4), 64–71.

Gibson, E. J., & Walker, A. S. (1984). Development of knowledge of visual-tactual affordances of substance. *Child Development*, 55(2), 453–460.

Gjersoe, N. (2013, October 12). The moral life of babies. *The Guardian.* Retrieved from https://www.theguardian.com/science/2013/oct/12/babies-moral-life

Goldstein, M. H., Schwade, J. A., & Bornstein, M. H. (2009). The value of vocalizing: Five-month-old infants associate their own noncry vocalizations with responses from caregivers. *Child Development*, 80(3), 636–644.

Gopnik, A. (1997). The scientist as child. *Philosophy of Science*, 63(4), 485–514.

Gopnik, A., Meltzoff, A., & Kuhl, P. (1999) *How babies think.* London: Weidenfeld and Nicolson

Gopnik, A., & Tenenbaum, J. B. (2007). Bayesian networks, Bayesian learning and cognitive development. *Developmental Science*, 10(3), 281–287.

Gordon, M. (2005). *Roots of empathy: Changing the world child by child.* Toronto, ON: Thomas Allen.

Goren, C., Sarty, M., & Wu, P. (1975). Visual following and pattern discrimination of face-like stimuli by newborn infants. *Pediatrics*, 56 (4), 544–549.

Gradisar, M., Jackson, K., Spurrier, N., & Gibson, J. (2016). Behavioral interventions for infant sleep problems: A randomized controlled trial. *Pediatrics*, 137(6), e20151486

Green, E. H. (1933). Friendships and quarrels among preschool children. *Child Development*, 4, 237–252.

Greenwood, C. (2009). Child's play: Mattel's Neil Friedman has built a career out of toying around – and making kids smile. *Success*, October 2009.

Gregory, A. (2018) *Nodding off.* London: Bloomsbury

Hall, G. S. (1898). Some aspects of the early sense of self. *The American Journal of Psychology*, 9(3), 351–395.

Hall, W., Hutton, E., Brant, R., & Collet, J. (2015). A randomized controlled trial of an intervention for infants' behavioral sleep problems. *BMC.* Retrieved from https://bmcpediatr.biomedcentral.com/articles/10.1186/s12887-015-0492-7

Hamlin, J. K. J., Mahajan, N., Liberman, Z., & Wynn, K. (2013). Not like me = bad: Infants prefer those who harm dissimilar others. *Psychological Science*, 24(4), 589–594.

Hamlin, J. K., Wynn, K., & Bloom, P. (2007). Social evaluation by preverbal infants. *Nature*, 450(7169), 557–559.

Harris, M. A., Brett, C. E., Johnson, W., & Deary, I. J. (2016). Personality stability from age 14 to age 77 years. *Psychology and Aging*, 31(8), 862–874.

Hart, B., & Risley, T. (1995). *Meaningful differences in the everyday experience of young American children.* Baltimore, MD: Brookes.

Hasson, U., Ghazanfar, A. A., Galantucci, B., Garrod, S., & Keysers, C. (2012). Brain-to-brain coupling: A mechanism for creating and sharing a social world. *Trends in Cognitive Sciences*, 16(2), 114–21.

Hawkes, K., O'Connell, J. F., & Jones, N. G. B. (1989). Hardworking Hadza grandmothers. *Comparative Socioecology: The Behavioural Ecology of Humans and Other Mammals*, 341–366.

Heap, I. (2017, July 4) *The happy baby song.* ImogenHeap.com Retrieved from http://imogenheap.com/home.php?article=2619

Held, R., & Hein, A. (1963). Movement-produced stimulation in the development of visually guided behavior. *Journal of Comparative and Physiological Psychology*, 56(5), 872–876.

Hepach, R., Vaish, A., & Tomasello, M. (2017). The fulfillment of others' needs elevates children's body posture. *Developmental Psychology*, 53(1), 100–113.

Hepper, P. G. P. (1991). An examination of fetal learning before and after birth. *The Irish Journal of Psychology*, 12(2), 95–107.

Herman, B. H., & Panksepp, J. (1981). Ascending endorphin inhibition of distress vocalization. *Science* (New York, NY), 211(4486), 1060–2.

Hochmann, J. R., Mody, S., & Carey, S. (2016). Infants' representations of same and different in match- and non-match-to-sample. *Cognitive Psychology*, 86 (March), 87–111.

Hoicka, E., & Akhtar, N. (2011). Preschoolers joke with jokers, but correct foreigners. *Developmental Science*, 14(4), 848–858.

Hoicka, E., & Gattis, M. (2011). Acoustic differences between humorous and sincere communicative intentions. *British Journal of Developmental Psychology*, 30(4), 531–549.

Hoicka, E., & Martin, C. (2016). Two-year-olds distinguish pretending and joking. *Child Development*, 87(3), 916–928.

Hollich, G., Golinkoff, R. M., & Hirsh-Pasek, K. (2007). Young children associate novel words with complex objects rather than salient parts. *Developmental Psychology*, 43(5), 1051–1061.

Horst, J. S., & Samuelson, L. K. (2008). Fast mapping but poor retention by 24-month-old infants. *Infancy*, 13(2), 128–157.

Howes, C., & Farver, J. (1987). Toddlers' responses to the distress of their peers. *Journal of Applied Developmental Psychology*, 8(4), 441–452.

Hrdy, S. (2010). *Mothers and others.* Cambridge, MA: Belknap Press.

Hurley, M. M., Dennett, D. C., & Adams, R. B. (2011). *Inside jokes: Using humor to reverse-engineer the mind.* Boston, MA: MIT Press.

Jakubowski, K., Finkel, S., Stewart, L., & Müllensiefen, D. (2017). Dissecting an earworm: Melodic features and song popularity predict involuntary musical imagery. *Psychology of Aesthetics, Creativity, and the Arts*, 11(2), 122–135.

James, W. (1890) *The principles of psychology.* New York: Henry Holt and Company.

Johanson, R., Newburn, M., & Macfarlane, A. (2002). Has the medicalisation of childbirth gone too far? *BMJ (Clinical Research Ed.)*, 324(7342), 892–895.

Johnson, M. H. (1990). Cortical maturation and the development of visual attention in early infancy. *Journal of Cognitive Neuroscience*, 2(2), 81–95.

Johnson, M. H., Dziurawiec, S., Ellis, H., & Morton, J. (1991). Newborns' preferential tracking of face-like stimuli and its subsequent decline, *Cognition*. 40, 1–19.

Johnson, M. H., & Morton, J. (1991). *Biology and cognitive development: The case of face recognition*. Oxford: Blackwell Scientific Publications.

Joseph, R. (2000). Fetal brain behavior and cognitive development. *Developmental Review*, 20(1), 81–98.

Kandel, E. R. (1976). *Cellular basis of behaviour: An introduction to behavioural neurobiology*. Oxford: W.H. Freeman.

Karp, H. (2002). *The happiest baby on the block: The new way to calm crying and help your baby sleep longer*. New York: Bantam Books.

Katz, L. (2016). Pleasure. In E. N. Zalta (Ed.), *The Stanford encyclopedia of philosophy* (Winter 2016 Edition). Retrieved from https://plato.stanford.edu/archives/win2016/entries/pleasure/

Keltner, D., & Ekman, P. (2015, July 3). The science of 'Inside Out.' *New York Times* Retrieved May 10, 2018, from https://www.nytimes.com/2015/07/05/opinion/sunday/the-science-of-inside-out.html

Kettner, V. A., & Carpendale, J. I. M. (2013). Developing gestures for no and yes: Head shaking and nodding in infancy. *Gesture*, 13(2), 193–209.

Kidd, C., Piantadosi, S. T., & Aslin, R. N. (2012). The Goldilocks effect: Human infants allocate attention to visual sequences that are neither too simple nor too complex. *PLOS ONE*, 7(5), e36399.

Kim, P. S., Coxworth, J. E., & Hawkes, K. (2012). Increased longevity evolves from grandmothering. *Proceedings: Biological Sciences*, 279(1749), 4880–4.

Kintz, J. (2011) *There Are Two Typos Of People In This World: Those Who Can Edit And Those Who Can't.* Amazon Media.

Kishi, T., Nozawa, T., *et al.* (2016). One DoF robotic hand that makes humans laugh by tickling through rubbing underarm. In *2016 IEEE/RSJ International Conference on Intelligent Robots and Systems (IROS)* (pp. 404–409). IEEE.

Klein, M. (1935). A contribution to the psychogenesis of manic-depressive states. *The International Journal of Psycho-Analysis.*

Knutson, B., Burgdorf, J., & Panksepp, J. (1998). Anticipation of play elicits high frequency ultrasonic vocalizations in young rats. *Journal of Comparative Psychology*, 112(1), 65–73.

Kobayashi, H., & Kohshima, S. (2008). Evolution of the human eye as a device for communication. In T. Matsuzawa (Ed.), *Primate origins of human cognition and behavior* (pp. 383–401). Tokyo: Springer Japan.

Koch, C. (2009). When does consciousness arise? *Scientific American Mind*, 20(5), 20–21.

Koestler, A. (1964). *The Act of creation*. London: Hutchinson.

Köhler, W. (1925*). The mentality of apes*. London: Routledge and Kegan Paul.

Kool A. D. (2015). Where's the baby? Retrieved 9 September, 2015, from http://www.vice.com/read/wheres-the-baby-183

Korzybski, A. (1933). *Science and sanity*. Lakeville, CT: The International Non-Aristotelian Library Pub. Co.

Kovács, A. M., & Mehler, J. (2009). Cognitive gains in 7-month-old bilingual infants. *Proceedings of the National Academy of Sciences of the United States of America*, 106(16), 6556–60.

Kuhl, P. K., Andruski, J. E., *et al.* (1997). Cross-language analysis of phonetic units in language addressed to infants. *Science* (New York, NY), 277(5326), 684–686.

Lancy, D. F. (2014). 'Babies aren't persons': A survey of delayed personhood. In H. Otto & H. Keller (Eds.), *Different Faces of Attachment* (pp. 66–110). Cambridge: CUP

Lancy D. F. (2015). *The anthropology of childhood.* Cambridge: CUP

Leach, P., & Matthews, J. (2010) *Your baby and child: new version for today.* London: Dorling Kindersley

Leclair-Visonneau, L., Oudiette, D., Gaymard, B., Leu-Semenescu, S., & Arnulf, I. (2010). Do the eyes scan dream images during rapid eye movement sleep? Evidence from the rapid eye movement sleep behaviour disorder model. *Brain*, 133(6), 1737–1746.

Lee, R. B. (1979). *The !Kung San: Men, women, and work in a foraging society.* Cambridge: Cambridge University Press.

Leong, V., Byrne, E., *et al.* (2017). Speaker gaze increases information coupling between infant and adult brains. *Proceedings of the National Academy of Sciences*, 201702493.

Leslie, A. M. (1987). Pretense and representation: The origins of 'Theory of Mind.' *Psychological Review*, 94, 412–422.

Leslie, A. M. (1992). Pretense, autism, and the Theory-of-Mind module. *Current Directions in Psychological Science*, 1(1), 18–21.

Lewis, M., Sullivan, M. W., & Brooks-Gunn, J. (1985). Emotional behaviour during the learning of a contingency in early infancy. *British Journal of Developmental Psychology*, 3(3), 307–316.

Longhi, E. (2003). *The temporal structure of mother-infant interactions in musical contexts.* (Doctoral dissertation, University of Edinburgh)

MacCorquodale, K. (1970). On Chomsky's review of Skinner's *Verbal Behavior*. *Journal of the Experimental Analysis of Behavior*, 13(1), 1333660.

MacNeilage, P. F. (2008). *The origin of speech.* Oxford: Oxford University Press.

Mahajan, N., & Wynn, K. (2012). Origins of 'us' versus 'them': prelinguistic infants prefer similar others. *Cognition*, 124, 227–233.

Manita, S., Suzuki, T., *et al.* (2015). A top-down cortical circuit for accurate sensory perception. *Neuron*, 86(5), 1304–1316.

Marcus, G. F. (2003). *The algebraic mind.* Cambridge, MA: MIT Press.

Marcus, G. F., & Davis, E. (2013). How robust are probabilistic models of higher-level cognition? *Psychological Science*, 24(12), 2351–2360.

Marcus, G. F., Vijayan, S., Bandi Rao, S., Vishton, P. M., & Ausubel, F. M. (1999). Rule learning by seven-month-old infants. *Science*, 283 (January), 77–80.

Marx, V., & Nagy, E. (2015). Fetal behavioural responses to maternal voice and touch. *PLOS ONE*, 10(6), 1–15.

Maurer, D., & Werker, J. F. (2014). Perceptual narrowing during infancy: A comparison of language and faces. *Developmental Psychobiology*, 56(2), 154–178.

McCabe, J. (1966) *Mr. Laurel and Mr. Hardy*. New York: Signet

Melhuish, E., Belsky, J., & Barnes, J. (2010). Evaluation and value of Sure Start. *Archives of Disease in Childhood*, 95(3), 159–161.

Meltzoff, A. N., & Borton, R. W. (1979). Intermodal matching by human neonates. *Nature*, 282(5737), 403–404.

Meltzoff, A. N., & Moore, M. K. (1977). Imitation of facial and manual gestures by human neonates. *Science*. 198(4312), 75-78.

Mennella, J. A., Jagnow, C. P., & Beauchamp, G. K. (2001). Prenatal and postnatal flavor learning by human infants. *American Journal of Pediatrics*, 107(6), e88.

Miller, L. (1989). *Closely observed infants*. London: Duckworth.

Mindell, J. A., Kuhn, B., Lewin, D. S., Meltzer, L. J., & Sadeh, A. (2006). Behavioral treatment of bedtime problems and night wakings in infants and young children. *Sleep*, 29(10), 1263–1276.

Mindell, J. A., & Lee, C. (2015). Sleep, mood, and development in infants. *Infant Behavior and Development*, 41, 102–107.

Moore, S. R., McEwen, L. M., *et al.* (2017). Epigenetic correlates of neonatal contact in humans. *Development and Psychopathology*, 29(05), 1517–1538.

Morris, P. H., Reddy, V., & Bunting, R. C. (1995). The survival of the cutest: Who's responsible for the evolution of the teddy bear? *Animal Behaviour*, 50(6), 1697–1700.

Nazzi, T., Bertoncini, J., & Mehler, J. (1998). Language discrimination by newborns: Toward an understanding of the role of rhythm. *Journal of Experimental Psychology: Human Perception and Performance*, 24(3), 756–766.

Oaksford, M., & Chater, N. (2007). *Bayesian rationality: The probabilistic approach to human reasoning*. Oxford: Oxford University Press.

Oatley, K., & Johnson-Laird, P. N. (2014). Cognitive approaches to emotions. *Trends in Cognitive Sciences*, 18(3), 134–140.

O'Higgins, M., James, R. I. S., Glover, V., Roberts, I., & Glover, V. (2008). Postnatal depression and mother and infant outcomes after infant massage. *Journal of Affective Disorders*, 109, 189–192.

Oller, D. K., Buder, E. H., Ramsdell, H. L., Warlaumont, A. S., Chorna, L., & Bakeman, R. (2013). Functional flexibility of infant vocalization and the emergence of language. *Proceedings of the National Academy of Sciences of the United States of America*, 110(16), 6318–23.

Oostenbroek, J., Slaughter, V., Nielsen, M., & Suddendorf, T. (2013). Why the confusion around neonatal imitation? A review. *Journal of Reproductive and Infant Psychology*, 31(4), 328–341.

Oostenbroek, J., Suddendorf, T., *et al.* (2016). Comprehensive longitudinal study challenges the existence of neonatal imitation in humans. *Current Biology*, 26(10), 1–5.

Oswald, D. L., Clark, E. M., & Kelly, C. M. (2004). Friendship maintenance: An analysis of individual and dyad behaviors. *Journal of Social and Clinical Psychology*, 23(3), 413–441.

Pan, B. A., Rowe, M. L., Singer, J. D., & Snow, C. E. (2005). Maternal correlates of growth in toddler vocabulary production in low-income families. *Child Development*, 76(4), 763–782.

Panksepp, J. (1998). *Affective neuroscience: The foundations of human and animal emotions*. Oxford: Oxford University Press.

Panksepp, J. (2001). The long-term psychobiological consequences of infant emotions: Prescriptions for the twenty-first century. *Neuropsychoanalysis*, 3(2), 149–178.

Panksepp, J., & Burgdorf, J. (1999). Laughing rats? Playful tickling arouses high frequency ultrasonic chirping in young rodents. In S. R. Hameroff, A. W. Kaszniak, & D. J. Chalmers (Eds.), *Toward a science of consciousness III* (pp. 231–244). Cambridge, MA: MIT Press.

Pearl, J. (1982). Reverend Bayes on inference engines: A distributed hierarchical approach. In *Proceedings of the AAAI National Conference on AI* (pp. 133–136).

Pearson, B. Z., Fernández, S. C., & Oller, D. K. (1993). Lexical development in bilingual infants and toddlers: Comparison to monolingual norms. *Language Learning*, 43(1), 93–120.

Penn, D. C., & Povinelli, D. J. (2007). On the lack of evidence that non-human animals possess anything remotely resembling a 'theory of mind'. *Philosophical Transactions of the Royal Society of London*. Series B, Biological Sciences, 362(1480), 731–44.

Petitto, L. A., & Marentette, P. F. (1991). Babbling in the manual mode: Evidence for the ontogeny of language. *Science*, 251, 1493–1496.

Piantadosi, S. T., & Kidd, C. (2016). Extraordinary intelligence and the care of infants, *Proceedings of the National Academy of Science*, 113(25) 6874-6879.

Piazza, E. A., Iordan, M. C., & Lew-Williams, C. (2017). Mothers consistently alter their unique vocal fingerprints when communicating with infants, 3162–3167.

Plooji, F. X. (1978). Some basic traits of language in wild chimpanzees?

In A. Lock (Ed.), *Action, gesture and symbol: The emergence of language* (pp. 111–131). New York: Academic Press.

Potegal, M., & Davidson, R. J. (2003). Temper tantrums in young children: 1. Behavioural composition. *Journal of Development and Behavioral Pediatrics*, 24(3), 140–147.

Potegal, M., Kosorok, M. R., & Davidson, R. J. (2003). Temper tantrums in young children: 2. Tantrum duration and temporal organization. *Journal of Developmental and Behavioral Pediatrics*, 24(3), 148–154.

Pratchett, T. (1987). *Equal rites*. London: Corgi.

Premack, D., & Woodruff, G. (1978). Does the chimpanzee have a theory of mind? *Behavioral and Brain Sciences*, 1(4), 515–526.

Provine, R. R. (2001). *Laughter: A scientific investigation*. London: Penguin.

Quine, W. V. O. (1960). *Word and object*. Cambridge, MA: MIT Press.

Ramaswamy, C. (2016). *Expecting: The inner life of pregnancy.* Glasgow: Saraband.

Ramsey, F. P. (1931). *The foundations of mathematics and other logical essays*. London: Routledge and Kegan Paul.

Ramsey, M. A., & Gentzler, A. L. (2015). An upward spiral: Bidirectional associations between positive affect and positive aspects of close relationships across the life span. *Developmental Review*, 36, 58–104.

Rathunde, K., & Csikszentmihalyi, M. *The developing person: An experiential perspective* (pp. 465–515). Hoboken, NJ: John Wiley & Sons.

Rauscher, F. H., Shaw, G. L., & Ky, C. N. (1993). Music and spatial task performance. *Nature*, 365(6447), 611.

Recchia, G., & Jones, M. N. (2012). The semantic richness of abstract concepts. *Frontiers in Human Neuroscience*, 6, 315.

Rechtschaffen, A., Gilliland, M., Bergmann, B., & Winter, J. (1983). Physiological correlates of prolonged sleep deprivation in rats. *Science*, 221(4606), 182–184.

Reddy, V. (2000). Coyness in early infancy. *Developmental Science*, 3(2), 186–192.

Reddy, V. (2001). Infant clowns: The interpersonal creation of humour in infancy. *Enfance*, 53, 247–256.

Reddy, V. (2008). *How infants know minds*. Boston, MA: Harvard University Press.

Reddy, V., & Mireault, G. (2015). Teasing and clowning in infancy. *Current Biology*, 25(1), R20–R23.

Reddy, V., & Trevarthen, C. (2004). What we learn about babies from engaging their emotions. *Zero to Three*, 24(3), 9–16.

Reissland, N., Francis, B., Mason, J., & Lincoln, K. (2011). Do facial expressions develop before birth? *PLOS ONE*, 6(8).

Repacholi, B. M., & Gopnik, A. (1997). Early reasoning about desires: Evidence from 14- and 18-month-olds. *Developmental Psychology*, 33(1), 12–21.

Rizzolatti, G., Fadiga, L., Gallese, V., & Fogassi, L. (1996). Premotor cortex and the recognition of motor actions. *Cognitive Brain Research*, 3(2), 131–141.

Robbins, A. M., Gray, M., Basabose, A., Uwingeli, P., Mburanumwe, I., Kagoda, E., & Robbins, M. M. (2013). Impact of male infanticide on the social structure of mountain gorillas. *PLOS ONE*, 8(11), e78256.

Rocha, S., & Mareschal, D. (2017). Getting into the groove: The development of tempo-flexibility between 10 and 18 months of age. *Infancy*, 22(4), 540–551.

Rocha, S., Southgate, V., & Mareschal, D. (2017). Infant spontaneous motor tempo. In P. M. C. Harrison (Ed.), *Proceedings of the 10th International Conference of Students of Systematic Musicology (SysMus17)* (p.86). London, UK.

Rochat, P. (1989). Object manipulation and exploration in 2-to 5-month-old infants. *Developmental Psychology*, 25(6), 871–884.

Rochat, P., & Striano, T. (2000). Perceived self in infancy. *Infant Behavior and Development*, 23(3–4), 513–530.

Rosch, E. H. (1975). Cognitive representations of semantic categories. *Journal of Experimental Psychology: General*, 104(3), 192–233.

Roth-Hanania, R., Davidov, M., & Zahn-Waxler, C. (2011). Empathy development from 8 to 16 months: Early signs of concern for others. *Infant Behavior and Development*, 34(3), 447–458.

Roy, B. C., Frank, M. C., DeCamp, P., Miller, M., & Roy, D. (2015). Predicting the birth of a spoken word. *Proceedings of the National Academy of Sciences*, 112(41), 12663–8.

Royal College of Obstetricians and Gynaecologists (RCOG) (2010). *Fetal awareness: Review of research and recommendations for practice.* London: RCOG Press.

Royal College of Obstetricians and Gynaecologists (RCOG) (2017). *Maternal Mental Health – Women's Voices*. London: RCOG Press.

Ruffman, T., Aitken, J., Wilson, A., Puri, A., & Taumoepeau, M. (2018). A re-examination of the broccoli task: Implications for children's understanding of subjective desire. *Cognitive Development*, 46 (December 2016), 79–85.

Ruffman, T., Lorimer, B., & Scarf, D. (2017). Do infants really experience emotional contagion? *Child Development Perspectives*, 11(4), 270–274.

Rustin, M. (2009). Esther Bick's legacy of infant observation at the Tavistock – Some reflections 60 years on. *Infant Observation*, 12(1), 29–41.

Saffran, J. R., Aslin, R. N., & Newport, E. L. (1996). Statistical learning by 8-month-old infants. *Science*, 274(5294), 1926–1928.

Saffran, J. R., Pollak, S. D., Seibel, R. L., & Shkolnik, A. (2007). Dog is a dog is a dog: Infant rule learning is not specific to language. *Cognition*, 105(3), 669–680.

Samson, D. R., & Nunn, C. L. (2015). Sleep intensity and the evolution of human cognition. *Evolutionary Anthropology*, 24(6), 225–237.

Savage-Rumbaugh, S., & Lewin, R. (1994). *Kanzi: The ape at the brink of the human mind*. London: John Wiley & Sons.

Schellenberg, E. G., & Hallam, S. (2005). Music listening and cognitive abilities in 10-and 11-year-olds: The blur effect. *Annals of the New York Academy of Sciences*, 1060(1), 202–209.

Schmidt, M. H. (2014). The energy allocation function of sleep: A unifying theory of sleep, torpor, and continuous wakefulness. *Neuroscience and Biobehavioral Reviews*, 47, 122–153.

Schonert-Reichl, K. A., Smith, V., Zaidman-Zait, A., & Hertzman, C. (2012). Promoting children's prosocial behaviors in school: Impact of the 'Roots of Empathy' program on the social and emotional competence of school-aged children. *School Mental Health*, 4, 1–21.

Sear, R., & Mace, R. (2008). Who keeps children alive? A review of the effects of kin on child survival. *Evolution and Human Behavior*.

Shapiro, C., Bortz, R., Mitchell, D., & Bartel, P. (1981). Slow-wave sleep: A recovery period after exercise. *Science*.

Shemella, P. (2013). Life in the baby universe. *Physics World* (September), 56.

Sherman, L. W. (1975). An ecological study of glee in small groups of preschool children. *Child Development*, 46(1), 53–61.

Shultz, T. R., & Zigler, E. (1970). Emotional concomitants of visual mastery in infants: The effects of stimulus movements of smiling and vocalizing. *Journal of Experimental Child Psychology*. 10(3) 390–402.

Sirois, S., & Mareschal, D. (2004). An interacting systems model of infant habituation. *Journal of Cognitive Neuroscience. Special Issue on Developmental Cognitive Neuroscience*, 16(8), 1352–1362.

Slater, A., Mattock, A., & Brown, E. (1990). Size constancy at birth: Newborn infants' responses to retinal and real size. *Journal of Experimental Child Psychology*, 49(2), 314–322.

Smith, L., & Yu, C. (2008). Infants rapidly learn word-referent mappings via cross-situational statistics. *Cognition*, 106(3), 1558–1568.

Southgate, V., van Maanen, C., & Csibra, G. (2007). Infant pointing: Communication to cooperate or communication to learn? *Child Development*, 78(3), 735–740.

Spelke, E. S., & Kinzler, K. D. (2007). Core knowledge. *Developmental Science*, 10, 89–96.

Spencer, H. (1859). The physiology of laughter. *Macmillan's Magazine*, 1, 395–402.

Stahl, A. E., & Feigenson, L. (2015). Cognitive development. Observing the unexpected enhances infants' learning and exploration. *Science* (New York, NY), 348(6230), 91–4.

Steiner, J. E., Glaser, D., Hawilo, M. E., & Berridge, K. C. (2001). Comparative expression of hedonic impact: Affective reactions to taste by human infants and other primates. *Neuroscience and Biobehavioral Reviews*, 25(1), 53–74.

Street, S. E., Navarrete, A. F., Reader, S. M., & Laland, K. N. (2017). Coevolution of cultural intelligence, extended life history, sociality, and brain size in primates. *Proceedings of the National Academy of Sciences*, 114(30), 7908–7914.

Stokoe, W. C. (1983). Apes who sign and critics who don't. In J. De Luce & H. T. Wilder (Eds.) *Language in Primates*. Springer.

Stumm, S. von, & Plomin, R. (2015). Breastfeeding and IQ growth from toddlerhood through adolescence. *PLOS One* 10(9), e0138676.

Sully, J. (1902). *An essay on laughter*. London: Longmans, Green and Co.

Sutcliffe, T. (1997). *Believing in opera*. Princeton University Press.

Tardif, T., Fletcher, P., Liang, W., Zhang, Z., Kaciroti, N., & Marchman, V. A. (2008). Baby's first 10 words. *Developmental Psychology*, 44(4), 929–938.

Téglás, E., Vul, E., Girotto, V., Gonzalez, M., Tenenbaum, J. B., &

Bonatti, L. L. (2011). Pure reasoning in 12-month-old infants as probabilistic inference. *Science*, 332(6033), 1054–1059.

Tenenbaum, J. B., Kemp, C., Griffiths, T. L., & Goodman, N. D. (2011). How to grow a mind: Statistics, structure, and abstraction. *Science*, 331(6022), 1279–1285.

Terrace, H., Petitto, L., Sanders, R., & Bever, T. (1979). Can an ape create a sentence? *Science*, 206(4421), 891–902.

Thomas, D. (1961) Poetic manifesto, *The Texas Quarterly*, Vol. IV, No. 4, 44–53.

Tomasello, M., Carpenter, M., & Liszkowski, U. (2007). A new look at infant pointing. *Child Development*, 78(3), 705–722.

Tononi, G., & Cirelli, C. (2014). Sleep and the price of plasticity: From synaptic and cellular homeostasis to memory consolidation and integration. *Neuron*, 81(1), 12–34.

Trainor, L. J. (1996). Infant preferences for infant-directed versus non-infant-directed playsongs and lullabies. *Infant Behavior and Development*, 19(1), 83–92.

Trehub, S. E., & Trainor, L. J. (1998). Singing to infants: Lullabies and play songs. In C. K. Rovee-Collier, L. P. Lipsitt, & H. Hayne (Eds.), *Advances in infancy research*, Volume 12 (pp. 43–64). Stamford, CT: Ablex Publishing Corporation.

Trevarthen, C. (2005). Stepping away from the mirror: Pride and shame in adventures of companionship. *Attachment and Bonding: A New Synthesis*, 55–84.

Trevarthen, C., & Reddy, V. (2017). Consciousness in infants. In S. Schneider & M. Velmans (Eds.), *The Blackwell companion to consciousness* (pp. 45–62). London: John Wiley & Sons.

Tronick, E., Als, H., Adamson, L., Wise, S., & Brazelton, T. B. (1978). The infant's response to entrapment between contradictory messages in face-to-face interaction. *Journal of the American Academy of Child Psychiatry*, 17(1), 1–13.

Turing, A. M. (1937). On computable numbers, with an application to the Entscheidungsproblem. *Proceedings of the London Mathematical Society*, s2-42(1), 230–265.

Vallortigara, G. (2012). Core knowledge of object, number, and geometry: A comparative and neural approach. *Cognitive Neuropsychology*, 29(1–2), 213–236.

Van Der Helm, E., Yao, J., Dutt, S., Rao, V., Saletin, J. M., & Walker, M. P. (2011). REM sleep depotentiates amygdala activity to previous emotional experiences. *Current Biology*, 21(23), 2029–2032.

Van der Meer, A. L. (1997). Keeping the arm in the limelight: Advanced visual control of arm movements in neonates. *European Journal of Paediatric Neurology*, 1(4), 103–108.

Victora, C. G., Bahl, R., *et al.* (2016). Breastfeeding in the 21st century: Epidemiology, mechanisms, and lifelong effect. *The Lancet*, 387(10017), 475–490.

Victora, C. G., Horta, B. L., de Mola, C. L., Quevedo, L., Pinheiro, R. T., Gigante, D. P., … Barros, F. C. (2015). Association between breastfeeding and intelligence, educational attainment, and income at 30 years of age: A prospective birth cohort study from Brazil. *The Lancet Global Health*, 3(4), 199–205.

von Zimmermann, J., Vicary, S., Sperling, M., Orgs, G., & Richardson, D. C. (2018). The choreography of group affiliation. *Topics in Cognitive Science*, 10(1), 80–94.

Vrontou, S., Wong, A. M., Rau, K. K., Koerber, H. R., & Anderson, D. J. (2013). Genetic identification of C fibres that detect massage-like stroking of hairy skin in vivo. *Nature*, 493(7434), 669–673.

Warneken, F. (2018). How children solve the two challenges of cooperation. *Annual Review of Psychology*, 69(1), 205–229.

Warneken, F., Chen, F., & Tomasello, M. (2006). Cooperative activities in young children and chimpanzees. *Child Development*, 77(3), 640–663.

Warneken, F., & Tomasello, M. (2006). Altruistic helping in human infants and young chimpanzees. *Science*, 311(5765), 1301–1303.

Wasserman, E. A., & Young, M. E. (2010). Same–different discrimination: The keel and backbone of thought and reasoning. *Journal of Experimental Psychology: Animal Behavior Processes*, 36(1), 3–22.

Waters, S. F., West, T. V., & Mendes, W. B. (2014). Stress contagion: Physiological covariation between mothers and infants. *Psychological Science*, 25(4), 934–942.

Watson, J. S. (1972). Smiling, cooing and 'The Game'. *Merrill-Palmer Quarterly of Behavior and Development*, 18(4), 323–339.

Watt Smith, T. (2015). *The Book of Human Emotions*. London: Profile Books.

Weaver, I. C. G., Cervoni, N., *et al.* (2004). Epigenetic programming by maternal behavior. *Nature Neuroscience*, 7(8), 847–54.

Weisberg, D. S., & Gopnik, A. (2013). Pretense, counterfactuals, and Bayesian causal models: Why what is not real really matters. *Cognitive Science*, 37(7), 1368–1381.

Werker, J. F., & Tees, R. C. (2003). Influences on infant speech processing: Toward a new synthesis. *Annual Review of Psychology*, 50, 509–535.

Whaley, K. L., & Rubenstein, T. S. (1994). How toddlers 'do' friendship: A descriptive analysis of naturally occurring friendships in a group child care setting. *Journal of Social and Personal Relationships*, 11(3), 383–400.

Whitehead, A. N. (1967). *The aims of education, and other essays.* Princeton, NJ: Free Press.

Wildgruber, D., Szameitat, D. P., Ethofer, T., Brück, C., Alter, K., Grodd, W., & Kreifelts, B. (2013). Different types of laughter modulate connectivity within distinct parts of the laughter perception network. *PLOS One*, 8(5), 10–13.

Wilhelm, I., Diekelmann, S., Molzow, I., Ayoub, A., Mölle, M., & Born, J. (2011). Sleep selectively enhances memory expected to be of future relevance. *Journal of Neuroscience*, 31(5).

Williams, D., & Colling, L. (2018). From symbols to icons: The return of resemblance in the cognitive neuroscience revolution. *Synthese*, 195(5), 1941–1967.

Williamson, L. (1978). Infanticide: An anthropological analysis. In M. Kohl (Ed.), *Infanticide and the value of life* (pp. 61–75). New York: Prometheus Books.

Winnicott, D. W. (1964). *The child, the family and the outside world.* Harmondsworth: Penguin.

Wulf, K. (1985). History of fetal heart rate monitoring. In W. Kunzel (Ed.), *Fetal heart rate monitoring* (pp. 3–15). Berlin: Springer-Verlag.

Xie, L., Kang, H., *et al.* (2013). Sleep drives metabolite clearance from the adult brain. *Science*, 342(6156).

Xu, F., & Kushnir, T. (2013). Infants are rational constructivist learners. *Current Directions in Psychological Science*, 22(1), 28–32.

Yoshida, H., & Smith, L. B. (2008). What's in view for toddlers? Using a head camera to study visual experience. *Infancy: The Official Journal of the International Society on Infant Studies*, 13(3), 229–248.

Zahn-Waxler, C., Robinson, J. A. L., & Emde, R. N. (1992). The development of empathy in twins. *Developmental Psychology*, 28(6), 1038–1047.

Zentner, M., & Eerola, T. (2010). Rhythmic engagement with music in infancy. *Proceedings of the National Academy of Sciences*, 107(13), 5768–5773.

Credits

Excerpt on pages 10–11 from *Expecting: The Inner Life of Pregnancy* © Chitra Ramaswamy, 2016, published by Saraband. Reproduced by permission of Saraband.

Excerpt on page 29 from *Ina May's Guide to Childbirth* © Ina May Gaskin, 2010, published by Ebury Publishing.

Quotations on pages 47 and 59 from *Making Babies* © Anne Enright, 2005, published by Vintage.

Excerpt on page 66 from *About the House* © W. H. Auden, 1965, published by Random House.

Quotation on page 149 from *Playing by Heart: The Vision and Practice of Belonging* © O. Fred Donaldson, 1994, published by Health Communications. Reproduced by permission of the author.

Quotation on page 151 from *Dummy: The Comedy and Chaos of Real-Life Parenting* © Matt Coyne, 2017, published by Wildfire. Reproduced by permission of Headline Publishing.

Lyrics on page 174 from 'One of These Things' © Joe Raposo and Bruce Hart. Reproduced by permission of The Joe Raposo Music Group, Inc.

Quotation on page 228 from *What We Learn About Babies from Engaging Their Emotions* © Vasudevi Reddy and Colwyn Trevarthen, 2004, published by Zero to Three. Reproduced by permission of Zero to Three.

Index

A Note on the Author

Caspar Addyman is a lecturer in psychology and director of the InfantLab at Goldsmiths, University of London. He has degrees in maths and psychology and completed his PhD at the world-renowned Birkbeck Babylab. He has investigated how babies acquire language, concepts and even their sense of time. Since 2012 he has been studying what makes babies laugh and why. His novel, *Help Yourself*, was published in 2013.

Unbound is the world's first crowdfunding publisher, established in 2011.

We believe that wonderful things can happen when you clear a path for people who share a passion. That's why we've built a platform that brings together readers and authors to crowdfund books they believe in – and give fresh ideas that don't fit the traditional mould the chance they deserve.

This book is in your hands because readers made it possible. Everyone who pledged their support is listed below. Join them by visiting unbound.com and supporting a book today.

Catherine Aithal
Sandra Armor
Sebastian Arndt
Nic Badcock
Daniel Baker
Haiko Ballieux
Nick Barnes
Rob Bartlett
Rachael Bedford
Paul Berg
Kasia & Jakub Bijak
Bluestone Childcare
Jacqueline Bonfield
Robert J Bonfield
Nigel Bonson
Isabelle Britten-Denniee
Belinda Brown
Philippa Bull-Diamond
Natalie Buschman
Christine Cairns
Anthony Carrick
Aurore Ceccaldi
Dani Cervantes
Rosie Clarke
Corinne Clarkson
John Connolly

Ben Cons
Jemima Cooper
Kelly Cooper
Fay and Tom Coster-Newsom
Abi Coutinho
Petrina Cutchey
Carina de Klerk
Cami O. Delaye
Kate Dent Rennie
Kate Devlin
Sarah Duguid
Alyson Elliman (née Dembovitz)
To Esme and the Cowles family. From uncle Imran.
Nicolas Farrugia
Roberto Filippi
Wilder, Coco, Aurelia and Florence Foxcroft
Catherine Francey
Chris French
Nathalia Gjersoe
Paula Góes
Ms L. Golubov
Chris Gray
Dan Greenberg
Abigail Greetham
Alice Gregory
Thomas Hamre
Rakel Hansen
Ceridwen Harris
Gwyneth Hibbett
Samantha Hills
Ben Hopper
William Horwood
Catherine Howard
Mo Hunter
Corinna Ilschner
Jenny Jacoby
Nicola Januszewski
Denny John
Ramiro Joly-Mascheroni
Helen Kanarbik
Cornelia Katrani
Dan Kieran
Helene Kreysa
Pierre L'Allier
Maria Lambert-Carter
Les LeLean
Leah Levy
Christina MacRae
Simon Makin
Jackie Martinez
Anyi Mazo-Vargas
Lucy McCahon
Janice McKinley
Jenny Mcloughlin
Evelyne Mercure
John Mitchinson
Kate Moore

Katy Moran
Katherine Morley
Matt Morris
Giuseppe Moschetti
Alan Murphy
Lasse Nielsen
Addison Niemeyer Billing
Owen O'Daly
Scott Pack
Roz Palethorpe
Zoe Palmer
Melanie Parham
Simon Parry
Pippa Percy
Justin Pollard
Ana Maria Portugal
JE Pourcho
Cat and Rob Quinn
Melissa Quinn
Christine Reed
Sarah Reilly
Zelda Rhiando
Tom Richards
Sara Riggare
Arne Robinson
Pippa Russell
Gabriela Rye
Alan Saunders
Jesus Mario Serna
Nik Snarey
Lili Soh
Ruby Sparklepants
Martin Spencer-Whitton
Tom Stafford
Jonathan Stamford
Jane Stevenson
Charlotte Stewart
Lauren Stewart
Graham Stock
Chloe Ella Stubbs
Kasia Tauzowska
Chelsey Taylor
Charlie Torrible
Sam Wass
Scott Weaver
Anna Williams
Melinda Williamson
Guy Windsor
Susi Wisniewski
Rupert Wood
Owain Wynne
Chris Yenter
Helen York
Jenny Young
Joanna Zimmerli